EUROPE IN TRANSITION: THE NYU EUROPEAN STUDIES SERIES

Series Editor: Martin A. Schain

Migrant Mobilization and Securitization in the US and Europe

How Does It Feel to Be a Threat?

Ariane Chebel d'Appollonia

First published in 2015 by
PALGRAVE MACMILLAN®
in the United States—a division of St. Martin's Press LLC,
175 Fifth Avenue, New York, NY 10010.

Where this book is distributed in the UK, Europe and the rest of the world,
this is by Palgrave Macmillan, a division of Macmillan Publishers Limited,
registered in England, company number 785998, of Houndmills,
Basingstoke, Hampshire RG21 6XS.

Palgrave Macmillan is the global academic imprint of the above companies
and has companies and representatives throughout the world.

Palgrave® and Macmillan® are registered trademarks in the United States,
the United Kingdom, Europe and other countries.

ISBN: 978–1–137–38804–9

Library of Congress Cataloging-in-Publication Data

Chebel d'Appollonia, Ariane.
    Migrant mobilization and securitization in the US and Europe : how
does it feel to be a threat? / Ariane Chebel d'Appollonia.
        pages cm.—(Europe in transition)
    Includes bibliographical references and index.
    ISBN 978–1–137–38804–9

    1. United States—Emigration and immigration—Government policy.
2. Europe—Emigration and immigration—Government policy.
3. Terrorism—United States—Prevention. 4. Terrorism—Europe—
Prevention. 5. Border security—United States. 6. Border security—
Europe. 7. National security—United States. 8. National security—
Europe. I. Title.

JV6483.C4573 2015
305.9'06912094—dc23   2014039845

A catalogue record of the book is available from the British Library.

Design by Newgen Knowledge Works (P) Ltd., Chennai, India.

First edition: April 2015

10 9 8 7 6 5 4 3 2 1

For Simon, as usual and for ever

Contents

Tables

Series Editor's Foreword

Ariane Chebel d'Appollonia's book on immigration, securitization, and mobilization in the United States and Europe focuses on the very heart of the politics of immigration on both sides of the Atlantic. During the past decade, issues of immigration have been increasingly tied to questions of state security. This is perhaps less surprising in Europe, where the majority of immigrants have been Muslim. At a time of increasing political chaos in the Islamic world, large and growing immigrant Muslim populations in Europe have been politically framed as threats both to national identity and to national security. It is more surprising in the United States, where it has taken considerably more political effort and creativity to link Latino and Asian immigration to challenges of security.

Moreover, the flow of immigration is very different on both sides of the Atlantic. The steady rise of legal immigration into the United States since 1965 has not been challenged. There have been no legislative efforts to halt or even cut back legal immigration since the 1990s, and recent proposals to "reform" immigration have all contained proposals to expand legal flows. Efforts to block entry have all dealt with undocumented migrants, or migrants who have overstayed their legal visas.

Although levels of legal entry into Europe have been roughly similar to those of the United States, the political opposition even to legal immigration has been strong, and has grown stronger during the past decade, as radical right political parties have achieved political breakthroughs. In contrast to the United States, countries in Europe have been politically sensitive to perceived challenges to their national identity, and, as Chebel d'Appollonia carefully notes, have taken action meant to deal with these challenges.

Despite these important differences, however, this book makes clear that the immigration-security nexus has been powerful on both sides of the Atlantic. The perceived threats to security may not be exactly the same in Europe and the United States, but the administrative and legislative actions have had surprisingly similar rationales. Moreover, the impact in each case has also been similar.

The core of this book is really about the impact of securitization programs, both on the targeted groups and on their social and political incorporation. Instead of facilitating incorporation, securitization measures raise obstacles that often cannot be met, and therefore exaccerbate the problem.

On the other hand, these measures tend to influence and shape patterns of immigrant/ethnic mobilization on both sides of the Atlantic. This is the most important part of the story in this book, since it involves, for the most part, those migrants who are now in fact European and American. The way that they integrate into the political system will be the other side of impact—the impact that immigrant populations have on electoral and more general political outcomes.

In this context, as Chebel d'Appollonia demonstrates in chapter four, securitization often has perverse effects. Rather than promoting deeper integration and social peace, these policies tend to promote greater ethnic identity and protest mobilization. In Europe, the impact appears to have deepened, rather than undermined multiculturalism, and politicized ethnic identities in important ways.

This is an important study. It both integrates a broad range of scholarly literature, and takes in new directions. I am very pleased that we have been able to publish it in the *Europe in Transition* series.

MARTIN A. SCHAIN
New York University

Acknowledgments

This book addresses some of the questions I listed in the conclusion of *Frontiers of Fear: Immigration and Insecurity in the United States and Europe* (2012). It constitutes part of a transatlantic research project on the Securitization of Migrant Integration (SOMI). It is a Sorbonne Nouvelle-Sciences Po initiative funded by Idex Sorbonne Paris Cité. The project, codirected by Romain Garbaye (Paris III) and myself, examines the relationship between security governance and subsequent forms of immigrant and minority mobilization in Europe and the United States. The central issues addressed by SOMI participants are threefold: First, the ways in which security governance affects migrants' and minorities' collective identities and actions; Second, how these effects vary among different migrant and minority groups, within and across countries; and finally, how various forms of mobilization may have a reciprocal impact on subsequent immigration and integration policies.

I am pleased to acknowledge the financial and logistical support provided in the writing of this book by Université Sorbonne Paris Cité (USPC), and the CEVIPOF (Center for the Study of Political Life) at Sciences Po—Paris.

I had the opportunity to present some of the arguments developed in this book when participating in conferences organized by the International Studies Association (ISA) in Toronto and the Council for European Studies (CES) in Amsterdam. I would like to specially thank Patrick Ireland and Anthony Messina for their comments at these conferences. I also thank my graduate assistant at Rutgers University, Meghan Sullivan, for her boundless energy and attention in helping me to collect the most relevant and recent materials.

I am pleased to have this opportunity to express my deepest thanks to Martin Schain who has supported my work and my morale for so many years. He has always provided me with valued guidance (except when it comes to trekking in the woods of upstate New York).

Finally I acknowledge the paradoxical contribution of Simon Reich—my beloved husband, best friend, and merciless critic. I benefited a lot from his multiple close reads of the manuscript in its various forms. This book is dedicated to him, with love and gratitude.

Introduction

In the early nineteenth century W. E. B. Du Bois vividly summarized the challenges that African Americans faced by asking "how does it feel to be a problem?" To come to terms with being treated as a "problem," he wrote, is a "strange experience," a "peculiar sensation" that leads to "double consciousness, this sense of always looking at one's self through the eyes of the others." Du Bois captured the feeling of stigmatization, noting that "the facing of so vast a prejudice could not but bring the inevitable self-questioning, self-disparagement, and lowering of ideals which ever accompany repression and breed in an atmosphere of contempt and hate" (1903, Chapter 1). He demonstrated that coping with the "color-line" problem had a dramatic impact on both self-identification and group categorization. "No Negro," he wrote, "has failed to ask himself at some time: What, after all, am I? Am I an American or am I a Negro? Can I be both? Or is it my duty to cease to be a Negro as soon as possible and be an American?" (1897).

The questions Du Bois raised a century ago are still relevant today. The color line continues to divide Western societies and severely undermines efforts to promote equality. The general population still perceives some ethnic minorities as being a "problem," mostly because of the persistence of racially based discrimination. Both Europe and the United States have, indeed, a long history of singling out specific groups who have been perceived and treated as a problem on the basis of their national origin, racial or ethnic identity, and religious or cultural distinctiveness (Schrag, 2010; Zolberg, 2006). Historically, specific immigrant groups were forced to ask themselves at various points if they could be American *and* Irish (when Irish immigrants were perceived as being "brown" and suspected of spying for the Vatican), American *and* Asian (when Asian Americans were "aliens ineligible for citizenship" until the McCarran-Walter Act of 1952 gave them the right to US citizenship), or American *and* Jewish (when Jews were not considered as fully Americans by "old line" US natives and denied voting rights in some states). Hostility to foreigners and racial nativism were popular in

European countries as well in the nineteenth and twentieth centuries, despite the European background of most immigrants, as illustrated by the racial riots between French workers and Italian immigrants in France in 1881 and 1893 and the anti-Semitic pogroms that took place in Russia in the 1880s and at the turn of the century. Racism and xenophobia reached a peak during the depression of the 1930s, as illustrated by the Holocaust and Nazi policies against other "un-German" populations.

Most minority groups have nevertheless achieved an initially hostile population's acceptance over time, as illustrated by the example of the "Irish who became White" in the United States (Ignatiev, 1995). The third-generation, native-born children of European migrants could afford to demonstrate signs of their ethnicity without their allegiance being questioned. As Douglas Massey's comprehensive research on assimilation demonstrated, this tendency broadened over time. By the 1980s, immigrants from Latin America and Asia assimilated in much the same way that European immigrants did before them. Indeed, today Asian Americans are commonly perceived as "model minorities." The dilemmas generated by the "double consciousness" described by Du Bois have been resolved by the multiplication of hyphenated American identities. Likewise, in Europe, children of European immigrants do not feel compelled to deny their cultural heritage in order to demonstrate that they are truly part of their society. Similarly, in most cases, integration in Europe has been a long, often painful process through which both immigrants and host societies have been transformed. Yet, like in the United States, ethnic communities of European descent found a way to assimilate while retaining part of their cultural identity.

Yet, not all immigrants integrate in the same fashion, or as successfully, on either continent. Some first- and second-generation immigrants perform poorly compared to both the native population and the children of other immigrant groups, as illustrated by Hispanics in the United States and Muslims in some European countries. Even more problematic is the fact that some groups are not considered "trustworthy" members of American, French, Italian, or other Western societies. Since the 1990s, the categories of "new comers," "illegal immigrants," "bogus" asylum seekers, and "suspicious minorities" have been increasingly conflated in the media and general public discourse. Western governments have responded to concerns raised by the so-called new immigration (itself a euphemism for "non-European") by linking immigration policy to other high profile issues, including the fight against drug trafficking, organized crime, and terrorism. The framing of immigration and integration as a "security issue" has been fuelled by a long-standing concern about the impact of immigration on job security, criminality, national identity, and social cohesion. Terrorist attacks in the United States and Europe have intensified this immigration-security nexus. The association between immigration and integration issues on one side, and insecurity on the other, are now deeply ingrained in public discourse and policy on both sides of the Atlantic. Collectively, they have produced what I have elsewhere characterized as the *securitization of immigration governance*. It is a process through which Western political elites—governments, leading political parties, and associated policy networks—rhetorically frame immigration as a security threat. This characterization produces a series of policies that justify an expansion of state powers, often at the expense of civil liberties. Immigrant and minority groups have responded to these policies negatively, expressing strong concerns about being singled out for increased surveillance, monitoring, racial profiling, and increased discrimination (Chebel d'Appollonia, 2012a).

A number of scholars have noted that immigration and integration policies have been deeply affected by the legislation introduced after 9/11 in the United States and Europe. Aristide Zolberg, for example, suggested at a meeting of the Board of Editors of the *International Migration Review* held in November 2001 that scholars should inquire as to the significance of the new security agenda and "share their reflections upon international migration in the wake of 9/11" (2002: 5). The journal subsequently published an article addressing the evolution of international migration flows and its economic and political impact, and another concerning the questions raised by "the meta-politics of migration and security."

Since then, various aspects of immigrants and the post-9/11 era have been documented from four perspectives. The first relates to studies in the field of migration policies and politics. Clustered under this heading, both US and European scholars have focused their attention on the combined effects of the evolution of borders controls, antiterrorism measures, and other related exclusionary legislation on migrants (Mittelstadt et al., 2011; Fraga, 2009; Luedtke, 2009; Alden, 2008; Schain, 2008a; Adamson, 2006; Collyer, 2006; Guiraudon, 2006; Rudolph, 2006; Lahav, 2004; Tirman, 2004; Boswell, 2003; Geddes, 2003); on immigration politics in the United States, in European countries, and at the EU level (Rubaii-Barett, 2011; Schuck, 2009; Newton, 2008; Schain, 2008b; Rosenblum, 2004; Guild, 2003; Messina, 2002; Tichenor, 2002);

and on migrant phobia and the rise to new prominence of anti-migrant groups (Mudde, 2007; Alexseev, 2006; Citrin and Sides, 2006).

A second perspective involves scholars from the field of security studies. Representatives of various new critical schools of security studies (such as the Aberystwyth, Copenhagen, and Paris schools) have provided new insights into the securitization process by exploring the questions of who securitizes, on what issues, for whom, under what conditions, and with what results (Booth, 2007; CASE, 2007; Buzan et al., 1998). Some scholars apply the theoretical insights of Myron Wiener in two areas: first, the study of the securitization of immigration policies (van Munster, 2009; Huysmans, 2006); and second, the impact of these policies on vulnerable populations (such as asylum seekers and refugees) with a focus on violations of civil liberties, basic freedom, and human rights (Badaccini et al 2007; Balzacq and Carrera, 2006; Thomas, 2006; Ivarsflaten, 2005). Other scholars examine the political, legal, and ethical issues raised by the "war on terror" in liberal democracies, in order to emphasize the controversial effects of counterterrorism (Crenshaw, 2010; Donohue, 2008; Cole and Lobel, 2007; Zimmermann and Wenger, 2006; Ignatieff, 2004; Cole, 2003; Haubrich, 2003).

Studies of migrant integration constitute a third component. Scholars working in this field have concurred that the securitization process has affected both the context of reception for immigrants, and the modalities of accommodation of ethnocultural minorities. They have disagreed, however, in evaluating the outcomes of these contextual changes. For some, security concerns and security-driven policies are an impediment to integration. As John Mollenkopf and Jennifer Hochschild noted, for example, "the specter of terrorism further complicates social incorporation" (2009: 9). For others, anti-immigrant legislation leads to higher mobilization rates—as illustrated by evidence drawn from prior periods during which immigrant rights were threatened (such as after immigration and welfare reform was introduced in the United States in 1996). According to Kristi Andersen and Elizabeth Cohen, "increases in naturalization have been seen in the wake of civil rights restrictions of non-citizens following the terrorist attacks of September 11, 2001" (Andersen and Cohen, 2005: 190). The only assumption shared by most scholars in this field is that specific immigrants and minorities have been further discriminated against since 9/11, although they provide little empirical evidence to support any conclusion regarding the actual effects of discrimination in terms of alienation at both the individual and group levels.

Finally, a fourth perspective—drawing on theoretical insights from social psychology, cross-cultural psychology, and cultural sociology—emphasizes the issues and challenges that immigrants face in host societies. As Rumbaut et al. noted well over a decade ago, "immigration researchers are increasingly crossing disciplinary boundaries…An interdisciplinary field or subfield of immigration is very much is the making" (1999: 1260). Proponents of this approach offer a complementary contribution to that made by political scientists in examining the complex factors shaping intergroup relations, acculturation, and migrants' mobilization in increasingly diverse societies (Howarth, 2008; Berry, 2001 and 1997; Dovidio and Esses, 2001). Some scholars adopting this interdisciplinary approach focus on the underlying psychological processes associated with (self) identification, the development of "groupness," and the effects of group boundaries (Todd, 2005; Jenkins, 1996). Others analyze the role of intergroup competition, intergroup prejudice, and different kinds of threats—such as "realistic threat," "social identity threat," or "symbolic threat" (Kosic and Phalet, 2006; Brown and Hewstone, 2005; Gaertner and Dovidio, 2000). New developments in cultural sociology have provided insights about the reaction of minorities to an adversarial environment. Michèle Lamont et al., for example, recently studied how members of stigmatized ethnoracial group manage that stigma through a range of "destigmatization strategies," how they negotiate social and symbolic boundaries, and how their responses are constrained by institutions, national ideologies, and cultural repertoires (2013).

These four perspectives provide useful insights for a better understanding of migrants and migration processes—whether in terms of new immigration policy, attitudes, or ideologies—in a post-9/11 era. Yet none directly address the impact of the securitization of immigration governance on patterns of integration and mobilization. This study, in contrast, focuses on the challenges that immigrants and minorities face today by asking what it means—*from their standpoint*—to be treated as a "threat."[1] I believe that this distinct kind of prejudice raises a specific yet novel category of concerns over integration and diversity management issues. Some of these certainly overlap with those related to other forms of exclusion. Since the publication of G. A. Allport's landmark book in 1954, negative ethnic prejudice has commonly been defined as an "avertive attitude" toward a person. This entails ascribing objectionable characteristics to a group member, simply by virtue of being a member of that group. This overcategorization is fueled by misconceptions and prejudgments resistant to all countervailing evidence (Allport,

1954, Chapter 1 purportedly entitled "What is the problem?"). As Linda Tropp and Thomas Pettigrew have argued, both members of minority and majority groups face contentious challenges as they approach cross-group interactions; "However, these challenges tend to be based in largely distinct concerns, corresponding with the groups' differences in status. In particular, the concerns of members of majority status groups typically involve being perceived as prejudiced by individuals lower in status, whereas the concerns of members of minority status groups involve becoming the target of prejudice from individuals higher in status" (2005: 951). Most research on integration, by inference, supports the contention that improving intergroup contact through optimal conditions can reduce prejudice (such as ensuring their equal status, providing educational programs, and introducing other institutional forms of support). One implication of this approach, according to John Dovidio, is that "if the problem, like a cancerous tumor, can be identified and removed or treated, the problem will be contained and the rest of the system will be healthy" (2001: 831). Governments have alternatively regarded the civil rights movement and various forms of affirmative action (in the United States), or of variants of multiculturalism (in Europe), as examples of initiatives that have stimulated positive intergroup attitudes and enhanced the inclusion of minority status groups.

Yet, there is a paradox in this kind of approach: while an integrative problem can be solved (at least hypothetically), a threat must be fought. Each respective governments' main rationale—in terms of public policies—is not to find ways to address discrimination if a group poses a threat. It is rather to use any means available to enhance domestic security, including measures that entail the further exclusion of targeted communities—as illustrated by the preemptive criminalization of "risk groups," expediting the process of deportation, and institutionalizing a process of stigmatization. The politics of fear, which has been evident in both the rhetoric and policies of decision makers since 9/11, has accentuated a cultural climate of fear (Linke and Smith, 2009; Jackson, 2007; Altheide, 2002; Furedi, 2002; Glassner, 1999). The growth of a climate of fear, reciprocally, affects the policy agenda as well as political attitudes and intergroup relations. Contributions from the fields of political psychology and developmental psychology provide evidence, for example, that native-born individuals predisposed to anxiety are more likely to espouse conservative political ideologies—as illustrated by the rise of ultraconservative and extremist right-wing parties in many European countries. Such fears also increase negative outgroup opinions, which manifest themselves politically in support for anti-immigration measures and pro-segregation attitudes (Lupia and Menning, 2009; Abramson et al., 2007; Jost et al., 2007; Brader, 2005; Skitka et al., 2004). Ethnocentric exclusion is coupled with "defensive exclusion" in support of a fearful nationalism, leading to some primal aggressive behaviors such as self-defense, preemptive violence against the 'enemy," and support for militias (from the Minutemen in the United States to the paramilitary groups in Italy who pursue "bogus" asylum seekers and Roma). As a result, immigrants (both legal and illegal) and some native-born minorities currently face high levels of insecurity. Security policies generate a long list of fears: of racial profiling, of being a victim of violence, of apprehension and deportation, and ultimately of being perceived as a threat (Cook, 2013; De Genova and Peutz, 2010; Varsanyi, 2010).

In this context of both actual and "ontological" insecurity, what are the options left for targeted groups in dealing with their suspect status? In the spirit of Du Bois, they may ask themselves: Can I be both Pakistani and British? Turk and German? Surinamese and Dutch? Algerian and French? Iraqi and American? Roma and Italian? Our efforts to answer such questions require us to consider the position of two kinds of respondents: those who belong to the majority group who express concerns about immigration and ethnic diversity; and those who are targeted by the effects of security governance. Doing so requires that we consider the structures, policies, and material resources that commonly frame integration, as well as the social and psychological factors that shape individual and collective behavior.

I examine both aspects in this book. In doing so, I argue that the securitization of immigration governance has dramatically altered the context of reception in the United States and Europe due to the effects of three interlocking new trends. The first is the introduction of security-driven public policies that tend to legitimize the use of "exceptional" measures designed to eradicate the alleged "threat" posed by immigrants and minority groups. These have led to a "permanent state of exception" (Agamben, 1998) that is designed to enhance homeland security by sacrificing the rights of "others." Politicians and bureaucrats view policies on the integration of migrants and of ethnic minorities as an instrument to counter threats. The politics of integration have therefore shifted from the traditional management of ethnic diversity to the protection of "us" against "them." Certainly, security measures that target immigrants and minority groups are nothing new, as illustrated in the United States by the Alien and Sedition Acts (1798–1801), the Immigration Act of 1917, the Alien Registration Act of 1940, and the internment of Japanese-origin residents of the West Coast during the Second World War. Comparably, various categories of "suspects" in Europe were the victims of criminalization, detention, and deportation, such as anti-Fascist refugees from Spain and Italy who were detained in French camps during the Vichy regime, and Jewish refugees who were categorized as "enemy aliens" by the British government and sent to internment camps in Australia and Canada. Most of these measures, however, were adopted during wartime and were terminated when hostilities ended. By contrast, the war on terror has no definitive time horizon and the corresponding securitization process potentially affects millions of people on both sides of the Atlantic.

The second trend is that the negative perceptions of immigrants and minority groups both fuel and are fueled by the media and politicians. They depict newcomers, domiciled migrants and their children as common criminals, urban rioters, and, occasionally, potential terrorists. There is strong evidence that this type of characterization goes beyond prior comparable cases of exclusion and discrimination. Their current construction of the "enemy inside" is the product of a combination of actual threats (the evidence being attacks committed by homegrown terrorists) coupled with an overestimation of symbolic threats—based on a variety of economic, social, and cultural concerns. Membership of a particular ethnic or religious community therefore constitutes, in itself, a security threat. In this context, the conception of integration has been changed: it actually means something approximating "conformity", "obedience," or "loyalty." Problematically, these are all intangible notions that traditional benchmarks of integration are unable to define or measure. What is currently expected from immigrants and minority groups extends beyond the traditional socioeconomic and cultural requirements required to become part of the mainstream to a compliance with security-defined social norms. Most European states, for example, have reformed their naturalization laws by introducing integration requirements explicitly related to security concerns. Some requisites include personal integrity clauses (such as "good character," "good civic conduct," or "respectable life"). These are often vaguely defined, sometimes inconsistently applied, but are always used in order to enhance national security against the "enemy within."

The third key trend concerns the responses of targeted immigrants and minorities to these varied measures. Much of the current literature treats them as objects rather than subjects of politics and policies. This limited interest in migrants as active participants in politics can be explained, as Davide Però and John Solomos pointed out, by the assumption that their behavior is either a "mechanistically determined reflection of the class structure...or a reflection of their ethnicity" (Però and Solomos, 2010: 8). Yet, immigrants and their children are clearly *not* simply passive receptors of policy. They engage in distinct forms of mobilization in response to the excesses of security governance. These span a huge spectrum. It is demarcated by indifference and passivity at one end. It then successively stretches from integration through pressure group politics, to nonviolent protest, civil disobedience, and violent protest. At the other end of this continuum lies radicalization. I thus argue that any effective understanding of the security governance process requires the study of the interplay between securitized immigration and integration policies and the choices that ethnic minorities make about *their preferred form of* mobilization.

No analysis should simply examine what governments do. That is only one part of the puzzle. Analyzing it as part of a larger "feedback" process is crucial: how migrants and minorities choose to respond, why they choose those options, and how their behavior subsequently affects immigration and integration policies.

The interactive effects of these three trends justify the need to reconceptualize how we define, analyze, and evaluate processes of integration. I will argue that scholars and policymakers need to pay more attention to the consequences of the increasing exclusion of various "others" on security grounds—independent from any objective measures of socioeconomic and cultural integration. Both Arab and white American Muslims, for example, are highly assimilated and approximate parity with other Americans in terms of income and educational achievements, positioning them among America's middle class. Yet, being members of a relatively affluent community does not insulate them against the suspicion of posing a threat either individually or collectively. More analytic and empirical work should focus on the perspective of immigrants and minorities, taking into account their perceptions of government policies and of integration in the context of securitization (such as, how do they define integration? Or how do they evaluate their level of integration?). We should also examine the evolution of their individual and collective identities (based on their perceptions of national identity, political, or religious identities) as the expression of new patterns of commonality in reaction to being perceived as a threat.

The potential number of questions to be addressed by such a research agenda is expansive. Does securitization push minorities who feel alienated toward or away from particular forms of political participation? Does the fear of being treated as a threat increase or decrease their willingness to integrate or participate in politics at all? Is there any connection between the participatory forms that immigrants and minorities adopt and their resentment of being discriminated against? Do Muslims in the United States and Europe feel more "Muslim" because they are identified and targeted as such? Ultimately, we need to examine the ways in which the effects of securitization and the patterns of organization and mobilization of migrants and minorities are related—with the central, foundational question being: Why have these policies fostered such diverse reactions among targeted migrant communities, extending across the entire spectrum of responses?

These are the issues that I address in this book, drawing from numerous research traditions in political science, sociology, and social psychology. In chapter 1, I provide a brief description of the main aspects of the current security governance. In the wake of 9/11, Western governments implemented security measures converging toward comparable objectives. The primary one was to prevent further terrorist attacks through the increased screening of suspicious individuals and groups (both foreign and native born). The second was to strengthen border controls and expulsion policies in order to fight illegal immigration. The third was to police minorities at national and local levels. I specify in greater detail the linkage between public discourse, security measures, and a variety of responses by targeted communities.

In chapter 2, I critically examine a common assumption supported by the existing literature on securitization: that discrimination increases a sense of alienation. That alienation, in turn, supposedly reinforces either group consciousness or an individual's sense of alienation, raising concerns about increased marginalization, political distrust and democratic disaffection, religious fundamentalism, and ultimately radicalization. In contrast, I argue that the relationship between expressions of prejudice and perceptions of discrimination on the one hand, and between perceived discrimination and responding attitudes toward society at large on the other hand, is complex. Data provided by numerous surveys and studies conducted for over a decade confirm that security-driven policies have had a strong negative impact: they fuel fear and resentment among all the selected groups (Hispanics and Muslims in the United States, Muslims in Europe). Yet concerns about the effects of securitization do not inevitably translate into high perception of discrimination and/or resulting negative attitudes toward a host society and the members of a dominant group.

Building upon the work of social psychologists, I examine variations in the respective impact of objective discrimination (as measured by traditional socioeconomic variables) and subjective discrimination (as expressed by immigrants and minorities targeted by security measures) among groups and across countries. I demonstrate that subjective discrimination plays a key role in the evolution of intergroup relations quite independent of objective discrimination. People who are objectively discriminated against by security measures but *do not feel subjectively* excluded have a positive attitude toward their host society, as illustrated by the attitude of both Hispanics and Muslims in the United States—and to a lesser extent Muslim immigrants in some European countries. Alternatively, people who are objectively discriminated against by security measures *but do feel subjectively* excluded have a more negative attitude toward their host society, especially when they are members of the second and third generation of immigrants. Being born and socialized in their host country, they feel entitled to the same treatment as members of the majority population. They are also more sensitive to discrimination, and less inclined to tolerate social marginalization. As a result, they are more critical of the society at large, and less trustful of national institutions. This trend, commonly labeled as "the paradox of integration," challenges some core components of the acculturation theory. It also prompts a careful examination of the actual effects of security governance on integration. Does being suspected of posing a threat preclude the integration of targeted populations? If so, in what fields and to what extent?

When addressing these questions in chapter 3, I critically analyze the importance of the context of migrant integration as emphasized by proponents of the political opportunity structure (POS) approach and the "new institutionalist" approach (Mollenkopf and Hochschild, 2009; Koopmans and Staham, 2000; Brinton and Nee, 1998; Tarrow, 1998; Ireland, 1994). The degree of receptivity toward immigrants vary from one country to another, along a continuum of receptivity that ranges from exclusion, passive acceptance, to supportive inclusion (or accommodation). The basic assumption of various context-bound perspectives is that integration is easier if the host society is ready to accommodate immigrants and their descendants in varied distinct domains (Crul and Schneider, 2012; Bowen, 2011; Connor, 2010; Suarez-Orozco et al, 2008; Crul and Vermeulen, 2006; Maussen, 2006; Portes and Rumbaut, 2006; Ireland, 2004). Each of these approaches has its own merits, but none adequately account for the varied forms of integration (or lack thereof) as a response to securitization measures. For the purpose of this study, I thus distinguish between a) integration as a process, taking place in an institutional framework, which includes citizenship regimes as well as various forms of diversity management (such as religious accommodation); b) integration assessed in terms of socioeconomic achievements, objectively measured by traditional indicators and subjectively perceived by immigrants and minority groups; and c) integration as defined by both the acculturation expectations of the receiving community and the acculturation orientations adopted by immigrants and minority groups. I analyze these various dimensions by making a distinction between objective integration (as defined by traditional socioeconomic indicators) and subjective integration (as perceived by members of both majority and minority groups).

As for discrimination, what really matters is the perception of how immigrants and minority groups "fit in"—from both the dominant group and minorities' perspectives. I thus focus on the impact of state policies (such as the reform of citizenship regimes and the introduction of assimilationist requirements, mostly in Europe) on both the opportunity structures of the receiving community and the integration patterns adopted by immigrants and minority groups. I demonstrate that the securitization of integration has redefined the boundaries between dominant and minority groups, thus resulting in a "clash of expectations" between members of the receiving society and immigrants targeted by security measures.

This finding prompts a question I address in chapter 4 and chapter 5: What are the actual effects of security governance on patterns of mobilization? My proposed analysis moves beyond the traditional conception of political participation as the main indicator of empowerment. Rather, I propose to analyze varied forms of mobilization by focusing on both conventional and unconventional forms of mobilization. The former includes electoral participation, ranging from naturalization and voting registration to political representation at the local and national levels. The latter relates to various types of nonelectoral activities such as making political donations, signing petitions, writing to officials, lobbying, membership of an organization (ethnic, mainstream, or mixed), and participating in demonstrations. I develop a typology of explanatory factors that are relevant from the immigrants' perspective in order to illustrate and analyze the increasing diversity of mobilization. This typology includes their subjective perception of the political and social arena, their form and degree of group membership, and their views of their own capacity for mobilization (or lack thereof). How immigrants and minorities deal with contextual changes must be considered through their experience and values, perceptions and expectations, emotions and feelings.

This typology also includes a list of institutional opportunities for mobilization in both Europe and the United States. It is commonly assumed that migrants and minorities in Europe have fewer such opportunities than their counterparts in the United States. Evidence suggests that their disenfranchisement in many European countries, as well as the lack of incentives for political parties to capture the support of ethnic voters, precludes the emergence of influential pro-migrant interest groups and migrant lobbies. I acknowledge, however, that the contrast between the United States and Europe should not be overstated, for several reasons. First, Hispanics and Muslims in the United States remain politically underrepresented, despite the potential electoral impact of ethnic politics and the resulting attempts by political parties to mobilize migrants and minorities as voters. Second, migrants and minorities in Europe are more mobilized than often acknowledged outside the realm of electoral politics. Third, there are alternative opportunities than those provided by national institutions—such as transnational networks (political and nonpolitical)—and civil society organizations.

I therefore argue that the excesses of securitization (such as xenophobic public discourse, racial profiling, denial of recognition, and violation of rights) have had a paradoxical effect on the mobilization of groups suspected of posing a "threat." Security governance has discouraged these targeted groups to fully engage in conventional politics; yet, it has also provided new incentives for unconventional mobilization— as illustrated by the 2006 Hispanic demonstrations as a response to a restrictive bill on immigration and the demonstrations in France against the 2004 law on the ban of the wearing "conspicuous" religious symbols in state schools. New, bifurcated responses to security governance have thus emerged: from active non-incorporation to violent protests, and ultimately radicalization. The vast majorities of aggrieved immigrants still want to participate in mainstream politics in traditional institutional ways. Yet some others tend to distance themselves from society at large and become more radical, despite—or as a response to—securitization measures.

In the book's concluding chapter, I consider the policy implications of these various forms of mobilization from two perspectives; one, entailing legal forms of the mobilization and the other, extralegal means. In the former case, targeted groups in Europe and the United States can influence the current framing of security measures, as illustrated by the reassessment of some governmental initiatives (such as the British PREVENT program or the NYC "stop and frisk" program). Muslims in Europe, as well as Hispanics and Muslims in the United States, have the current capacity to mobilize through a feedback process and to affect security governance. They are thus both legitimate political actors and, to some extent, successful promoters of desecuritization policies within the confines of the process. In the latter case, security governance still fuels a vicious circle by increasing a sense of alienation among a segment of minorities. A sense of threat leads a small fraction of them to pose a physical threat. The dynamics of this bifurcation is still poorly understood. But understanding this trend is relevant to both academics and policymakers.

Note

1. For the sake of simplicity, the term "immigrant" refers to foreign-born individuals and their children (that is members of the 1st and 1.5 generation) who may have—or not—been naturalized. It also refers to both legal and illegal "newcomers," as well as asylum seekers. The term "minority" includes native-born members of ethnic/racial groups who are settled for two generations and more. Except for African Americans in the United States, this study does not address the issue of "national minorities" (such as Bretons in France or Basques in Spain). I expand on this later in this book.

CHAPTER 1

The Securitization of Immigration and Integration Governance

The immigration and counterterrorism policies implemented after 9/11 have had severe consequences for specific groups identified as "security threats" by the general public. These policies have collectively produced what has become known as the "securitization of immigration governance." It is a process through which Western political elites (such as governments, leading political parties, and associated policy networks), public opinion, and the media construct immigration as a security threat. Typical aspects of securitization measures include the introduction of restrictive border controls intended to fight terrorism, accompanied by those intended to curb illegal migration flows and to police minorities. The security-immigration nexus is therefore apparent, visible in the ways in which politicians and bureaucrats view policies on the integration of migrants and of ethnic minorities as a means to counter threats. This nexus is further consolidated by negative stereotypes propagated by the mass media and official public discourse that, in turn, fuels concerns about the willingness of immigrants to integrate into their host societies. Furthermore, the securitization process has given legitimacy to a range of narrative frameworks that, as Sarah Scuzzarello noted, "have strong normative implications for how we conceive of a society, its citizens and the values that are honorable in it" (2011: 4). From the state's perspective, these normative implications are translated into the distinction between "wanted" and "unwanted" immigrants, as well as "good" and "bad" citizens. From society's perspective, the relationship between immigrants and members of the receiving country is based on acculturation attitudes that represent beliefs about the "best way" for minorities to adapt to the culture of the dominant group. From the perspective of immigrants and minorities suspected of being a threat, the main challenge is to achieve integration despite the presence of discrimination.

Pointedly, and perhaps paradoxically, these three agendas since 9/11 may clash as part of the changing policy landscape. In substantiating this claim, I focus on three interrelated trends in evaluating the recent changes in institutional structures that today channel trajectories of integration. The first trend is that government officials and minority groups do not share the same conception of integration: The former focus on loyalty (a law-and-order approach) and, notably in Europe, on conformity (by which a minority group's identity is replaced by an identification with the dominant culture). The latter anticipate full acceptance into the mainstream political process, better socioeconomic inclusion, and cultural integration (in which minority identity is retained while valuing the dominant culture). Discrepancies between these two conceptions of integration are illustrated by a "clash of perceptions" and fuel debates about the willingness of immigrants and minorities more generally to join the mainstream. The second trend is that the process of the securitization of integration has led to mismatches between what immigrants want and what the dominant group in several host societies expects from them. This, in turn, affects the adaptive strategy adopted by immigrants and the complexities they encounter in attempting to do so—as illustrated by the polarization of identities and the increasing social distance between majority and minority groups. The third and final trend is that concerns about "societal cohesion" and disintegration have fostered the adoption of further integrative policies that may have exclusionary effects. This cycle is potentially problematic in that it reinforces the pattern it seeks to address.

Setting the Context

The security-driven measures adopted by the US and European governments since 9/11 have strengthened the policy linkage between terrorism and immigration, leading to a huge expansion in border and interior enforcement. In the United States, the war on terror was conducted on a basis of a new legislation authorizing law enforcement with broad powers to investigate all offenses related to terrorism. The USA Patriot Act (2001), the REAL ID Act (2005), and the Protect America Act (2007) expanded the definition of "terrorism" and enlarged the federal government's power to conduct criminal investigation. The laws allowed the detention of suspected aliens if there were "reasonable grounds" to believe suspects were involved in terrorist activities. The main objectives of the new legislation were to increase the number of suspects apprehended (using "sneak and peak" searches) and detained, and to expedite the process of deportation (by limiting judicial review). These and additional measures (such as the "mass interviews" program and the "special registration" program) have targeted specific groups, mostly persons of Arab ethnicity or of the Muslim faith. The State Department imposed a mandatory 20-day suspension of all visa applications submitted by men aged 18 to 45 from 26 Arab and Muslim countries. Under the "absconder apprehension initiative," noncitizens from Middle Eastern countries were tracked down and deported. Finally, delays in the naturalization process were implemented for Arabs and Muslims. The intensification of domestic antiterrorist activity involved an extensive use of racial profiling, as well as significant infringement upon civil liberties in the name of security. The enactment of new statutory provisions designed to identify and apprehend foreign terrorists was actually followed by a "catch-up strategy" that targeted all Muslims (and persons who "look like" Muslims) living in the United States. In the New York area, a surveillance unit was created in 2004 in order to collect information about mosques and Muslim civic associations by recruiting informants among Muslims arrested for minor offenses. The New York Police Department (NYPD) also monitored North East universities between 2006 and 2012 by sending undercover agents to spy on students who were members of Muslim student associations.

Other measures have addressed the perceived security risks generated by immigrants though enhanced border security and interior immigrant enforcement. Legislation designed to improve border security and prevent the entrance of unauthorized immigrants included the reorganization of the federal policy system under the Department of Homeland Security (DHS) in 2003, and the Intelligence Reform and Terrorism Prevention Act of 2006. Under DHS, US Customs and Border Protection (CBP) was given the task of intercepting terrorists, enforcing immigration laws, and collecting custom duties at the ports of entry and preclearance stations. Increasing staffing has been accompanied by huge spending on supporting technologies such as radar, sensors, and unmanned aerial vehicles (Meissmer et al., 2013; Totten, 2013). In December 2005, the House of Representatives adopted the Border Protection, Antiterrorism, and Illegal Immigration Act (HR 4437) that required the federal government to take custody of undocumented aliens detained by local authorities and mandated employers to verify workers' legal status. It made it a felony to be in the country without proper documents or to assist someone to attempt to enter or remain illegally in the United States. It made a conviction of drunk driving a deportable offense as well. Finally, it called for an estimated $2.2 billion worth of fences to be erected along part of the southern border. The Act was strongly opposed by a broad range of organizations and NGOs. Huge protests took place in 2006 in Los Angeles, New York, Chicago, and other cities—with at least a million marchers nationwide. The HR 4437 did not pass the Senate. The Congress, instead, passed the Secure Fence Act of 2006 that allocated funds for 700 miles of fencing along the southern border. It deployed thousands of National Guard members to assist the CBP and added thousands of new beds in detention facilities.

The militarization of border controls has been complemented by tougher enforcement of immigration laws within the country, as illustrated by the 287(g) program and the Secure Communities Program. The former expanded the role of state and local authorities in immigration enforcement under the supervision of DHS. In December 2012, more than 1,300 state and local officers in 19 states were involved in this program. The latter, created in 2008, was expanded by the Obama administration to nearly all the nation's 3,200 jails. Under this initiative, law enforcement authorities have been asked to submit the fingerprints of arrestees to immigration databases in order to better manage the deportation process of illegal immigrants—even when they are not violent criminals or do not pose a threat to public safety. As a result, deportations have risen to record levels in recent years, from 165,168 in 2002 to 391,953 by 2011 (DHS, 2011). Other measures included new change of address requirements, restrictions on the issuance and acceptance of identification documents, and a renewed emphasis on worksite enforcement.

A number of states and local governments have pursued their own enforcement strategies, including anti-vagrancy laws, mandatory verification of employment eligibility for new hires through the E-Verify program, training of state troopers to arrest illegal immigrants, and reassigning troops to the Mexican border. The Clear Law Enforcement of Criminal Alien Removal (CLEAR) expanded state and local police immigration enforcement authority. A report from the National Council of State Legislatures indicated that 30 states enacted restrictive measures under the guise of preventing terrorism in 2006. Since then, states such as Alabama, Arizona, and Oklahoma have passed laws that go as far as making it a criminal offense for an immigrant to fail to carry official documents. The adoption in 2010 of the law SB 1070 in Arizona ignited a national controversy. Its key provision gives police the authority to check the immigration status of individuals during a "lawful stop, lawful contact, detention or arrest" where there is "reasonable suspicion" they were not in the country legally—a provision upheld by the US Supreme Court in 2012. Three dozen copycat bills facilitating racial profiling against Hispanics and others presumed to be "foreign" have been introduced in state legislatures across the country since 2010.

In Europe, the linkage between terrorism and immigration was illustrated by a series of initiatives at the EU level, such as the Common Position of December 2001 and the Framework Decision of June 2002. Designed to strengthen cooperation among member states, the EU legislation expanded cross-border operational initiatives, such as the European arrest warrant, Europol, and Eurojust. The EU Counter-Terrorism Strategy was adopted in November 2005, partly as a response to the London bombings. It listed the main measures under the four headings of Prevent (radicalization), Protect (EU citizens and European values), Pursue (terrorists and other criminals), and Respond (to threats). It stated that the EU had to enhance the protection of its external borders to make it harder for suspected terrorists to enter and operate within the EU. Many European states added their own counterterrorist packages to the EU framework. These packages gave broad powers to law enforcement agencies for the surveillance of individuals suspected of being members of terrorist groups, as well as the prosecution of anyone promoting or assisting a terrorist organization. In addition to the creation of new criminal-law offenses related to terrorism, varied national legislations extended the period of detention without formally charging suspects who have been arrested (for up to 28 days in Great Britain). As in the United States, Muslims have been targeted by security-driven measures such as increased police surveillance, banning of groups, and deportation.

In the meantime, the securitization of immigration policy was reinforced at the EU level with the creation of the European Agency for the management of Operational Cooperation at the External Borders (Frontex) in 2005. A number of EU information systems were developed, such as Eurodac in the field of asylum; the Schengen Information System in the field of police and judicial cooperation; and the Europol Information System in the field of criminal law. All these new measures reflected the linkage between terrorists, immigrants, asylum seekers, and refugees. They also significantly contributed to the militarization of border controls. EU member states introduced their own legislation in order to tighten immigration and asylum procedures. In Germany, for example, provisions introduced in 2005 created the option of issuing a deportation order on the basis of an "evidence-based threat prognostic." The British government implemented new regulations design to refuse asylum to anyone with "possible terrorist connections" the same year. A comparable tendency to ease the terms whereby aliens could be removed was illustrated by the adoption in Italy of Law 144. It provided for deportation if there was any reason to believe that aliens might pose a security threat. Furthermore, efforts to attract highly skilled workers both at the national and EU levels were balanced by additional restrictive measures designed to make family reunification more difficult, as well as access to citizenship and social benefits for the "unwanted" immigrants. This latter category has been expanded over time and now includes immigrants (either legal or illegal) who are perceived as a threat to societal cohesion and public security. Issues raised by discriminatory practices against Roma (citizens and EU nationals alike) provide a dramatic example of the varied restrictionist policies currently implemented in Europe.

The Immigration-Security Nexus

Security governance has been consolidated by the development of a framework of communicative actions (public discourse, images, stereotypes) involving political leaders, state and local agencies, political parties, and the media (Balzacq, 2005; Williams, 2003). The securitization and politicization of the discourse on immigration has included the formulation of a systematic linkage between immigrants and all the "dangers" any nation might ever experience—such as the erosion of national identity, threats to employment, public order, and domestic security (Korkut et al., 2013; Bird et al., 2010; Warner, 2005; Ceyhan and Tsoukala, 2002). In the United States, "security concerns" were raised by restrictionists opposed to a comprehensive reform agenda during the immigration debates of 2005–2006 and 2007. The most virulent controversies focused on undocumented immigrants—often depicted as taking jobs away from Americans, as welfare dependents, criminals, or potential terrorists. In his book entitled *In Mortal Danger: The Battle for America's Borders and Security* (2006), Tom Tancredo, then Republican member of the House of Representatives, actually synthesized the common arguments made by leaders of the Tea Party and some other Republicans in language reminiscent of Pat Buchanan's pamphlets about Mexicans nearly two decades earlier. After his unsuccessful candidacy for the 2008 Republican presidential nomination, Tancredo endorsed Mitt Romney—who supported a similar anti-migrant agenda.

Anti-migrant propaganda has been more effective at the state level, as illustrated by the election of Jan Brewer (who garnered national attention by signing the SB 1070) as governor of Arizona in December 2010, and the adoption of laws banning Islamic Sharia law in various states (including Oklahoma, North Carolina, Kansas, South Dakota, and Tennessee).

In Europe, Alessandra Buonfino noted, "immigration as a threat and a security concern has become the hegemonic discourse in government policy" (2004: 24). This discourse targets all categories of "others": legal and illegal immigrants, resident foreigners, asylum seekers and refugees, as well as cultural and religious minorities (such as native-born Muslims and Roma). Political leaders instrumentalized fears raised by immigration not only to legitimize their security-driven policies but also, and above all, to secure the electoral support of their constituents. Political parties, mainly from the far right but from the center as well, have played a key role into the construction of immigrants as "enemies," by claiming that immigration was connected with many security problems (from petty delinquency to fundamentalist jihadism) in addition to posing a threat to national culture and identity. In Germany, for example, Chancellor Merkel took a harder line toward immigrants who showed a "resistance to being integrated," stating in October 2010 that attempts to create a multicultural society have "utterly failed." This statement reignited a controversial debate initiated by Thilo Sarrazin, a prominent Social Democrat and then member of the German Central Bank. In his book, *Deutschland schafft sich ab/Germany does away with Itself,* he argued that Muslim immigrants were undermining national prosperity and the national stock of human capital (because of their "low intelligence quotient").

In Great Britain, Prime Minister David Cameron presented his immigration reform proposals in March 2013. He contrasted immigrants who deserve acceptance (mostly highly skilled workers, the "brightest and the best") to those people "who take advantage of our generosity without making a proper contribution to our country," and who "put pressure on public services"—low-skilled workers who come with their dependents, illegal immigrants, bogus refugees, and bogus foreign students (Cameron, 2013). In Spain, the dramatic growth of the immigrant population (from 1.5 million in 2000 to 6.5 million in 2009) did not lead to a significant backlash. However, the economic crisis that began in 2007 increased anti-migrant sentiments and led political parties to adopt a tougher immigration platform. The Popular Party (PP), for example, put anti-immigrant rhetoric at the center of its electoral propaganda, notably in Catalonia where the main targets have been Romanian Roma and Muslims. In 2011, a PP candidate was elected as mayor of Badalona (near Barcelona) on a xenophobic platform— one that was approved a year later by the entire Catalan branch of the PP. The question of urban insecurity has dominated recent electoral campaigns in France, Belgium, and Italy—leading mainstream parties to support a "zero tolerance" policy designed to control "minorities at risk." According to Fabio Quassoli, "governments and their power apparatuses seem to find in the fight against insecurity and crime an opportunity to act strong—or at least to show a strong determination to do so—against all the threats to their voters' security" (Quassoli, 2004: 1176). Whether this strategy actually improves security remains to be seen. But it certainly reinforces negative stereotypes and generates a climate of social anxiety.

Finally, the media has regularly fueled the fear of foreigners, supporting the claims of some political parties in the search for sensationalism. A review of British media since 2000, for example, found that two-thirds of its coverage has focused on Muslims as a terrorist threat, a cultural threat, or both (Moore et al., 2008). As a result, Anastassia Tsoukala argues, "we witness the establishment of a dialectical relation between political and media discourses, which are thus mutually reinforced." Furthermore, "the media structure 'a' reality that ends up influencing, to various degrees, public opinion" (Tsoukala, 2005: 168, 173). This "securitarian" discourse in turn fuels, and is fueled by, concerns expressed by public opinion—which affects the type of policies a government will initiate. In addition, governmental rhetoric, social discourse, and media discourse have, as noted by Maurice Crul and Jens Schneider, "an influence on the political and social climate, directly affecting immigrants' and their children's quest for a place and position in the host society" (2012: 117). The vicious cycle is thus complete and is likely to last if we consider the evolution of public opinion in the United States and European countries.

Immigration indeed remains an important source of anxiety for natives who regard it as more of a societal problem than an opportunity. Fifty-three percent of US respondents and 50 percent of European respondents shared this negative perception of immigrants according to a German Marshall Fund Report issued in 2011 (up to 68 percent in the United Kingdom). Sixty percent of respondents in the United States and the United Kingdom then believed that immigrants take jobs away from native workers and additionally depress wage levels. Majorities on both sides of the Atlantic believed that most immigrants were in the host countries illegally (a perception shared by 58 percent of respondents in the United States, 59 percent in France, 74 percent in Spain, and up to 80 percent in Italy) (GMF, 2011). These findings are consistent with those provided by previous studies. A survey conducted by the Pew Hispanic Center in 2006 revealed that 48 percent of US respondents believed that the growing number of newcomers threaten traditional American values and beliefs (Pew, 2006).

Perceptions of immigration are not uniform in the 28 EU member states, but there is evidence that the overall sentiment has been increasingly negative throughout Europe. A report from the European Monitoring Center on Racism and Xenophobia (EUMC) suggested that the dominant perception of immigrants and minorities in Western and Central Europe (58 percent of respondents) was that they constitute a "collective ethnic threat." Furthermore, 60 percent of the respondents expressed a "resistance to multiculturalism" (Coenders et al., 2005). Consistent with these findings, an Ipsos MORI poll conducted in 2011 found that 77 percent of respondents in Russia, 72 percent in Belgium, 71 percent in Great Britain, and 67 percent in Italy agreed that there are "too many" immigrants in their respective countries. Large majorities believed that "immigration has placed too much pressure on public services" (including 76 percent in Great Britain, 70 percent in Spain, and 66 percent in Belgium) (Ipsos Mori, 2011). Another study conducted in 2011 by Andreas Zick and his colleagues in eight European countries found that 50 percent of respondents condemned Islam as a "religion of intolerance." A range spanning from 17 percent in the Netherlands to more than 70 percent in Poland believed that Jews "seek to benefit from their forebears' suffering during the Nazi Era"; and about one-third believed "there is a natural hierarchy of ethnicity" (Zick et al., 2011).

These findings, like those provided by numerous other surveys conducted during the course of the last decade, point to the conclusion that such public perceptions are framed by a series of negative stereotypes and misperceptions that are the foundation for the support of the securitization process. These include a widespread confusion between legal and illegal immigrants; an overestimation of the size of the foreign-born population; fears about the socioeconomic and the cultural impacts of immigration; and an underestimation of the actual levels of immigrant integration. British respondents, for example, estimate the foreign-born population living in their country at 31.8 percent while only 11.3 percent of the population is actually foreign-born. American respondents estimate a foreign-born stock of 37.8 percent while the actual foreign-born population represents only 12.5 percent of the total population

(GMF, 2011). The actual percentage of migrants in Italy in 2010 was around 7 percent. Yet polls showed that the population estimated this percentage to be around a staggering 25 percent (IOM, 2011). As Canoy et al. (2006: 15) noted, "the lack of accurate information strengthens public perception of migration as a dangerous phenomenon beyond the control of the national authorities and enhances suspicion of official statements on the matter...The media coverage of immigration and the political discourse on immigration feed the perception of a crisis." Other scholars reach a similar conclusion about the exclusionary outcomes of the discursive construction of immigrants as posing a threat. For Ted Brader and his colleagues, who analyzed the situational triggers affecting support for immigration in the United States, "public debates about immigration, like those in other domains, often suggest the interests, values, or lifestyles of citizens are in harm's way. Elite discourse tends to emphasize adverse consequences for jobs, taxes, crime, schools, cultural norms, or social harmony" (2008: 959). This language fuels public anxiety that, in turn, fuels prejudice (Sniderman et al., 2004; Kinder, 2003).

Perceptions of the impact of migration are so distorted in some countries that the belief that immigrants take jobs away from natives is widespread—independent of the actual level of unemployment. As a result, opposition to immigration is mostly unrelated to contextual factors, such as the actual size of migrant communities or the overall state of the economy (Citrin and Sides, 2006; Kehrberg, 2007; McLaren and Johnson, 2007). The impact of "symbolic threats" is, by contrast, far more significant. Negative perceptions of immigration are mostly fueled by existential fears that immigrants and some minorities are threatening national integrity and societal security in both the United States and Europe (Mukherjee et al., 2013; Schneider, 2008; Leong and Ward, 2006; Coenders et al., 2005; Gijsberts et al., 2004; Semyonov et al., 2004; Scheepers et al., 2002). The characterization of immigrants as a threat to national culture and identity relies on the assumption that specific groups fail to assimilate due to their ethnicity, religion, or culture of origin. In the United States, for example, there are continuing concerns raised about the linguistic integration of largely Spanish-speaking immigrants. As Benjamin Newman et al. note, "The problem for many monolingual Americans is that the presence of non-English speakers creates barriers to interpersonal communication and challenges what is perceived to be a core aspect of American identity. As a result, many individuals experience a degree of disorientation or "culture shock" without ever leaving their home country (Newman et al.,

2012: 2). Exposure to a foreign language thus increases the probability of anti-immigrant sentiments and support for restrictive immigration measures (Citrin and Wright, 2009; Schilkraut, 2007; Paxton and Mughan, 2006).

In Europe, concerns focus on Muslims (both foreign and native-born) who are mostly perceived as irredeemably "other" and therefore posing a threat to the alleged ethnocultural homogeneity of Western societies. In Spain, for example, 30 percent of Spaniards believe that Muslim immigrants are integrating "very poorly" and another 34 percent "poorly" (GMF, 2012). In France, majorities believe that immigrants integrate poorly (56 percent) as a result of their insufficient efforts to adjust to French society (60 percent). North-African immigrants and Muslims are perceived as forming a "separate and partitioned group" by 42 percent and 55 percent respectively. The general population's fear that French culture is under siege focuses on Islamic religious and cultural practices. Eighty-nine percent of French respondents, for example, believe that wearing a Muslim veil constitutes a threat to French values; and 55 percent believe that public policies should not facilitate Muslim religious practices (such as the building of mosques, carrying out Islamic funerals, and the ritual slaughtering of animals) (CNCDH: 2012). Majorities in other countries also worry that Muslims "have an increasing sense of Islamic identity" (66 percent in Germany, 63 percent in Great Britain, and 60 percent in the Netherlands) (Pew, 2005).

Unsubstantiated concerns about a potential "clash of civilizations" have been reinforced by actual threats such as the terrorist attacks of 9/11, the murder of Theo van Gogh in the Netherlands in 2004, the Madrid (2004) and London (2005) bombings, the violent controversy over the prophet Mohammed cartoons in 2005–2006, the Boston bombing in 2013, as well as numerous failed terrorist plots on both sides of the Atlantic (e.g., at the Glasgow airport in 2007 and at Times Square in NYC in 2010). My point is not to deny that Western societies are facing serious threats, nor to dismiss the continuing issue of urban violence, as illustrated by the French riots of 2005. As Rafaela M. Dancygier demonstrates, immigration is actually a source of two kinds of conflict. The first one, immigrant-native conflict, consists of "violent and non-violent native opposition to immigrants, such as the local electoral success of xenophobic parties or physical attacks directed against migrant settlers." The second one, immigrant-state conflict, involves confrontation between immigrants (and their children) and state actors, most often the police (Dancygier, 2010: 4). It is worth noting, however, that countering the assumptions that ground securitization, most terrorists are not immigrants while the vast majority of immigrants are not terrorists. The majority of them are not criminals either, despite the common belief that they are more prone than natives to commit crime (Rumbaut and Ewin, 2007; Martinez and Valenzuela, 2006). It is also noteworthy that immigrants and minorities are more often the targets of violence than its perpetuators (CAIR 2010; HRF, 2008; EUMC, 2005). Yet, the security measures targeting immigrants and minorities have strengthened the stereotypes of the "criminal immigrant" and "terrorist alien."

Debates over (Dis)integration

Integration is often broadly defined as "the process by which immigrants become accepted into society," which suggests, according to Rinus Penninx, that there are two parties involved: "the immigrants, with their characteristics, efforts and acceptance, and the receiving society, with its interaction with these newcomers. It is the interaction between the two that determines the direction and the ultimate outcome of the integration process" (2003: 1). This assumption that integration is a two-way process has become widespread in the United States and Europe. In developing their "new assimilation theory," Richard Alba and Victor Nee pointed out that "the historical reality is that the majority changes too, and that the American mainstream has been continually reshaped by the incorporation of new groups" (2003: 65). In Europe, EU institutions promote today a comparable approach. Common basic principles for immigrant integration were adopted in 2004. They emphasize the importance of a holistic approach, and the fact that "integration is a dynamic, two-ways process of mutual accommodation by all immigrants and residents of Member States (Council of the EU, 2004). This approach has been reaffirmed by the Commission's Common Agenda for Integration (2005), the Stockholm Program (2009), the Europe 2020 Strategy (2010), and the European Agenda for the integration of non-EU nationals (2011). In a similar vein, the Global Commission on International Migration (created by the United Nations Secretary-General in 2003) defined integration as a multidimensional process: "Both migrants and non-migrants need to be committed to the process and respect each other, and prepared for the naturally occurring changes in the perceptions and cultural structures of each society as a result of integration" (2005: 44).

This conception of integration implies that the responsibility for integration is shared by immigrants and the receiving country, although "these two are unequal partners: the receiving society, in terms of its institutional structures and the way it reacts to newcomers, has much more to say in the outcome of the process" (Penninx, 2003: 1). However, one of the main results of the immigration-security nexus is that large numbers of policymakers and a swathe of US public opinion tend to believe that immigrants want to live lives disconnected from the mainstream—thus posing a threat to national cohesion. In the United States, for example, 44 percent of the general population said in 2006 that today's immigrants were less willing to adapt to the American way of life compared with those who arrived in the early 1990s; and 58 percent complained that recent immigrants did not learn English within a reasonable period of time (Pew Hispanic Center, 2006). The US public remains unconvinced that most Muslim immigrants want to adopt American ways. About half (51 percent) think that Muslim immigrants are reluctant to assimilate (Pew, 2011). This view is widely shared in many European countries, including Germany (88 percent), the Netherlands (65 percent), and Great Britain (61 percent) (Pew, 2005). Specific groups are suspected of being "unwilling" to assimilate. Roma in France, for example, are accused of living in segregated geographic areas (mostly shantytowns or camps), begging or stealing instead of working, and refusing to obtain proper official identification documents. Manuel Valls, then French Interior Minister, suggested in September 2013 that Roma should thus "return to Romania and Bulgaria" because "these populations have a way of life that is extremely different to ours, and they are obviously in confrontation with local populations... We are not here to welcome these people" (BBC, September 25, 2013). It is worth noting that Roma from Bulgaria and Romania represent a tiny minority of the Roma community in France (about 15,000 out of 500,000—of which the large majority has French citizenship). They are EU nationals and thus legally enjoy the rights to work and to live within the EU—rights limited by the French government, which has imposed additional restrictions in terms of housing, education, and health care. A similar trend is noticeable in Italy where Roma represent the tiny fraction of 0.25 percent of the total population—(about 60,000 people, 50 percent of them being Italian citizens). Here they are unable to integrate because most Roma are forced to live in camps (such as in Lazio, near Rome), with no access to transportation, schools, or health care services. They are subsequently poorly integrated. This, in turn, fuels the unfounded suspicion that they are unable to integrate.

Yet, majorities among the general population in most European countries believe that effective integration is the sole responsibility of the immigrants. Most French (61 percent) and German (67 percent) respondents to an IFOP survey, for example, believe that the "poor" integration of Muslims was largely a result of their refusal to integrate. Potential barriers to integration, such as unemployment (20 and 10 percent respectively) and racism (18 percent and 15 percent respectively) were overlooked (IFOP, 2010). A 2011 study conducted by the European Commission in 14 member states found that the general population believed "that the main obstacle to integration was the migrants' lack of desire to integrate and the subsequent formation of 'ghettos' which was limiting integration into society." Non-EU immigrants, by contrast, mentioned the attitude of the general public "as a key obstacle to integration," notably feelings of distrust among society and institutional prejudice (Qualitative Eurobarometer, 2011: 42, 46). Other obstacles mentioned by immigrants include discrimination in the labor market; restrictions or difficult procedures to gaining access to citizenship; costs of certain integration programs; and limitations to voting rights.

This "clash of perceptions" has been widely documented, notably in the cases of Hispanics in the United States (Citrin et al., 2007; Waters and Jiménez, 2005;) and Muslims on both sides of the Atlantic (Cesari, 2013; Allen, 2010; Nyiri, 2010; Mogahed, 2007; Modood et al., 2005; Fetzer and Stoper, 2004). Aristide Zolberg and Long Witt Woon persuasively argued that intolerance toward Islam in Europe is quite similar to anti-Hispanic sentiment in the United States. Islamic populations and Hispanics have become "metonyms for the dangers that those most opposed to immigration perceive as looming ahead: loss of cultural identity, accompanied by disintegrative separatism or communal conflict" (1999: 7).

The Securitization of Integration

Despite a growing volume of scholarship on integration, S. Karthick Ramakrishnan has noted that "there is still no standard set of terms to characterize the outcomes and processes being analyzed—witness the use of terms as varied as assimilation, adaptation, incorporation, and integration" (2013: 29). These concepts often lack clarity and consistency in meaning. They are defined and measured in numerous ways, which makes it difficult to compare findings from different national contexts. Furthermore, there is a "widely assumed difference between the concept of assimilation, taken to be dominant in the US debate, and integration in Europe" argued Jens Schneider and Maurice Crul. They added that, "while the American notion of 'mainstream' does not preclude variety and diversity, European 'integration' predominantly carries the implicit ideal of (a minimum degree of) cultural homogeneity" (2012: 2). Convergence theorists emphasize that Western Europe and the United States have become increasingly similar in terms of citizenship policies, cultural practices, and welfare benefits regardless of these different "philosophies of integration." (Freeman, 2011 and 1995; Joppke and Morawska, 2003). Others scholars employing transatlantic comparisons insist instead on the resilience of variation in national contexts, as illustrated by substantial differences in citizenship regimes, electoral politics, social welfare regimes, and school systems (Mollenkopf and Hochschild, 2010; Alba and Foner, 2009).

How states actually define and pursue integration still varies widely. In addition to a lack of "integration policy" per se, the United States has remained relatively immune from the temptation to revise its naturalization regime. Restrictionist groups have tried to repeal the Fourteenth Amendment that affirms that all persons born in the country are US citizens regardless of their parents' citizenship. Several bills have been introduced to fight against "anchor babies" but all failed in state legislatures and the US Congress. A comparison with Europe will therefore still have to admit that greater tolerance exists toward cultural and religious diversity in the United States, despite the implementation of more stringent regulation of immigration.

Fears of "disintegration" by contrast, fuel a dominant restrictive trend in Europe based on concerns about "societal disunity allegedly associated with ethnic minority separatism in general, and Muslim alienation and estrangement (and ultimately violent extremism) in particular (Triandafyllidou et al., 2012: 3). What Tariq Modood and Nasar Meer called a "renationalization of citizenship" (2012: 34) has been accelerated and hardened as states have reacted to 9/11 coupled with the alleged "failure to integrate" on the part of Muslims. According to Per Mouritsen, "the introduction and public controversy about language requirements, knowledge tests and screening for self-support, clean criminal records and non-radical leanings now specifies what constitutes 'good' citizenship . . . Citizenship is increasingly viewed as a club to be protected from politically alien or culturally inadaptable outsiders" (2012: 95). In Great Britain, official reports identified a lack of "community cohesion" as key in explaining the urban disorders that occurred in several northern towns in the summer of 2001 (Cantle, 2001; Clarke, 2001; Denham, 2001). Likewise, the French riots of 2005, and similar episodes of urban unrest involving migrant communities across Europe, strengthened the idea that discrimination, segregation, and alienation were strong predictors of violent protest and ethnic tensions. As Paul Bagguley and Yasimin Hussain argued, "the binary opposition between social cohesion and segregation has become the dominant frame which the riots are 'read' with segregation now seen as exemplifying a dysfunctional community" (2006: 4).

Furthermore, the terrorist attacks of July 7, 2005 (7/7) and other incidents involving "homegrown terrorists" in European countries have transformed concerns about integration into security concerns among policymakers, both at the national and EU levels. This shift has been illustrated by a greater emphasis on integration by European institutions and agencies. The EUMC stressed the connection between "fear and suspicion," the "feeling and experience of not belonging," alienation, and "violent urban disturbances" (EUMC, 2006b). The EU Strategy for combating radicalization, adopted in 2005, identified prejudice and discrimination as vectors for terrorist recruitment, and emphasized the need to improve the implementation of the 2000 Directives on Racial Equality. The document emphasized that the prevention of violent radicalization should include a focus on a variety of issues: employment, social exclusion and integration issues, equal opportunities and nondiscrimination, as well as broadcast media, the Internet, education, and youth engagement. According to the Council of the EU, "to ensure the long-term integration of minority groups, the EU should 'target inequalities and discrimination where they exist and promote inter-cultural dialogue and long-term integration where appropriate'" (EC, 2005). In 2012, the Organization for Security and Cooperation in Europe (OSCE) adopted a consolidated framework for the fight against terrorism. In it the organization argued that antidiscrimination policies are essential in countering "violent extremism and all forms of radicalization that lead to terrorism—the so-called VERLT" (OSCE, 2012).

What Rogers Brubacker (2001) identified as "the return of assimilation" has been illustrated by the new "integration requirements" introduced under the guise of enhancing national integrity. Many European states have introduced language and civics tests as a condition for immigration, family reunion, access to long-term residence status, and naturalization. Pre-entry requirements are often an instrument for the selection of newcomers—as illustrated by the legislation passed in the Netherlands in 2006, which then served as a model for Denmark, Germany, France, and the United Kingdom. The common objectives are to limit the number of low-skilled immigrants and to restrict family immigration. Newly arriving migrants are now obliged to follow a course of programs and/or to sign "integration contracts" designed to enhance their assimilation—both in traditional assimilationist countries such as France, and in pluralist and multiculturalist countries such as the Netherlands and Great Britain. The introduction of integration requirements in the host country, long after immigrants arrived and settled, has been officially justified on the basis of concerns about the promotion of active participation in the polity and civic society. In the Netherlands, the shift from "pillarization" (the Dutch version of multiculturalism) to assimilation was then accentuated with passage of the Dutch Nationality Act of 2003 and the New Integration Act of 2007 (van Oers, 2010). Successfully completing an integration examination has become a condition for permanent residency and naturalization. "Social orientation" courses (for which immigrants have to pay) focus on Dutch values and norms—including questions about gay marriage and church-state relations, which, as Ricky van Oers notes, raises the specter of it being a litmus test for immigrants with specific religious backgrounds (2009).

In the United Kingdom, the Nationality, Immigration, and Asylum Act of 2002 introduced integration tests to the domain of naturalization. Linguistic and civic education requirements became mandatory for immigrants wishing to obtain a long-term residence permit and to apply for naturalization. The basic premise is that immigrants have to "earn" their residence and thus their British citizenship—a premise reinforced by the Borders, Citizenship, and Immigration Act of 2009. The fault line of this new agenda is "the perceived incompatibility between British society and Muslim communities in which supposedly alien values are embedded" (Kundnani, 2007: 29). This agenda has blurred the distinction between immigrants and "tolerated" ethnic communities. An "integration contract" was introduced in France in 2003, integration being assessed in terms of sufficient knowledge of French and the principles that govern the Republic (such as equality between men and women, and secularism). Acceptance of this contract became compulsory in 2006, and was extended in 2007 to migrants' families (with courses on parents' rights and duties). Similar legislation was passed in many other European countries, officially justified in terms of promoting an ethnocentric conception of integration.

For those who support the shift toward assimilationism in Europe, multiculturalism has encouraged immigrants and minorities to separate themselves and live according to their own values, resulting in a lack of social cohesion and—ultimately—have helped foster the threat of homegrown terrorism. This means that "openness" is no longer viewed as strengthening integration (as defined by the state on the basis of security concerns) but rather encouraging societal dislocation—if not national balkanization, and thus should be restrained. The retreat of multiculturalism has been officially endorsed in statements made by several European leaders, such as German Chancellor Angela Merkel, British Prime Minister David Cameron, and former French President Nicolas Sarkozy. They have all accused the so-called multicultural model of being the main cause for residential segregation, low socio-economic integration, a lack of national identity, and inadequate community cohesion—although it is unclear whether, in doing so, they were referring to the same conception of multiculturalism. As Anna Triandafyllidou et al. noted, the concept of multiculturalism has become polysemic, a "portemanteau term" that encapsulates a variety of contested meanings (2012: 4). In France, official concerns relate to the protection of "Frenchness" defined in terms of secular values and principles. A good example of this phenomenon is provided by 2006 French legislation that introduced the notion of "defective assimilation" (*défaut d'assimilation*). This was defined as "values," "lifestyle," or the "radical practice" of a religion (such as wearing a hijab) that are incompatible with the essential principles of French society. In Germany, national identity is increasingly defined in terms of Christian heritage even though the government has never formally adopted a multicultural policy agenda. In Great Britain, the new identity politics has led to a "panicky retreat to a liberal public-private distinction," which is supposed to address issues of racism, segregation, and religious discrimination (Modood, 2009b).

What Should We Expect?

Concerns about the impact of security governance fuel an ongoing debate, one that has produced various theoretical and empirical studies that offer conflicting arguments and conclusions. Pessimists commonly assume that racial profiling and other exclusionary practices (such as surveillance, visa prohibitions, tougher immigration enforcement, excessive use of force, and "stops and searches") all increase the level of perceived discrimination. Immigrant perception of high levels of discrimination, in turn, supposedly fuels fears, anger, resentment, and a sense of relative alienation. These practices can generate social isolation, cultural estrangement, a heightened sense of political distrust, negative feelings toward the host society, and ultimately, separatism or radicalization.

Contributions by social psychologists suggest that discrepancies between migrants' acculturation attitudes and perceived attitudes of the majority group may negatively influence intergroup relations. The concordance model of acculturation and the belief congruence theory illustrates this trend. (Piontkowski et al., 2002; Rokeach, 1969). Annette Rohmann et al., for example, found that cultural discordance and contact discordance contributed to intergroup anxiety for host society members and immigrants, which in turn, fueled perceived symbolic threats. For immigrants, they noted, "the most threatening scenario is when they want to maintain their culture to a higher degree than they think is accepted by the host community" (2006: 686).

Another scenario includes the strengthening of boundaries between immigrants and natives who try to insulate themselves from future hostilities, a climate of fear that precludes collective engagement, and a weaker degree of civic participation (Garcia and Keyes, 2012). This scenario relates to the polarization of identities. A "reactive ethnicity" (Rumbaut, 2008) is typical of minority groups that have cultural characteristics perceived as oppositional to the culture of the majority. A related effect is the emergence of an "ethnic hierarchy" that reflects the increased social distance between majority and minority groups. The Dutch, for example, have an ethnic scale in mind when they think about the social acceptance of ethnic minorities in their country: Contacts with Spaniards are preferred over contacts with Surinamese, then Turks, and finally Moroccans (Hagendoorn and Pepels, 2003).

Prolonged integration problems are not just a menace for those who are discriminated against but also one for society at large. Timo Makkonen argues that in a worst-case scenario, "on the societal level, widespread discrimination triggers a vicious circle where the different forms of discrimination lead to the accumulation of material disadvantages on the part of the minority and immigrant groups, which increases social distance and reinforces stereotypes and negative attitudes, which then again increases the likelihood of discrimination" (2012: 88–89). A number of American scholars, in identifying this vicious circle, have pointed out that discrimination reduces the opportunities for immigrants and minorities to achieve social mobility and eventually leads to alienation (Stepick and Dunton Stepick, 2012; Gans, 2007; Portes et al., 2005; Schildkraut, 2005; Sizemore and Milner, 2004). In the same vein, a 2004 report of Amnesty International on the effects of racial profiling listed the "community-levels costs" of security governance in the United States. These include a fear and mistrust of the police, the alienation of minorities, a reinforcement of the segregation of minority communities, and emotional and psychological distress among victims (Amnesty International, 2004: 22).

There is relatively strong support among European scholars for the view that discriminatory practices lead immigrants and their children to perceive greater bias by both the majority group and public institutions. Their findings suggest that this hampers their integration into the society and fosters intergroup conflicts (Brenick et al., 2012; Kamans et al., 2009. Döring, 2007; Salentin, 2007). Studies on Muslims show that discrimination increases disaffection, social distance, and the risk of violent radicalization (Joppke, 2009; Sniderman and Hagendoorm, 2007; Philipps, 2006). Subsequent issues have been tentatively identified, such as the strengthening of group boundaries and increased prejudice among minority groups. In their analysis of perceived permeability of group boundaries, Ursula Piontkowski et al. noted that, "an assimilation attitude presupposes that members of the out-group find access to the dominant group. If there is no possibility for leaving one's group and becoming a member of the other group, staying separate is predetermined" (2000: 5). This trend fuels both suspicion among the dominant group about the motivation of migrants and resentment among minority groups. As Zick et al. (2001) have noted, attitudes of minority groups are also affected by prejudice. The assimilation orientation is more likely to be selected by those who tend to show less prejudice against the majority than those who preferred separation. Negative perceptions of natives thus undermine the acculturation process and increase opportunities for societal conflict (Barry and Grillo, 2003; Koopmans, 2003).

More optimistic scholars demonstrate that the majority of the members of migrant and minority groups—including Muslims in Europe—seek peaceful integration into the mainstream where they live despite encountering discrimination (Abbas, 2011 and 2007; Maxwell, 2010b; Nyiri, 2010; Brouard and Tiberj, 2008; Klausen, 2005). There is strong evidence to support the claim that most immigrants want to be part of the mainstream culture. A 2012 survey of non-EU-born immigrants conducted in 15 cities across seven member states found that large majorities wanted to become long-term residents and adapt to their respective host country. They prioritized speaking a common language as the most important factor in facilitating integration and were thus eager to improve their language proficiency. Immigrants expressed an eagerness to gain access to citizenship, and a greater interest in voting than the general population (ICS, 2012). This is also true in the United States: immigrants are learning English today faster than the previous waves who arrived at the beginning of the twentieth century. Their willingness to integrate has led to significant progress in various dimensions, such as socioeconomic attainment, political participation, and social interaction with host communities. The effects remain uneven. Hispanics, for example, have experienced very rapid improvements according to several socioeconomic indicators, but third and subsequent-generation Hispanics are still not matching the performance of their non-Hispanic, white counterparts. Yet, overall, the gap between immigrants and the rest of the society has narrowed over time in terms of educational performance, occupational status, wealth, and home ownership. Remarkably, Tomas Jiménez noted, "the progress has unfolded almost entirely without the help of policy intervention. With the exception of refugees, immigrants receive relatively little federal funding for integration programs." Notably, fears about immigrants' ability to integrate have not been assuaged, even though this laissez faire approach has been quite effective, and "even though immigration is a prominent part of the country's DNA" (2011: 1).

This brief review suggests that there is clearly no consensus about the effects of securitization on the perceptions and attitudes of immigrants and minorities. The optimistic and pessimistic perspectives differ widely in their evaluation of the effects of discrimination and alienation. These two options are examined in detail in the following chapters, including the possibility that securitization may result in a self-fulfilling prophecy: the effects of securitization may accentuate what is perceived as threatening on the part of immigrants and minorities (such as stronger ethnic identification and religiosity). In doing so, I analyze the effects of security governance on discrimination and intergroup relations, acculturation strategies and identificational integration.

CHAPTER 2

Securitization and Discrimination

The optimistic and pessimistic scenarios sketched out in the previous chapter differ widely in their evaluation of the effects of securitization on immigration and integration governance. The former focuses on discrimination as the main result of securitization, but forecasts that immigrants and minority groups can achieve integration despite facing prejudice and socioeconomic inequalities. The latter also assumes that security-driven measures increase discrimination, which leads to disintegration and potential radicalization. Neither of these scenarios, however, is explicit about the nature and scope of discrimination. The current debate among policymakers and scholars therefore raises more questions than it answers.

Focusing on three groups that are especially targeted by security-driven measures—Hispanics and Muslims in the United States, Muslims in Europe—I critically explore in this chapter the potential linkage between discrimination, alienation, and perception of the host society in two realms. The first relates to the relationship between objective discrimination (as measured by socioeconomic and political indicators) and subjective discrimination (as perceived by those who are discriminated against). The second involves the various effects of discrimination (both objective and subjective) on intergroup attitudes. As John Dovidio and Victoria Esses noted, "issues of immigration are fundamentally psychological" (2001: 377). Building upon the contribution of social psychologists, I argue that subjective discrimination plays a key role in the evolution of intergroup relations. I analyze data provided by numerous surveys and studies conducted over the last decade. These confirm that security-driven policies have had a strong negative impact: they fuel fear and resentment among all the selected groups.

Concerns about the effects of securitization, however, do not inevitably translate into high perception of discrimination and/or negative attitudes toward the host society and members of the dominant group. I provide evidence of crucial variations among groups and among countries—which paradoxically validate both the optimist and pessimist positions. Concerns about security governance do not always fuel a global sense of alienation and do not preclude the will to integrate into the host society; yet, resentment and distrust among the most targeted groups increase over time and are positively correlated with socioeconomic and cultural integration.

The Discrimination Conundrum

There is a large consensus among experts that immigrants and minorities suffer from objective discrimination. Socioeconomic indicators show that immigrant groups and minorities live in disproportionate numbers among the ranks of the unemployed, the underpaid, and the undereducated (Makkonen, 2012 and 2007). Mexicans, for example, are more likely than other immigrants to come to the United States with less education and with no ability to speak English. Once in the country, they are more likely to earn low incomes, lack health care, and have higher school dropout rates. Furthermore, Hispanics, as well as African Americans, are less likely than whites to receive a job offer (Bertrand and Mullainathan, 2004). There is a similar pattern in Europe. The children of Moroccan and Algerian immigrants suffer from unemployment rates at twice the national average in France (Silberman and Fournier, 2006). The impact of discrimination in the job market is felt in other areas such as housing and health. According to the EUMC, Muslims in Europe are "often disproportionately represented in areas with poor housing conditions, while their educational achievement falls below average" (EUMC, 2006b: 8). In Great Britain, findings from the census show that Muslim unemployment stood at 16 percent (compared to 4.7 percent nationally), 52 percent owned their own home (68 percent nationally), and 30 percent were considered to be in poor health, nearly double the national average.

Yet, when it comes to evaluating the impact of objective discrimination on immigrants' attitudes toward society at large, we are left facing a series of conflicting findings that should be treated with caution for at least four reasons. First, discrimination remains difficult to measure and evaluate despite the introduction of antiracist and antidiscrimination regulations. Existing evidence relies mostly on reported incidents, complaints, and court cases. Precise statistics are often not available, especially in Europe where states either do not have an adequate system to record incidents or do not properly implement EU Directives (HRF, 2008). Reputedly, 82 percent of those who were targets of discrimination did not report their experience, for example, across all groups surveyed by the EU Agency for Fundamental Rights (FRA) survey in 27 EU member states—up to 100 percent of Sub-Saharan Africans and 98 percent of Brazilians in Portugal (EU FRA MIDIS, 2009).

Second, data on participation rates in the labor market, educational attainments, or housing conditions are problematic as well. Muslims in Great Britain, for example, are on average three times more likely to be unemployed than the Christian majority and have the highest level of economic inactivity (OSI, 2004). Yet, it would be misleading to attribute this socioeconomic exclusion only to religious discrimination. Other related factors must be taken into account, such as level of education, language fluency, and other components of social capital. This begs a crucial question: Are immigrants and minorities discriminated against because of their race, their ethnicity, their religion, their level of education, their gender, or their culture? It is difficult to disentangle these factors because they are not mutually exclusive. Muslim African Americans, for example, appear to bear a double burden in that they face racial as well as religious discrimination. Furthermore, discriminatory factors vary across time. We can safely assume, for example, that discrimination based on linguistic abilities fades over successive generations while racial discrimination may prove more enduring.

Third, discrimination is multidimensional, with uneven levels in different spheres. For instance, a study conducted by the Open Society Institute (OSI) on Muslims in 11 European cities confirmed that these populations were not integrated into the mainstream labor market. Their level of educational achievement, however, varied. In some countries, Muslims achieved reasonable living standards once their socioeconomic background was taken into account (OSI, 2010). To complicate matters further, immigrants and minority groups do better sometimes than the general population in terms of employment and educational attainment. Asians in the United States, for example, are the most educated racial group, with a very high percentage having at least a college degree (44 percent compared with 27.5 percent for the general population) (US Department of Education, 2010). Societal indicators also show that there are significant variations among migrant and minority groups. On average, US Muslims perform much better than Hispanics in terms of employment and median income. In Great Britain, by contrast, Pakistani and Bangladeshi immigrants have higher levels of unemployment than other ethnic groups.

Finally, most studies focus on intergroup discrimination without considering the issue of intragroup discrimination. Immigrants entering the United States, Michael Jones-Correa argued, "might experience discrimination from a number of sources: from native-born white, from native-born blacks, from other immigrants, and not least from their native born co-ethnics. To assume that native-born whites are the sole source of discrimination is an oversimplification at best" (Jones-Correa, 2005: 86). Among Latinos who perceived "some type of discrimination," about 13 percent of the 2006 Latino National Survey (LNS) respondents said it was from another Latino. Intragroup discrimination involving various Muslim communities is widespread in many European countries. In France, for example, 61 percent of the perpetrators of assaults and threats are from the same ethnic group (compared with 12 percent from the majority population) (EU FRA, 2008). Tension between migrant groups also leads to violence. In Greece, for instance, migrants from the former Soviet Union report discrimination incidents more frequently than other groups. Yet, they report less Greek perpetrators (40 percent) than Albanian (79 percent) and Romanian (77 percent) ones (Marvakis et al., 2004).

Furthermore, the relationship between objective discrimination and perceived discrimination is complex, as illustrated by the conflicting findings generated by different theoretical approaches. From the standpoint of "integrated threat theory," the most common assumption is that both individuals and groups who are not part of the mainstream will perceive themselves to be the subject of a higher level of discrimination than those who are more integrated. Its proponents anticipate that newcomers (notably illegal immigrants) are more vulnerable to varied forms of discrimination and thus perceive discrimination more often than the majority population. Likewise, lower-status groups (as defined by income and education) are more likely than higher-status groups to perceive discrimination (Stephan et al., 2008).

However, according to proponents of the "contact hypothesis," immigrants who have more contact with natives are expected to perceive less in-group discrimination and be less likely to experience threat on the grounds that it leads to greater familiarity and understanding. Intergroup contact is supposed to increase with educational level: better-educated minority groups have more voluntary contact with the native population than lesser-educated ones. They thus feel more accepted and perceive less discrimination against them. These trends have been demonstrated by studies testing the contact hypothesis (André et al., 2010; Stephan et al., 2009; Pettigrew and Tropp,

2006; Snellman and Ekehammer, 2005; Verkuyten, 2005; Dovidio et al., 2003; Pettigrew, 1998).

Yet, countervailing studies have found that immigrant perceptions of discrimination increase over time. According to the "theory of exposure," for example, more educated immigrants are more likely to be aware of discriminatory practices. Education enables them to become more sophisticated critics of social inequalities and more sensitive to prejudice (Wodtke, 2012). Results of the 2006 LNS conducted by Michael Jones-Correa (2012) showed that perceptions of experiences of being treated unfairly increase from first-generation immigrants (28 percent) to later generations (44 percent for the second generation, 45.8 percent for the third, and 52 percent for the fourth). A similar trend is noticeable among other groups in the United States, confirming the relation between perceived discrimination and a greater sense of entitlement (Hirsch and Lyons, 2010). Studies conducted in Europe show that the higher the level of an immigrant's assimilation, the more they report perceived discrimination. The amount of perceived discrimination thus increases with the length of residence, better socioeconomic status (SES), educational attainment, and "well-being" (Jasinskaya-Lahti et al., 2006).

Variations in subjective perception of discrimination can be partially explained by any bias introduced by the language employed in surveys, and/or in sample selection. Furthermore, most studies do not clearly investigate the roots cause of perceived discrimination. Do immigrants feel discriminated against for reasons of race, ethnicity, religion, language, education, or income? Answers can vary from one group to another, as well as over time. When asked to evaluate discrimination based on religion, black Muslims are less likely to report intolerance than white Muslims do (42 percent and 61 percent respectively). Hispanics are increasingly aware of discrimination based on immigration status (up from 23 percent in 2007 to 36 percent in 2010) but they do not consider racial discrimination to be a major issue (Pew Hispanic Center, 2010). The FRA study found that one-third of Muslims reported experiencing discrimination based on ethnicity alone, while 10 percent identified religious discrimination alone. A plurality (43 percent) encountered discrimination on the grounds of both race and religion (EU FRA, 2008).

Another option is to deny, or at least minimize personal discrimination which, according to Crosby (1984 b), allows victims to maintain some positive illusions about themselves. This commonly leads to the so-called personal-group discrepancy, an ambivalent approach by which people perceive lower levels of personal discrimination than group discrimination (Kessler et al., 2000). A last typical behavioral response is the strategy of avoidance when the person concerned avoids situations in which the likelihood of discrimination is high (Tropp, 2003).

In order to examine the detailed effects of security governance as it relates to the impact of discrimination (both objective and perceived) on intergroup attitudes, most studies emphasize the importance of the identification process, both at the individual and group levels. There is an abundance of research in this field; yet, the results are often contradictory. Social identity theorists, for example, have argued that people who experience discrimination react to unfair treatment by increasing their feelings of identification with their in-group (Tajfel and Turner, 1986). According to the "uncertainty-identity theory," people can mitigate the effect of personal discrimination by identifying more strongly with the groups with whom they belong (Hogg, 2000). In line with this argument, studies based on the Rejection-Identity Model (RIM) have found that the individual level of rejection leads to higher levels of group identification—this identification having a positive impact on self-esteem (Schmitt and Branscombe, 2002). Some studies have expanded the RIM to the question of the perception of group discrimination. In some cases, they demonstrate the positive relationship between perceived discrimination and ethnic or religious identification that, in turn, can motivate minority groups to distance themselves from the values and norms of the host society (Chryssochoou and Lyons, 2010; Hogg et al., 2010). Perceived discrimination discourages immigrants from identifying with the majority group and results in a process of dis-identification, a development that may result in increased hostility toward the out-group (Jasinskaja-Lahti et al., 2009; Verkyuten, 2007; Berry et al., 2006).

Other studies show that discrimination (both at the group and personal levels) and identification are largely independent from each other (Cameron and Lalonde, 2001). According to Bourguignon and his colleagues in a study of African immigrants in Belgium, perceived group discrimination is positively related to self-esteem and can be protective for stigmatized people who may believe they are not alone in their plight. Yet, they found no relationship between perceived group discrimination and in-group identification. The seemingly disparate results might be partly explained by the variety of measures for self-identification used in existing studies. As noted by Bourguignon et al., "different facets or definitions of identification could in fact be differently related to discrimination" (2006: 785). Another explanation relates to the complexity of in-group identity that includes cultural, social, and religious dimensions. As noted by Inga Jasinskaja-Lahti and her colleagues, "the correlation between national and ethnic identity may be positive, negative, or zero, depending on the structure of the immigrant identity in the particular context" (2009: 109). In his analysis of political trust and satisfaction across successive generations in Europe, Rahsaan Maxwell found evidence that first-generation migrants are more likely than native and second-generation migrant-origin individuals to have positive views of their host societies. He argued that evaluations of the host society are shaped by subjective factors related to an individual's migration status: "Regardless of their difficulties, migrants will have positive evaluations about the host society institutions in comparison to natives who may have higher expectations" (2010b: 103). Therefore, other variables that should deserve attention relate to individual factors, such as a person's history of migration, whether they are native or not, their age, and legal status. It is worth noting that these variables can produce different outcomes depending on the group's size, status, and the nature and context of intergroup contact.

Furthermore, ethnic identification does not necessarily imply negative attitudes toward the majority group and may even be associated with more positive attitudes (Phinney et al., 2007). As Stephan et al. noted, "threats sometimes trigger positive behavior towards out-group members. Positive behaviors are likely to emerge when people are motivated to appear non-prejudiced and hence maintain a positive image of themselves or their in-group" (2009: 52). Research in the field of the common in-group identity model, for example, demonstrates that more favorable attitudes toward out-group members may be produced by shifting cognitive representations of membership (in both in-groups and out-groups) to a single inclusive social identity. As M. B. Brewer (2000) suggested, this process does not require each group to forsake its group identity because individuals can possess multiple identities while belonging simultaneously to several groups.

Finally, a growing body of research suggests that "successful socio-economic and cultural integration does not always lead to positive political or attitudinal integration" (Maxwell, 2010a: 31). This trend is illustrated by the "integration paradox." It describes the phenomenon whereby immigrants and minorities who are relatively well educated and successful on the labor market are more sensitive to prejudice. Thus, as Irene ten Teije and her colleagues argued in their study on immigrant groups in the Netherlands, "experiences and perception of non-acceptance and discrimination, despite successful integration in society, would make them turn away from the host society, for example by developing more negative attitudes toward the native population" (2013: 78). Researchers have emphasized varied dimensions in addressing this paradox, such as the effects of relative deprivation (Smith et al., 2011); the relationship between educational attainment; level of expectations; or negative attitudes toward the host society (Van Doorn et al., 2012; Martinovic et al., 2009; Van Tubergen and Van de Werfhorst, 2007). According to De Vroome et al., the negative relationship between levels of education and the perception about a host society can be explained by three factors. First, "the theory of exposure suggests that higher educated immigrants may actually experience more discrimination and lower subgroup respect in everyday life"; a second, "related argument is that higher education implies more cognitive sophistication, which can mean that higher educated immigrants are more aware of the lack of respect for immigrants in society;" and, third, "the theory of rising expectations suggests that higher educated immigrants tend to be more sensitive to (in)equality and respect by the majority population" (2013: 5). Alejandro Portes and Ruben Rambaut (2006) confirmed that in the United States, the more acculturated immigrants have high expectations and therefore have greater perceptions of discrimination. Antje Röder and Peter Mühlau demonstrated that low assimilation into the host society was linked to a higher trust level in institutions by testing the acculturation hypothesis. They argued that an immigrant's optimism stems from their lower expectations about institutional performance based on their experiences in their countries of origin. Yet, "the 'frame of reference effect' weakens over time and with increased acculturation in the country of residence" (2012: 777).

Securitization and Intergroup Relations in the United States

The current state of the literature illustrates the complexity of the interplay between perceived discrimination, identification, and attitudes toward the majority group. Perceptions of the host society can be evaluated in different ways, generating different findings. Attitudes toward the national out-group are mostly measured by social psychologists in terms of social interaction with out-group members—including the willingness to be friendly with out-group members (Liebkind et al., 2006). As Jan Pieter Van Oudenhoven and his colleagues argued, "social psychologists have too often developed and tested theoretical paradigms referring to isolated parts of intergroup relations whereas acculturation research has been very broad and in many cases largely descriptive" (2006: 645). Political scientists, by contrast, focus on varied dimensions of political participation, levels of trust in institutions, and social values—in order to test structural theories (such as the segmented assimilation view) and explain positive ("second-generation advantage") or negative ("generations-of-exclusion") outcomes (Portes and Rivas, 2011). They deal minimally with the psychological dimensions of integration.

We thus need to combine these various approaches in order to address three questions raised by the securitization of immigration governance: How does perceived discrimination translate into perceptions of the host society (in terms of values, institutions, and policies)? Does perceived discrimination actually create disenfranchised communities unwilling to adjust to the dominant values, customs, and ways of life? Does it increase a sense of alienation among targeted groups pushing them toward isolation? In addressing these questions, I utilize measures of attitudes toward the host society, employing various indicators such as "perception of society," "trust in institutions," "values compatibility," and "life satisfaction" developed by a variety of scholars. These relate to what Richard Alba and Victor Nee called "the immigrants' subjective world," including their "perceptions of society, perceptions of discrimination against their own group, and patterns of social relations within and beyond their respective ethnic community" (2003: 198). Four trends actually emerge, as summarized in table 2.1.

Table 2.1 Relation between perception of securitization, worry, perceived discrimination, and attitudes toward host society (by groups)

	Perception of securitization	Level of perceived group discrimination	Level of perceived personal discrimination	Attitudes toward the host society
Hispanics in the United States	Negative	High	Low	Positive
Muslims in the United States	Negative	Low	Low	Positive
Muslim immigrants in Europe	Negative	High	High	Positive
Second-generation (and more) Muslims in Europe	Negative	High	Low	Negative

Source: Author's own

Both foreign-born and native-born Hispanics and Muslims in the United States feel unfairly targeted by the securitization of immigration governance. Yet, their respective perception of discrimination differs significantly, notably among members of the first generation, although they all share a positive attitude toward the United States.

Hispanics are especially concerned about increased immigration enforcement, as illustrated by their negative evaluation of the 287(g) program, the Secure Communities program, and local initiatives (such as the Arizona law SB1070). Large majorities disapprove workplace raids (up to 76 percent), and criminal prosecution of illegal immigrants working without authorization (73 percent) (Pew Hispanic Center, 2008). The issue of deportation is the most important source of worry. According to a nationwide survey, 52 percent of Hispanic respondents say they worry "a lot" or "some" that they, a family member, or a close friend could be deported. Understandably, the most fearful are foreign-born respondents (68 percent) and, among them, those who are undocumented (84 percent). It is worth noting that 80 percent of the estimated 11.1 million illegal immigrants in the United States are of Hispanic origin. Concerns about deportation affect other categories as well, such as legal immigrants (71 percent), foreign-born citizens (58 percent), and native-born ones (32 percent) (Pew Hispanic Center, 2010). This can be explained by the fact the Hispanic population is becoming less immigrant-based. According to the 2010 census, 62 percent of Hispanics are native-born while approximately 85 percent of immigrant families are "mixed-status"—including citizens, legal, and illegal immigrants.

Other studies have confirmed that Hispanics, both those who are documented and those who are not, regard the increased enforcement of immigration laws that have occurred since 9/11 as fearful and discriminatory (Thronson, 2008; Adler, 2006; Hernandez, 2005). A study conducted by the University of Illinois at the local level in four US cities (Chicago, Houston, Los Angeles, and Phoenix) indicates that the increased involvement of police in immigration enforcement has significantly heightened fears among Hispanics. When asked to evaluate security-driven policies, 38 percent of respondents reported they felt like they are under more suspicion now that local authorities have become more involved (including 26 percent of US-born, 40 percent of foreign-born, and 58 percent of undocumented respondents). Additionally, 38 percent of all respondents said they were afraid to leave their homes (Theodore: 2013). A study conducted in the Phoenix metropolitan area identified interactions with border patrol and immigration enforcement officers as a major source of fears that, in turn, decreased trust in the local police (Menjivar and Bajarano, 2004).

Hispanics combined strong concerns about various aspects of security governance with high levels of perceived discrimination against them. In 2010, the Carnegie Corporation of New York (CCNY) conducted a survey among foreigners born of South Asian, East Asian, Middle Eastern, and Latin American (mostly Mexicans) heritage. The survey was completed through interviews with six focus groups in five cities (New York, Atlanta, Los Angeles, San Francisco, and Detroit). Table 2.2 summarizes the key findings related to perceived discrimination.

Hispanics in the United States tend to report higher levels of discrimination than other groups. As table 2.2 illustrates, 75 percent of Mexican immigrants believe that there is a "great deal" or "some" discrimination against immigrants in the United States. This view, by contrast, was held by only 62 percent of other immigrants. Furthermore, 73 percent believe they are discriminated as a group (compared to only 43 percent of all immigrants surveyed). These findings seem to contradict the assumption that first-generation immigrants are usually less likely than members of subsequent generations to believe that they suffer from high levels of discrimination. However, these findings should be treated with caution for at least two reasons: first, opinions vary according to the political context. Attention on whether Hispanics face unfair treatment has intensified since 2006, as illustrated by national controversies about the enactment of HR Bill 4437 in 2005 as well as other restrictive measures at the state level; national coverage of the 2006 street protests against Bill 4437, in which over five million people

Table 2.2 Levels of perceived discrimination in the United States (Q: Would you say that there is a great deal or some discrimination in the United States today against the following?)

(%)	All immigrants	Mexicans	Muslims
Immigrants	- great deal: 22 - some: 40 = 62	- great deal: 32 - some: 43 = 75	- great deal: 3 - some: 24 = 27
Immigrants from your birth country	- great deal: 15 - some: 28 = 43	- great deal: 34 - some: 39 = 73	- great deal: 4 - some: 16 = 20
You personally	- great deal: 9 - some:16 = 22	- great deal: 7 - some: 16 = 24	- great deal: 1 - some: 25 = 26

Source: Adapted from Carnegie Corporation/Public Agenda, 2010

participated, and national debates about the Development, Relief, and Education for Alien Minors (DREAM) Act, and other proposals designed to reform the immigration system. These events have reinforced the idea that immigration enforcement laws specifically target Hispanics. Other surveys confirm that Hispanics perceive themselves as the most discriminated group in the United States, a view shared by other ethnic groups. An Associated Press-Univision poll conducted in 2010 found that 61 percent of American respondents said that Hispanics face significant discrimination, compared with 58 percent who said blacks do (Fram, 2010).

Second, Hispanics are more likely to say that their group is discriminated against than to say they have personally been victims of discrimination. As table 2.2 indicates, the perception of personal discrimination is quite low among Mexican respondents (24 percent) and virtually the same as for other immigrants. This trend may relate to the "personal-group discrepancy" by which the number of personal discrimination cases reported is always inferior to the episodes of group discrimination. Another related, perhaps more plausible, explanation is that Hispanics, like the general population and other minority groups, tend to overestimate threats against their group while being fully aware of their actual level of personal insecurity. It is worth noting that Hispanics do not report an increase of personal discrimination, despite the strengthening of immigration enforcement. The 2008 National Survey of Latinos found that only 8 percent of native-born and 10 percent of foreign-born Hispanics reported that the police or other authorities have stopped them and asked about their immigration status (Pew Hispanic Center, 2008). About 49 percent said that Americans were less tolerant toward immigrants in the wake of the controversy over measures such as AZ SB1070, but only 5 percent of both native- and foreign-born respondents reported in 2010 that they had been stopped by police, questioning their immigration status (Pew Hispanic Center, 2010). This "personal insecurity" hypothesis is confirmed by surveys asking Hispanics to rank the issues that are personally most important to them. According to the Hispanic Federation, for example, 25 percent are personally concerned about "jobs and the economy," and 24 percent about "immigration reform." Only 10 percent mention discrimination, racism, and prejudice (Hispanic Federation, 2010).

Positive attitudes toward the United States are shared by large majorities of Hispanics, despite their high sensitivity to group discrimination. Fears generated by the increased involvement of police in immigration enforcement measures, as well as concerns about discrimination based on immigration status, do not translate into negative views of American society or suspicion toward the white population. Two-thirds of Hispanic immigrants (66 percent) say their group gets along with whites either "very" or "pretty" well. This figure is higher among second-generation Hispanics, of whom 81 percent say their group gets along very or pretty well with whites (Pew Research Center, 2013). Furthermore, Hispanics are deeply invested in the American dream. An overwhelming majority (87 percent) believe the opportunity to get ahead is better in the United States than in their country of origin or ancestry. Some 44 percent say that moral values are better in the United States than in their country of origin. Approximately 72 percent say the United States is also a better place for raising children (up to 81 percent for second-generation Hispanics), and 79 percent say that if they had to do it all over again, they would come to America (up to 87 percent for second-generation Hispanics) (Pew Research Center, 2013; Pew Hispanic Center, 2012b). These positive views have been stable for the last decade. In 2003, 80 percent of Mexican immigrants, for example, believed that the United States was a "unique country that stands for something special in the world"—with a legal system you can trust (81 percent), good health care (82 percent), and good education (70 percent) (Public Agenda, 2003). Hispanics, especially first-generation ones, tend to have more positive political and institutional attitudes than natives (Escobar, 2006; Wenzel, 2006; Michelson, 2003). Charles Weaver compared the attitudes of Mexican Americans and non-Hispanic whites toward 13 major social institutions in the United States. He found that the assumption that Mexican Americans lack trust in institutions had no basis and that they were, in many instances, more trustful than were non-Hispanic whites. He also demonstrated that feelings of being discriminated against had a negative impact on trust in people but had no significant effect on social trust (2006; 2003).

A large majority of Hispanics have a positive view of the United States, despite the negative effect of acculturation on those who are native-born, who tend to be less trusting than foreign-born. Their life satisfaction, for example, as well as the intent to remain in the country and acquire US citizenship, increase over time. Furthermore, Hispanics define the "American dream" in similar terms to those used by the general US population. Their life goals are having good paying and steady jobs, living in safe neighborhoods with high-quality schools for their children, enjoying basic freedoms, and to be treated fairly and respectfully by others. More importantly, the "Latino optimism for the attainability of the American dream" increases over time.

Second- and third-generation members are more aware of the barriers to upward mobility, and more sensitive to discriminatory practices. Alejandro Portes and Ruben Rumbaut, in their study of Hispanic integration, concluded that "the more educated, proficient in English, and informed immigrants are, the more critical their views and the greater their perceptions of discrimination...In other words, the more they come to understand American society as it actually is, including its various shortcomings and the lingering reality of discrimination" (2006: 198). They remain, nonetheless, more optimistic about their prospects for achieving the "Americano dream" than their American counterparts (Fraga et al., 2010: 39, 181).

A majority of American Muslims, like their Hispanic counterparts, feels extremely insecure, but the nature of their concerns differs slightly. In the aftermath of 9/11, the most severe measures "produced a very frightening world for Arab and Muslim Americans" who "lived with a lurking fear that any impropriety committed at any time in their lives might be brought forth to impugn them" (Cainkar, 2009: 3). By late 2003, mass arrests, special registration, and expedited deportations had ended but, since then, Muslims have been confronted with the issue of intolerance. There is little empirical evidence that foreign-born Muslims worry about the specific issue of deportation. Most studies and surveys focus exclusively on various aspects of Islamophobia and do not address issues of immigration enforcement—although 63 percent of Muslims in the United States are foreign-born. There is plentiful evidence, by contrast, that Muslims worry today about government surveillance, being singled out by security measures, and being harassed in public. At the local level, a 2003 study conducted by the New York City Commission on Human Rights (CCHR) found that 79 percent of respondents felt their lives have been negatively affected. "Many spoke of being scared, stared at, intimidated, fearful, alienated, depressed, uncomfortable, cautious, hurt, ridiculed, insecure, scrutinized, and emotionally stressed" (CCHR, 2003: 14). A study of Muslims in Phoenix (Arizona) found that the most common terms used to describe the change in their lives and in the community's collective self-image were "afraid," "scared," "being suspect," and "have to be careful." Up to 85 percent of respondents believed that 9/11 had a negative impact on their lives, and over 68 percent agreed that their civil rights were either less protected, or not protected at all since 9/11 (Ali, 2011). A 2011 nationwide study found that 55 percent of all American Muslims said it had become more difficult to be a Muslim in the United States since 9/11. A majority (52 percent) believed that security-driven policies single out Muslims for increased monitoring (up to 72 percent among African American Muslims). Experiences of intolerance were reported by pluralities, such as being treated with suspicion (28 percent), being called offensive names (22 percent), and singled out by airport security (21 percent) and by police (13 percent). It is worth noting that the perception of "being singled out" was very high among native-born Muslims (up to 71 percent compared to 41 percent among those who were foreign born), and increased with the level of education and income (Pew Research Center: 2011).

Unlike Hispanics, American Muslims express a relatively low level of perceived discrimination. As shown in table 2.2, Muslim respondents to the Carnegie Corporation of New York (CCNY) survey are less likely to perceive a "great deal" or "some" discrimination in the United States than other groups, both at the individual and group levels (20 percent and 27 percent respectively). These findings suggest that concerns about security-driven discriminatory practices do not translate into a more global sense of alienation. Minimally, three reasons can explain this puzzling trend. The first relates to the characteristics of the Muslim sample: they were all foreign-born respondents; 75 percent immigrated before 2001; and 43 percent came from Pakistan and the Middle East. This is an important point as other studies have confirmed that nativity, immigration experience, and generational status contribute to explaining variations in perceived discrimination (Halim, 2006; Haddad and Esposito, 2000). First-generation immigrants, who represent about 65 percent of the Muslim population, tend to be less sensitive to discrimination because they are "more prepared to accept difficult circumstances as the price to pay for moving into their chosen society" (Maxwell, 2010a: 30). This is consistent with the "frame of reference effect": they have lower expectations due to their lack of social capital, and thus tend to be more tolerant toward their host society. Findings from the Pew survey confirm that the belief that life has become more difficult for Muslims after 9/11 is shared by only 51 percent of those who are foreign-born (compared to 61 percent among native-born), and by 49 percent of those who arrived after 1990 (compared to 58 percent for those who came pre-1990 (Pew Research Center, 2011). However, what surveys rarely measure is the tendency to underreport feelings of discrimination by Muslim immigrants who may minimize the obstacles they have to face in order to maintain positive illusions about their future in their new host country. Furthermore, studies in Europe found that one of the reasons why Muslims did not report their experience of victimization was that they thought "it was too trivial, not worth reporting—which serves to highlight the 'normality' of victimization for many Muslims respondents" (EU FRA, 2009: 12). The same may be the case in the United States.

The second reason deals with the effect of different standards of comparison. Attitudes toward US society vary according to a migrant's levels of dissatisfaction with their homeland—which vary according to the region of origin. The 2011 Pew survey, for example, found that among foreign-born Muslims, those born in the Middle East and Pakistan are less likely than those born in South Asia to say they have been victims of discrimination (41 percent, 30 percent, and 51 percent respectively). Yet, majorities of foreign-born (68 percent) and native-born (62 percent) respondents agreed that life in the United States is better than in most Muslim countries—72 percent among South Asians who nonetheless express higher levels of perceived discrimination than other groups.

The third reason relates to the process of intergroup comparison in the evaluation of discrimination. American Muslims are nearly identical to the general US public in terms of education and household income, performing better than other groups in some categories. According to one Gallup study, 40 percent have a basic college degree or higher, which makes them the second most highly educated religious group after Jews. Muslim Americans are also more likely to report being employed than the general US population (70 percent and 64 percent respectively) and nonworking Muslims are more likely to be students (31 percent)—far higher than the general population (10 percent) (Gallup, 2009).

Like Hispanics, a majority of Muslims have a positive view of the United States. The Carnegie Corporation of New York study found that they embrace American ideals more than other groups. About 61 percent reported that they were "extremely happy" in the United States (compared with only 33 percent of other immigrants). A stunning 92 percent said the United States would be their permanent home, compared with 69 percent of other immigrants (CCNY: 2010). Nearly three-quarters of Muslims (74 percent) expressed faith in the American dream, saying that most people can achieve it through hard work (compared with 62 percent of the US public overall). In terms of their habits and hobbies, 48 percent watch professional or college sport (similar to Americans overall) and 44 percent display the flag (up to 50 percent among those who are foreign-born). The majority of foreign-born Muslims (58 percent) responded that American people are friendly toward them, including large majorities of those born in Pakistan, the Middle East, and North Africa (Pew Research Center, 2011).

Several studies confirm that US Muslims do not differ significantly from the general American public in their view of the importance of hard work, community health, and financial satisfaction (CAIR, 2006). Furthermore, American Muslims and Christians have very similar views on the importance of religion (Gallup, 2009; ARIS, 2008). As Matthew Neumeyer noted, "American Muslims are finding the American dream economically while European Muslims are not, forcing them to reconcile the ideals of Western prosperity and their plight" (2008: 36). On the less sanguine side, African American Muslims are slightly less enthusiastic about the American dream. When compared with other Muslims, they are the most acculturated. Yet, they are less educated, earn less, suffer more from spatial segregation, and express a strong sense of alienation combined with lower levels of trust. Only 20 percent of them, for example, believe that American people are friendly to Muslim Americans—compared to 37 percent among other native-born Muslims (Pew Research Center, 2011). In his study of the American mosque, Ihsan Bagby found that African American mosque-goers are the more critical of America, with 74 percent agreeing that "America is immoral" (compared with 35 percent among Muslim immigrants) and only 41 percent agreeing that "America is better" (compared with 61 percent for Muslim immigrants). However, Bagby pointed out that "alienation with American society is not necessarily an indication of hostility that might lead to extremism" (2009: 485).

Securitization and Intergroup Relations in Europe

Like Muslims in the United States, European Muslims constitute an extremely diverse group. Demographics and immigration patterns illustrate Muslim diversity in race, ethnicity, and socioeconomic status, as well as language and cultural traditions, and religious practices and beliefs. Muslims communities have lived in various parts of Europe for centuries (such as in Spain, Cyprus, the Baltic and Balkans regions). Most Muslims who currently live in Europe arrived during the 1960s, later joined by their families during the 1970s and 1980s. There are now second- and third-generation European-born Muslims who have acquired the citizenship of their country of birth—notably in the United Kingdom, France, Belgium, the Netherlands, and Sweden. Former colonial ties played a key role in settlement patterns. In France, for example, immigrants came from the former North African colonies and protectorates, while in the United Kingdom, immigrants came mainly from Pakistan and Bangladesh. Since the early 2000s, Southern European countries have received large number of new Muslim immigrants, nota-bly Albanians, Moroccans, and Sub-Saharan Africans, as well as those more recently forced to migrate because of the turmoil created by the "Arab Spring." The national origin of these groups often conceals a vari-ation of ethnic backgrounds. Muslims from Turkey include both Turks and Kurds, Moroccans include those with Arab and Berber heritage, and Pakistanis include Punjabis, Kashmiris, and Pathans. According to the EUMC's National Focal Point (NFP) reports, "the majority of Muslims in Europe are Sunnis, although there is also a small Shiite minority, as well as other strands, like Alevis and Sufis. There are also significant differences among Sunnis along ethnic lines, as there are several schools of law within Sunni Islam" (EUMC, 2006c: 24).

What Muslims in Europe share in common is that they feel under intense scrutiny and are treated as a suspect community. Majorities of Muslims express strong concerns about being targeted by security-driven policies such as restrictive border controls, police stops, and racial profil-ing. The EUMC, Eurobarometer, FRA, OSI, and Amnesty International have all conducted different surveys and pilot "discrimination studies." Although their findings are not directly comparable, they provide use-ful background information that assist in identifying major patterns. In 2008, experts from the FRA/EU-MIDIS interviewed North Africans (from Algeria, Egypt, Libya, Morocco, Sudan, Tunisia, and Western Sahara) in five European countries (Spain, France, Italy, the Netherlands, and Belgium). Respondents included immigrants and native-born (citi-zens and noncitizens), aged 16 to 55 years or more. Findings confirmed the intensity of police activity with regards to North Africans. About half of respondents, for example, reported having some contact with the police in the prior 12 months in France and Spain (and one in five in Spain was stopped more than ten times). In Italy, 31 percent were stopped once and 30 percent were stopped at least four times (EU FRA MIDIS, 2009). Another study conducted in 2010 looked at the frequency of police stops experiences by minority and majority respondents in ten European countries. Minority respondents were significantly more likely than majority respondents to be stopped by the police, such as in Spain where 81 percent of North Africans reported contact with the police when using public transport, compared with only 30 percent of majority respondents. Furthermore, majority respondents tended to state that the police were respectful toward them during a stop, whereas large plurali-ties of minority respondents indicated that the police were disrespectful (up to 35 percent of North African and 20 percent of Turkish respon-dents in Belgium) (EU FRA, 2010b).

The FRA study on immigrants and native-born people who identified themselves as Muslims in 14 EU member states confirmed the impact of racial profiling. On average, the police stopped 40 percent of Muslims in the prior 12 months, and 40 percent believed that this occurred because of their immigrant or minority status (up to 74 percent of Muslims in Italy, 72 percent in Spain, and 66 percent in France) (EU FRA, 2009). Large majorities also reported discriminatory treatment by immigration/border control personnel. The most targeted were reputedly North Africans living in Italy (79 percent) and France (76 percent) while about 50 percent of those living in Belgium were stopped as well (EU FRA, 2008). On average, 37 percent of Muslim respondents stopped by customs or border controls believed it was specifically because of their ethnic background (up to 86 percent in Italy and 81 percent in Spain). In comparison, 19 percent of non-Muslim minority respondents considered this to be the case (EU FRA 2009).

Reports at the national level confirm these trends. Muslims in the United Kingdom, for example, consistently report some form of hostility directed toward them, such as being singled out (the actual figures range from 20 to 38 percent), being the object of hostility (32 percent), and being the object of suspicion (42 percent) (Blick et al., 2006). On the organizational level, similar concerns are reported by Muslim-led organizations. According to the Muslim Council of Britain, for example, "Muslims in the United Kingdom feel particularly vulnerable, insecure, alienated, threatened, intimidated, marginalized, discriminated and vilified since the 11 September tragedy" (Mirza et al., 2007: 30).

Muslims in Europe express concerns about the direct effects of security measures, legislation, and policies restricting the wearing of religious or cultural symbols, and restrictions on the establishment of Muslim places of worship (Amnesty International, 2012). Muslims interviewed by EUMC representatives in 2006 expressed anger and frustration about official policies such as the ban on headscarves. According to the EUMC's report, "Although such a ban can be framed by the authorities in terms of a general ban on religious symbols, many Muslims feel it is targeted at them"—legitimizing discrimination in other areas such as employment (EUMC, 2006c: 9). Their experiences were particularly negative when related to antiterrorism policing. Members of Muslim organizations (both religious and nonreligious) reported "instances of police entering mosques wearing shoes, and with police dogs" (EU FRA, 2009: 55). In many countries, Muslims also felt unfairly treated by the justice system, arguing that security-driven actions were counterproductive and did not help to generate trust.

Table 2.3 Levels of perceived discrimination in Europe (Q: Is discrimination widespread? Very or fairly widespread)

(%)	Belgium	Spain	France	Italy	Netherlands
Ethnic discrimination	76	54	88	94	72
Religious discrimination	75	32	77	84	66

Source: Adapted from EU-MIDIS (2009)

Predictably, majorities of Muslims in Europe believe that widespread discrimination exists in their respective countries. Findings from the OSI survey showed that a total of 75 percent of Muslim respondents said there was "a lot" (30 percent) or "a fair amount" (45 percent) of ethnic/racial prejudice in the country they lived. About 80 percent believed that there was "a lot" (43 percent) or "a fair amount" (37 percent) of religious prejudice (OSI, 2010). North Africans surveyed by the EU-MIDIS experts expressed very high levels of group discrimination, with some variations across the five countries included in the study—as illustrated by table 2.3.

It is worth noting than European-born Muslims, collectively, are more likely to perceive high levels of group discrimination. According to the OSI, 34 percent of them felt that there was "a lot" of racial discrimination in the country in which they lived. By contrast, only 28 percent of Muslims born outside of Europe shared this belief. Whether someone is native-born also affects the likelihood that they will perceive religious prejudice. About 50 percent of European-born Muslims felt there was "a lot" of religious discrimination, compared with 39 percent of those born outside the EU. Muslim immigrants in Europe expressed lower levels of group discrimination when they compared their life in Europe with the situation in their country of origin. For example, those with negative experiences of police corruption in their countries of origin tend to have more trust in the police than those born in Europe. However, Muslim immigrants in Europe remain much more sensitive to group discrimination than foreign-born Muslims in the United States.

Like Hispanics in the United States, Muslims in Europe are more likely to say that their group is discriminated against than to report a high level of personal discrimination. This "personal group discrepancy" is illustrated by findings from EU and national studies. On average, 30 percent of Muslim respondents to the FRA study reported personal experiences of discriminatory treatment—compared to 51 percent who believed that group discrimination was "very" or "fairly" widespread (FRA, 2009). Findings from the OSI study illustrated a similar discrepancy between group discrimination (34 percent) and personal discrimination (16 percent) on the ground of ethnic profiling, as well as group perception (43 percent) and individual perception (51 percent) of religious prejudice (OSI, 2010). This trend has proven consistent over the last five years. Substantial majorities of Muslims living in Europe in 2006 said they have not personally had any bad experiences attributable to their race, ethnicity, or religion (Pew Research Center/Global Attitudes Project, 2006).

This trend can be partly explained by the overestimation of levels of group discrimination, such as in the case of Hispanics in the United States. The multiplication of controversies such as "headscarf affairs" and debates about the potential prejudicial effects of security policies, have focused the political and media attention on discrimination against Muslims in Europe. As a result, both Muslim and non-Muslim groups agree that religious discrimination is widespread—a belief shared by 70 percent of non-Muslim respondents to the OSI survey. Seventy-one percent of Muslims surveyed, and a similar proportion of the general population (70 percent), felt that there was either "a lot" or "a fair amount" of religious prejudice in the United Kingdom. Among all religious groups, 85 percent believed that prejudice against Muslims has increased (Communities and Local Government, 2010). Another explanation for the gap between experiences of personal discrimination and a perception of group discrimination relates to the underestimation of personal discrimination by respondents. For example, 38 percent of Muslims surveyed by the FRA indicated that their experience of victimization was so banal that it was not worth reporting (FRA, 2009). This "avoidance behavior" can be expected to lower the rate of personal discrimination experienced by Muslims. Another strategy consists of being "invisible," although most current studies show that wearing traditional/religious clothing only marginally affects the likelihood of encountering personal discrimination.

In the United States, foreign-born Muslims tend to report lower levels of personal discrimination than native-born ones. In Europe, by contrast, Muslim immigrants are more aware of prejudicial treatment than those born in Europe or those who have become citizens. According to an OSI study, 23 percent of Muslim males born outside the EU said they experienced religious discrimination "almost all the time" or "a lot of time"—compared with 21 percent of those born in the EU. Approximately 19 percent of Muslim immigrants reported experiences of racial discrimination, compared to 16 percent of those born in the EU. The moderating impact of citizenship is quite significant, particularly among men and among young people (aged between 16 and 24 years). For example, 41 percent of Muslim male noncitizens indicated they had experienced discrimination (both religious and ethnic) in contrast to 27 percent of Muslim male citizens. Among young people, 29 percent who are citizens and 48 percent who are not citizens experienced personal discrimination (FRA, 2009). Finally, among North Africans, 30 percent who are citizens express high levels of personal prejudice, compared to 43 percent of those who are not citizens (EU FRA MIDIS, 2009). Being born in Europe and having access to citizenship thus mitigates against discrimination at the individual level. Furthermore, the length of stay in the country for immigrants is correlated with a decreasing feeling of being personally discriminated against. On average, 26 percent of those who were in the country for more than 20 years experienced discrimination in contrast to 50 percent who were in the country for one to four years. This trend confirms the "contact hypothesis."

Yet, other findings illustrate that the "integration paradox"—the perception of personal discrimination tends to increase with higher levels of language proficiency, education, and income. Immigrants who are not fluent in the national language, for example, are the least likely to have encountered discrimination (28 percent) while 40 percent of those who are fluent and have a foreign accent reported personal experiences of discrimination. A high level of education may also run a higher risk of discrimination. People with five or fewer years of education are the least likely to report discrimination (16 percent) while those with 14 years or more express a high feeling of being discriminated against (40 percent) (EU FRA MEDIS, 2009). This trend tallies with findings from national studies. In Germany, for example, the Federal Ministry of Interior conducted a study on the feelings and attitudes of Muslims in 2007. The study showed more than 60 percent of Muslim students declared that, as foreigners, they had been discriminated against by the police or administrative agencies (compared to one-third of all non-Muslims). Furthermore, 43.2 percent of Muslim students felt rejected by the German population, which clearly illustrated the connection between linguistic-practical integration and the magnitude of personally experienced slights (FMI, 2007).

The integration paradox also plays a key role when it comes to evaluating the perception of host societies by Muslims. Muslims born outside the EU tend to express higher levels of personal discrimination than those born in the EU. But they remain quite positive toward their host societies and express higher levels of trust than members of the second and third generation (Röder and Mühlau, 2011). A study by Ulrich Wilamowitz-Moellendorff found, for example, that Turkish immigrants had strong trust in German democracy and German institutions although they perceived a significant degree of discrimination. He argued that, "experiences at the individual level do not impact negatively on attitudes at the level of society" (2001: 9). Rahsaan Maxwell (2010b) demonstrated that British Muslims were more likely than Christians to have high levels of trust in government—a sign of general political satisfaction that was higher among Muslim immigrants than Muslims born in Britain. By contrast, second- and third-generation Muslims have less positive feelings toward society and native majority despite the fact that they report lower levels of personal discrimination than "new comers" born outside the EU. According to the EUMC, "even when Muslims are citizens of a member State, they can still feel a sense of exclusion. They feel that they are perceived as 'foreigners' who are a threat to society and treated with suspicion . . . While the second and third generation are in many ways more integrated than the first, at the same time their expectations are greater and so the consequent exclusion is more keenly felt" (EUMC, 2006c: 7). As a result, they tend to trust institutions less than immigrants and non-Muslim native-born, as illustrated in table 2.4.

Furthermore, findings for various studies confirm that there appears to be a negative relationship between levels of education and trust in institutions. Muslims with no formal education have higher levels of trust than those with secondary education in relation to parliament (36.5 percent versus 28.4 percent), and government (37.5 percent versus 25.3 percent) (OSI, 2010). In Germany, data gathered by the Federal Ministry of Interior showed that "distance to democracy" and "distance to the rule of law" positively correlated with levels of education. Among the university students surveyed in Hamburg, Augsburg, Cologne, and

Table 2.4 Levels of trust (a lot and fair amount) in the police and parliament in Europe (breakdown by if native-born and whether Muslims)

%	Trust in the police	Trust in national Parliament
Muslims born outside the EU	57	36
Muslims born in the EU	51	25
Non-Muslims	60	41

Source: Adapted from OSI (2010)

Berlin, about 30 percent declared a moderate distance to democracy combined with a low willingness to accommodate, strong tendencies toward isolation, and high levels of religious prejudice against Jewish and Christians groups. The report identified three groups susceptible to radicalization: the well-educated Muslims who reported low levels of personal discrimination, but expressed empathy with "the position of Muslims in the world"; Muslims with little education who faced strong socioeconomic discrimination; and a tiny residual group including people with a traditional religious orientation (FMI, 2007).

Several factors are commonly listed in explaining the global disenchantment expressed by members of the second and third generation. The first relates to life satisfaction. Recent immigrants do not report different levels of life satisfaction compared to natives. However, feelings of well-being decrease after a few years of residence and remain low for a long time. Mirna Safi, for example, demonstrated that members of the second generation had a lower level of life satisfaction than natives with nonimmigrant parents. She argued that "no evidence is detected for the inter-generational hypothesis of assimilation" because perceived discrimination has a significant negative effect on the anticipation or the perception members of minority groups may have of their life chances (2010: 167). Furthermore, native-born Muslims get particularly frustrated by demands that they "integrate further" while they feel they have done all they can in that process. As the EUMC's report noted, "they feel although integration is a two-way process, yet the constant pressure on Muslims to integrate means that in practice only one side is emphasized" (EUMC, 2006c: 8). The pessimism of second- and third-generation Muslims comes from what they perceive to be unreasonable demands put on them, in addition to suffering from hostile government acts and media distortion. This trend is illustrated, for example, by what a French Muslim explained to the EUMC representative: "The second generation has been asked by society to integrate itself, and it's done this well. In many ways, we respect France more than native French people; but what else to they want? . . . We've probably done all we can. I've got qualifications, I work, I live like a normal French person, but I'm not sure I'm a Frenchman in the eyes of my compatriots" (EUMC, 2006c: 26). Haleh Afshar reported a similar sense of frustration and discouragement among British-born Muslims. What they had hoped, he wrote, "was to have found their own place in a multicultural Britain where communities could live side by side in harmony and mutual respect. But, in the context of an orchestrated sense of public crisis, as 'Muslims' they suddenly found themselves redefined in a one-dimensional notion of 'others' and the enemy within... In this context, it is unreasonable to demand them to 'conform' and be 'absorbed' in a community that fears and denigrates them" (2013: 22).

Negative attitudes toward the majority group are magnified by socioeconomic inequalities that affect the majority of Muslims in many European countries. Unlike most American Muslims—who shared the American dream—Muslims in Europe economically lag behind natives and some other ethnic/religious groups. Roxane Silberman et al. noted that "were the Maghrebins an immigrant group in the US, they would be identified as a group at risk of 'downward' assimilation and an instance of the value of the concept of segmented assimilation" (2007: 23). Even when Muslims reach the top of the social ladder, they are still partially excluded from full acceptance—as illustrated by the "beurgeoisie" whose members felt treated as "French in the second degree." As Jean Beaman explains, "only partial assimilation is possible for them," because they are denied cultural citizenship, "a claim to belonging that is accepted by others, that would enable children of North African immigrants to traverse the cultural/symbolic boundaries of French identity and be considered truly French" (2012: 48).

Implications

The positive perceptions of the host society expressed by a majority of those who are most targeted by securitization tend to validate the optimistic scenario. This is notably the case for the majority of both Hispanics and Muslims in the United States—and to a lesser extent Muslim immigrants in some European countries. The fears and resentment generated by immigration and counterterrorism policies since 9/11 have not been translated into high political distrust, rejection of the host society, and enmity according to a wealth of survey research. This finding contrasts with the expectations espoused by politicians, anti-migrant groups, and the popular press. Some scholars confirm these reassuring findings, noting, for instance, the rather limited impact of some measures, or the uneven actual implementation of anti-immigrant regulations at the local level (including Arizona where municipal officials are not so keen to chase after immigrants) (see Provine et al., 2012). Aristide Zolberg, for example, noted that "it is remarkable that despite the overwhelming support for tighter border control and significant inroads into the civil liberties of resident aliens, notwithstanding continuing pressure by dedicated restrictionists who argue that security considerations mandate a reduced intake... the United States refrained from severely tightening its immigration policy" (2006: 448). Martin Schain offers a similar conclusion: "defined in relation to a multicultural society after 1965, immigration policy has remained relatively open through good and bad economic times. The core of this policy has resisted nationalist challenges in the 1990s, and the more recent challenges of September 11 security" (2008b: 34). Research on threats and other forms of oppression reaches an equally optimistic conclusion from an alternative perspective. It reveals that a hostile environment can provide opportunities for immigrants to increase their sense of solidarity, collectively mobilize, and thus achieve full social citizenship in order to protect their interests (Okamoto, 2010; Almedia, 2003).

Yet, numerous findings nonetheless confirm the negative impact of the integration paradox which—mostly in the case of native-born Muslims in Europe—leads to negative perceptions, political and institutional distrust, and a strong sense of alienation. In the extreme, both advantaged and disadvantaged people can be vulnerable to feelings of relative deprivation when they perceive a discrepancy between their expectations and actual attainment. In his analysis of Islamic radicalism in Great Britain, for example, Tahir Abbas purportedly noted that "alienation and disenfranchisement are significant starting points, but a few of the so-called 'radical-jihadi' leaders have emerged from communities that are not necessarily poor—with some who are graduates and middle class" (2011: 128–129). Notably, the events of 7/7 were not the product of "unassimilated Muslim youth." In the United States, Major Nidal Malik Hasan (Fort Hood rampage, 2009) and the 2013 Boston bombers (Dzhokhar and Tamerlan Tsarnaev) were also relatively integrated. These findings support the proposition that the actual context of integration plays a key role in the processes of identification and subsequent behavior. I examine this question in the next chapter by focusing on two dimensions: What Western governments expect from immigrants and minorities when they design and implement security-driven policies of integration; and how those targeted as a potential "threat" react to suspicion and evaluate their degree of integration.

CHAPTER 3

Securitization and Integration

D o security-driven policies serve the goal of enhancing immigrant integration or do they act as a mechanism for exclusion? Does securitization enhance a sense of national belonging, and more importantly in the current context of "ontological insecurity," does it secure the loyalty of immigrants and natives born of foreign descent? Or does it push immigrants and their children toward separation, marginalization, and, ultimately, radicalization? In addressing these questions, I analyze the actual outcomes of securitization in the context of reception in various host societies. I argue that the paradox of the securitization of integration is that more integrative policies have been implemented (because of the fears raised by a lack of integration as a source of insecurity): yet these actually provided fewer opportunities to integrate (fuelling suspicion against immigrants and their descendants). Furthermore, the "integration paradox" suggests that the common indicators for integration (such as educational achievements, occupation, or ethnoracial and cultural factors) do not—and cannot—fully explain the behavior of those who are suspected of posing a threat. Targeted immigrants and minorities are not "passive agents" whose actions are determined by the host society context (e.g., immigration policies, treatment of illegal immigrants) and the societal context (e.g., institutional arrangements in education, the labor market, housing, religion, and legislation). They are also "active agents" and reactive to the current context of suspicion and prejudice. I thus advocate an approach that expands to examine how migrants and their children define and perceive their own level of integration in the current context of securitization. Variables measuring self-perceptions of integration by targeted groups should include their self-identification and sense of belonging; sense of empowerment; and sociability and organizational membership. Comparing *objective* integration (from the state's perspective), *subjective* integration (from migrants'/minorities' perspective), and the relationship between the two provides a better understanding of complex behavioral trends.

Concerns over the Retreat from Multiculturalism

It remains to be seen whether the retreat of multiculturalism will solve the issues of socioeconomic inequality and residential segregation—and thus will effectively address the root causes of "disintegration." Conversely, it generates concern as to whether the securitization of integration is not aggravating the problems that it is supposed to solve. Opponents to the retreat of multiculturalism argue that policies based on fears of disintegration actually run counter to the so-called promotion of integration. As Ricky van Oers et al. noted, "multiculturalism and the politics of recognition have been superseded by a model of integration that shifts the attention away from issues such as equal treatment, non-discrimination and social inclusion toward conditional sociopolitical membership, the preservation of core national norms and values and towards social cohesion" (2010: 4). Other scholars have suggested that integration policies in Europe are "turning into a legislative duty for the immigrants, not a natural result of their participation in society" (Bodemann, and Yurdakul, 2006: 5). Hence, "the focus of integration policy is no longer on the equalization of opportunity, but rather on the discouragement and penalization of migrants who do not possess certain attributes" (Ryan, 2008: 312). Ralph Grillo has identified a "backlash against diversity" that combines "disenchantment with multiculturalism, concerns about social cohesion, and, not least, about Islam" (2005:8). According to van Oers et al., this reflects a "certain ideological configuration which associates foreignness with 'objective deficiencies' in need of remedy" (2010: 7). In that same vein, Anna Triandafyllidou et al. argued that "the upsurge of international terrorism during the past decade and the global financial crisis of the last couple of years have provided fruitful ground for the securitization of migration and integration agendas, one the one hand, and the condemnation of previous 'multicultural integration' approaches as harmful to social cohesion on the other" (2012: 1).

A few empirical studies have tested some of the main arguments that justify the retreat of multiculturalism. First, there is no evidence to support the proposition that policies of "cultural recognition" undermine social inclusion and political engagement. Matthew Wright and Irene Bloemraad convincingly demonstrated that "the claim that multiculturalism undermines immigrants' socio-political integration appears largely without foundation" (2012: 77). Using data from the ESS (2002–2008) and the US Citizenship, Involvement, Democracy survey (2005), they found no evidence that immigrants in countries with stronger policies of cultural recognition are less attached to the political community. They concluded that "the most important rationale for the political backlash against multicultural policies appeared unfounded empirically" (Ibid: 88). Other cross-national studies reached the same conclusion (Bloemraad, 2011; Koopmans et al., 2005). According to John Mollenkopf and Jennifer Hochschild, the obvious counterargument to the claim that multicultural policies preclude integration is provided by a comparison between Europe and the United States— where immigrant political incorporation occurs more rapidly. Two of the explanatory factors they suggested relate to the "openness" of the US system. First, naturalization laws for legal immigrants have been less stringent and complicated than in most European states, resulting in higher rates of naturalization. Second, "Americans' long history of racial discrimination may, ironically, now make it easier to incorporate immigrants" because "American immigrants' children have found a way to benefit from affirmative action mechanisms set up decades ago to help native born minorities to attain higher education or training for some public service jobs" (2010: 27). In contrast, immigrants in Europe suffer from a lack of robust affirmative action laws, minority advocacy groups, and a variety of organizational strategies intended to mitigate the effects of discrimination. Jack Citrin et al. (2001), in their study of the meaning of national identity, found that the US liberal theory of national identity has not lead to "ethnic balkanization" in America. Rather, levels of chauvinism, patriotism, and pride were strikingly similar among blacks, whites, Asians, and Hispanics.

Second, there is no evidence that multiculturalism has increased the level of incompatibility between national, ethnic, and religious identities. Several studies have demonstrated that ethnic and national identities are not seen by immigrants as incompatible (Chryssochoou and Lyons, 2010; Verkuyten and Thijs, 2002). In the United States, findings from the 1996 GSS national survey showed that "national and ethnic identities tend subjectively to be experienced as complementary rather than competing" (Citrin et al., 2001: 86). In France, Colette Sabatier investigated the identification process among second-generation adolescents from five distinct ethnic backgrounds. She found that ethnic and national identity affirmations were independent, whereas relationship with parents and perceived discrimination reflected the dynamics of acculturation among immigrant families (2008). At the European level, Kathleen Dowley and Brian Silver relied on the 2006 European Social Survey in 21 countries in studying support for the EU among ethnic, religious, and immigrant minorities. They found that minority populations were nearly universally more likely to favor a further integration of Europe than majorities. The support for continued European integration was strongest among Muslims despite tensions between "visible and practicing Muslims and increasingly secular and security concerned Europe" (2011: 333).

Third, the focus on language proficiency as an incentive for migrants to adjust to the dominant culture of the receiving society is based on a confusion between socioeconomic integration and cultural integration. Evidence suggests that there indeed exists a positive relation between acculturation and economic benefits. Speaking the language of the destination country has a positive effect on integration. Yet, the linguistic tests for newcomers have produced uneven results. High failure rates were noticeable in some countries, such as Germany where 50 percent in 2008 did not reached level B1—a requisite for permanent residence and naturalization. In Denmark, the requirements of language competencies at level 3 barred most non-Europeans from gaining citizenship. Large majorities passed the test in other countries but the results were biased to some extent by the characteristics of the candidates. In France, for example, only 25 percent failed the test in 2008, explicable by the fact that the majority of candidates originate from former French colonies in North Africa and thus have a high level of proficiency. Yet, given that these Maghrebis are not socioeconomically integrated well, the effectiveness of using a linguistic test as a barometer of integration is questionable. Ricky van Oers, in his comparative study of the effects of these tests, convincingly argued that "the idea that knowledge of language and society is a reflection of someone's integration has become generally accepted. It is, however, at least questionable whether conclusions regarding someone's integration can be drawn from her test results" (2010: 103). By contrast, as Arend Odé and Justus Veenman (2003) noted, more culturally and socially integrated minority groups are not always socioeconomically better off because there is no causality between the ethnocultural position and the socioeconomic position. Immigrant and minority socioeconomic and sociopolitical integration are not parallel processes. They may occur independently, or even have an inverse relationship with each other. Certain minority groups may have full citizenship rights, but remain located by the majority group outside the national community—which suggests that the relationship between citizenship, (self) identification, and national belonging is complex, not straightforward.

The fourth aspect relates to the decline of naturalization rates (in absolute terms) in some countries where linguistic and civic tests have been used as an efficient mechanism for controlling immigration, in addition to other restrictive measures. In Austria, for example, naturalization was made dependent on ten years of legal settlement by the 2006 Nationality Act. The naturalization of foreigners married to Austrians was made dependent on six years of uninterrupted legal residence, and processing and filing fees were considerably raised. As a result, naturalizations dropped by 46.5 percent in 2007. The interaction between citizenship policies and naturalization rates is admittedly a complex one. Other factors than naturalization laws play a key role, such as conditions in the country of residence, those in the country of origin, and individual characteristics of the immigrants. Utilizing several citizenship policy indexes, many researchers have nonetheless found a positive and significant correlation between naturalization policies and the behavior of potential applicants. Eurostat's bivariate analysis, for example, found that naturalization policies explain 50 percent of the variation in member states' naturalization rates (European Commission, 2013: 24). Other scholars provided evidence that stricter naturalization regimes hinder naturalization that, in turn, negatively affects an immigrant's sense of membership in their adoptive nation (Dronkers and Vink, 2012; Sartori, 2011; Reichel, 2011).

The Clash of Expectations

The perspective of immigrants and minority groups on the securitization of integration should be additionally considered, by drawing on a range of studies that emphasize both the changes in context of reception and the behavioral responses to these changes. Building upon the contribution of acculturation theory, we may wonder if a "clash of expectations" is currently damaging the relationship between immigrants and differing components of receiving societies.

Acculturation research identifies two central dimensions that determine not only the level, but also the quality of integration: cultural maintenance (the degree of cultural identity manifested by each group); and contact and participation (the degree of intergroup contact and the resultant participation of each group with each other) (Berry, 2001, 1997). These two central dimensions, in turn, define four strategies based on the expectations expressed by majority and minority

Table 3.1 Acculturation expectations and strategies

	Majority's strategies toward minority	Minority's acculturation strategies
Integration (inclusive pluralism)	- Willingness to allow minorities to participate - Acceptance of immigrants' retention of their original culture	- Wish to participate in the society at large - Wish to maintain their original culture
Assimilation (inclusive monism)	- Willingness to allow minorities to participate - Pressure on minorities to abandon their original culture	- Wish to participate in the society at large - No wish to maintain their original culture
Separation (exclusive pluralism)	- Unwillingness to allow minorities to participate - Acceptance of minorities' cultural autonomy	- Wish to avoid interaction with other groups - Wish to maintain their original culture
Marginalization (exclusive monism)	- Unwillingness to allow minorities to participate - Pressure on minorities to abandon their original cultural	- Wish to avoid interaction with other groups - No wish to maintain their original culture

Source: Adapted from Berry (2001) and Zick et al. (2011)

groups. As table 3.1 illustrates, the *integration* strategy is expressed by the receiving society in its acceptance of immigrants' retention of their original culture and willingness to allow them to participate. This strategy is supported by immigrants when they have an interest in both maintaining their cultural identity and engaging in interactions with other groups. If the members of the dominant group make participation conditional on immigrants' abandoning their original culture, what they are striving for is *assimilation*; whereas the opposite strategy (conceding cultural autonomy but refusing participation) leads to *separation*. From the immigrants' perspective, assimilation signifies a wish to join the mainstream by abandoning their original culture. By contrast, separation means that immigrants want to maintain their cultural identity as well as avoid interaction with others. If a society neither allows immigrants to maintain their original culture nor to participate in the society, the outcome is *marginalization*. This strategy, from the immigrants' perspective, is often the result of little interest (or possibility) in cultural maintenance and little interest (mostly for reasons of exclusion and discrimination) in having relations with other groups.

The respective strategies preferred by the dominant group and by minority groups may or may not coincide. The "best case" scenario relates to mutual accommodation, especially if integration is the strategy pursued on both sides. This strategy, John Berry argued, "requires immigrants to adopt the basic values of the receiving society, and at the same time the receiving society must be prepared to adapt national institutions (e.g., education, health, justice, labor) to better meet the needs of all groups now living together in the larger plural society" (2001: 619). Berry added other preconditions, such as the widespread acceptance of the value to a society of cultural diversity (e.g., multiculturalism); low levels of prejudice; positive mutual attitudes among cultural groups; and a sense of attachment to (or identification with) the larger society by all groups. The importance of mutual accommodation has been stressed by several scholars including Bourhis et al. (1997), van Oudenhoven et al. (2006), and Zick et al. (2011). The "worst case scenario," by contrast, relates to mismatches between what immigrants want and what members of the dominant group expect from them. "When the dominant group enforces certain norms of acculturation," Berry noted, "or constrains the choices of non-dominant groups or individuals," then "it becomes like a Pressure Cooker" (1997: 10).

It is clear from the research based on the current securitization climate that the acculturation expectations of receiving societies have changed dramatically in Europe, and to a lesser extent in the United States—where no official "retreat of multiculturalism" has been promoted on the top of the agenda. Integration remains the dominant trend, despite some tentative moves toward imposing assimilation on immigrants and their children. The ability to speak English, a key component of traditional Americanism, is not an ethnocentric criterion. According to Citrin et al., "this is an achieved rather than an ascribed trait. In fact, language minorities and foreign-born residents are as likely as white or black Americans to emphasize the linguistic criterion for national identity." Furthermore, while a majority (58 percent) of US natives favor the maintenance of cultural diversity, there is simultaneously considerable confidence about the prospects for assimilation. Many Americans "may seem to feel that assimilation and maintaining connection to one's ethnic heritage are mutually compatible" (2001: 82). Findings from the 21st Century Americanism survey conducted in 2004 showed that 97 percent of US respondents believed in "respecting other people's cultural differences" and 93 percent believed that "seeing people of all backgrounds as American should rank high in making someone a true American" (Jiménez, 2011; Schildkraut, 2007). In Europe, by contrast, there is an increased discrepancy in terms of acculturation between natives and immigrants. In their study of the acculturation strategies of nonimmigrants in eight European countries, Andreas Zick and his colleagues found that majorities or large pluralities of respondents chose integration (defined as "immigrants should maintain their own culture and also adopt the country's culture"). This attitude was held by more than 50 percent of respondents in Portugal and Great Britain (55 and 54 respectively); about half in Italy and the Netherlands; 42 percent in France; and 38 percent in Germany. Considerably fewer respondents called for immigrants to assimilate by abandoning their original culture (between one-third and one-quarter in the Netherlands, Great Britain, Germany, and France; only 20 percent in Portugal; 18 percent in Italy; and 15 percent in Poland) (2011: 108).

Should we assume from these findings that the assimilationist policies implemented in the name of security weakly translate into assimilationist expectations from members of the dominant group? The study actually included several caveats that preclude jumping to any conclusion. First, respondents often vacillated between integration and assimilation when multiple responses were permitted, and many respondents called for separation (defined as immigrants should maintain their culture of origin and not mix it with the country's culture). This form of separation was supported, for example, by 43 percent of respondents in France and by about one-third in Germany and Italy. Second, respondents who supported assimilation or separation were more likely to express prejudice toward minority groups. On the question of future relations with immigrants, only one-third of respondents were optimistic. The British and Portuguese respondents were more pessimistic (more than 40 percent). Zick et al. also found that those who predicted a deterioration of relations tended more strongly toward prejudice against minorities (Ibid: 114). Finally, the willingness to grant immigrants the rights for participating in society (such as access to citizenship and the right to vote) was rather limited. Large pluralities (about 45 percent overall) of respondents opposed general voting rights (up to 55 percent in Italy), as well as the idea of making naturalization easier for long-term residents (Ibid: 112). Other findings illustrated that the members of the majority group in various countries wanted to distance themselves from immigrants. Forty-one percent of all European respondents, for example, said they would not send their child to a school where a majority of the pupils are immigrants (up to 55.6 percent in the Netherlands); and 49 percent would prefer not to move to an area where many immigrants live (Ibid: 116).

Studies conducted at the national level have confirmed that accultura-tion preferences from receiving societies are moving toward assimilation (as related to ethnocentrism) or separation (in order to facilitate sending immigrants back to their home countries). In Germany, Andreas Zick et al. identified a preference for assimilation among nationals. They argued that, "as further evidence of ethnocentrism, this preference is related directly to their prejudice which is connected to ideologies about the subjectively assumed 'best way' that minorities should relate to the culture of the dominant majority" (2001: 542). Dalia Mogahed and Zsolt Nyiri, in their analysis of data provided by a Gallup survey conducted in three European cities (Paris, London, and Berlin) found that assimilation was seen by members of receiving societies as a vital defense against the "threat" posed by Muslims (2007).

In contrast to host society members who generally prefer assimila-tion or separation, immigrants have adopted integration as their favorite acculturation strategy. Studies conducted in the Netherlands, as well as in Germany and Finland, showed that large majorities of immigrants preferred integration, followed either by separation or assimilation (Jasinskaja-Lahti et al., 2003; Zagefka and Brown, 2002). Some studies reported variation of strategies across life domains. Immigrants favored multiculturalism more than natives, and preferred cultural mainte-nance in private domains more than in public ones. This distinction illustrates the bidimensional nature of acculturation: increased iden-tification with one culture in one sphere does not necessarily required decreasing identification with another culture in another sphere. As Arends-Tóth and van de Vijver suggested, "cultural maintenance and adaptation to the larger society are relatively independent options that do not exclude each other" (2003: 263). Mirna Safi, in her study of the immigrant integration process in France, found interesting variations among immigrant groups. Turkish immigrants have been following a "cultural pluralist" strategy in which the attachment to the commu-nity is a means of becoming socioeconomically integrated into French society through active networks and civic organizations. North African immigrants have become more assimilated. They are more likely than other groups to intermarry, apply for naturalization, and be involved in civic organizations. Their French linguistic skills are also superior to Turkish or Asian immigrants. Yet, they are perceived as being reluc-tant to assimilate by French natives while suffering from downward social mobility. Portuguese immigrants, by contrast, are perceived as being extremely assimilated although they tend to express "identitary resistance despite their high integration level in several other areas.

Portuguese immigrants remain strongly attached to their country of origin, staunchly refusing to seek French naturalization (76 percent have taken no steps in this direction)" (2008: 25). These findings illustrate the complexity of the integration process: those who are perceived as "well integrated" may not have a strong sense of national belonging, while those who are suspected of being a "threat" may actually express a strong attachment to their host society.

Aspects of Identificational Integration

Integration trajectories involve functional and cognitive aspects. Functional aspects relate to the extent to which individuals participate in the major institutions of a society, mostly through education, work, and political participation. Cognitive aspects involve self-identification and collective identity, as well as feelings of belonging and loyalty (Engbersen, 2003). These cognitive aspects relate to the context of reception through the notion of social capital, a "centrally important, disturbingly opened, and ubiquitous notion" (Kay and Johnston, 2007: 17) that is used to describe networks of affiliation, or the psychological orientations that stem from affiliation, or both (Bjørnskvo, 2006; Putnam, 1995). Social capital thus includes solidarity, social trust, civic engagement, reciprocity, as well as other forms of capital (such as human capital). Various trends have been identified by scholars who applied the concept of social capital to the integration of migrant and minority groups. According to Meindert Fennema and Jean Tillie (2001,1999), differences in political participation of ethnic minorities are linked to differences in "civic community" defined as the level of "ethnic social capital" reached by minority groups through participation in ethnic associational life. Jean Tillie (2004) emphasized the role of the interaction between individual and group level social capital in order to explain various degrees of political participation of ethnic citizens. Social capital is also invoked to explain educational achievements among immigrants and minority groups, access to employment, involvement in social activities, and the development of ethnic business enclaves.

Another common proposition is to emphasize the dual aspect of social capital that can be either inclusive (bridging) or exclusive (bonding). Bridging social capital promotes solidarity and reciprocity by uniting different social and/or ethnic groups (as illustrated by the civil rights movement, ecumenical religious organizations, and multiethnic communities). Bonding social capital refers to exclusive organizations and networks that bond their members together but isolate them from others. It is worth noting that bonding social capital is not the preserve of the dominant group as it can also include, for example, ethnic fraternal organizations and ethnic business enclaves (Portes, 1998). Yet, when immigrants and minorities focus on bonding (instead of bridging to the surrounding society), it often raises concerns about national cohesion and the alleged "clash of civilizations." In many European countries, "bridging has thus become the primary object of government policy, urging immigrants to become 'good citizens' and preventing the formation of minority groups that might turn their backs on society" (Scholten and Holzhacker, 2009: 82).

Building upon these studies, I identify several potential effects of securitization on individual and collective identification, group consciousness, and sense of national belonging. First, it is commonly assumed that the effects of securitization fuel a strong sense of commonality and thus reinforce group consciousness among Hispanics in the United States, as well as Muslims in the United States and Europe. According to Dennis Chong and Reuel Rogers, "group identification refers to an individual's sense of belonging or attachment to a social group. Group consciousness, in contrast, combines basic in-group identification with a set of beliefs about the group's status and alternative means to improving it" (2005: 47). As noted by Matt Baretto and his colleagues in their study of Muslim Americans, "it is possible that common experiences with discrimination, feelings of alienation from government in the US, and shared religiosity lead to the formation of group identity for this population similar to other pan-ethnic communities such as Asians or Latinos" (2008: 1). There are, however, other options (that may not be exclusive). The identification process can be transnational when immigrant experience involves maintaining cultural, economic, and social ties with the homeland. At the individual level, strategies of acculturation are also available, such as a distancing from in-group membership or opting for bicultural forms of identity integration.

Second, it is commonly assumed that targeted groups have only two options in the current context of securitization: either to prove their loyalty by embracing national values (sometimes to the detriment of their ethnic/religious identity) or to choose segregation as a way to protect themselves against discrimination. Most studies inspired by the rejection-identification model assumed that ethnic-based rejection is associated with stronger identification with ethnic groupness while there has been some disagreement about the causal relationship between ethnic identification and national identification. Some scholars argue that ethnic identification is inversely related to national identification (Armenta and Hunt, 2009) but others provide evidence that ethnic groups do not always identify less with the host country (Gong, 2007).

Since 9/11, debates on both sides of the Atlantic have focused on concerns about the potential relationship between ethnic and/or religious identification, national identification, and loyalty. It is thus important to evaluate the role played by ethnic, religious, and national identities in the processes involved in the incorporation into the national polity. In doing so, key aspects of "subjective integration" should be included, such as subjective social status (Kelley and Kelley, 2009), and self-esteem (Cihangir et al., 2010; Cassidy et al., 2004; Mayor et al., 2003). What matters here is people's subjective belief that they are moving up or down in the host society. It is commonly objectively measured by intergenerational mobility, but subjective scales also play a key role in the integration process (Robins et al., 2001; Bagley et al., 1979). For each group selected in the United States and Europe, I thus analyzed three sequential trends: the effect of discrimination on self-identification and group consciousness; the impact of group consciousness and self-identification on national identification; and the relation between national identification and naturalization rates.

Security, Identity and Loyalty in the United States

In the case of Muslims and Hispanics in the United States, there is some evidence that speaks to the question of how compatible ethnic, religious, and national identifications actually are. First, perceptions of discrimination do not automatically translate into a negative view of the United States, as analyzed in the previous chapter. Hispanic and Muslim immigrants are extremely positive about the "American dream" and remain optimistic about their ability to achieve it. Second, as illustrated in table 3.2, there is no trade-off between blending into American society and maintaining a strong minority group identity.

Table 3.2 Major identification trends among Hispanics and Muslims in the United States

	Religious/ethnic identification	Group consciousness	National identification	Naturalization rate
Hispanics	High	Low	High	Low
Muslims	High	High	High	High

Source: Author's own

In their study of group identity among Muslim Americans, Matt Barreto and his colleagues demonstrated that Muslims were able to combine an extreme social diversity (in terms of origins, traditions, languages, and political beliefs), a high degree of group consciousness (mostly fuelled by perceptions of discrimination), and a resilient national identification (despite discrimination). About 44 percent of the respondents felt they shared a "great deal" in common with other Muslims, and 43 percent a "fair amount," while only 11 percent said "only a little." The impact of securitization was illustrated by responses to a question on "linked fate": 67 percent strongly agreed that their individual fate was linked with other Muslims. This suggests that "as Muslims become integrated into American society, they begin to view themselves as a distinct group and are more aware of their minority status, and shared commonality with other fellow Muslims" (2008: 19).

A high sense of commonality is thus part of the Americanization process, and does not preclude a high sense of national belonging. When asked how strongly they identified with various groups (such as the United States, ethnic background, religion, or religious community), American Muslims most identified with the United States (69 percent), followed by their religion (65 percent), and their ethnic background (60 percent) (Gallup, 2011). Findings from the Muslim American Public Opinion Survey (MAPOS) confirmed these trends. A large majority of Muslim respondents said their fate was linked to what happens to other Muslims in the United States—leading to a "great deal" (44 percent) or a "fair amount" (43 percent) of commonality with other US Muslims. Most respondents (about 65 percent), however, believed that the teachings of Islam do not conflict with participation in the American political system (Dana, 2011).

Like Muslims, Hispanics express a strong sense of ethnic identification. However, this identification is based on their countries of origin rather than group commonality. According to a 2012 Pew survey, 51 percent identified themselves by their family's country of origin. More said that they have different cultures (69 percent) than said they shared a common culture (29 percent). As a result, only 24 percent defined themselves by using a pan-ethnic label (Hispanic or Latino). This pan-ethnic identification decreased across generations, from 28 percent among first-generation members to 21 percent among third- and higher-generation members (Pew Hispanic Center, 2012b). These findings are consistent with other studies. As noted by Luis Fraga and his colleagues, "while Latinos largely share a common language and religion—both important cultural markers that might facilitate identification—they remain divided by national origin, generation, immigration history and status, and even by their formal relation to the US polity" (2010: 147). It is thus important to make a distinction between pan-ethnicity identification and the instrumental construction of a "Hispanic community" for political purposes.

There is a high level of common political interest among Hispanics, but this political communality does not reflect a strong sense of linked fate. Unlike Muslims, Hispanics do not defined their group consciousness by their "discrimination experience." They refer instead to their "immigration experience" (Masuoka and Sanchez, 2008). However, as noted by Michael Jones Correra, "for discrimination to lead to mobilization, it must not only be similarly experienced, but also similarly interpreted" (2005: 86). All Hispanics have a more positive view of illegal immigration than do non-Hispanic white or blacks, Yet, a "close the door behind me" attitude is noticeable among Hispanics. About 31 percent believe that illegal immigration has a negative impact on Hispanics living in the United States; 43 percent of those who are English dominant believe that illegal immigration hurts the US economy; and 28 percent believe that illegal immigrants should be deported (Pew Hispanic Center, 2010). Lisa Martinez analyzed the "fissures between newcomers and native-born Latinos" that have not been surmounted, except during the 2006 demonstrations. However, she argued, "the question remains whether Latino ethnic solidarity will be enough to sustain the momentum and energy of the mobilizations" (2008: 574). These findings suggest that the relationship between group identification and group consciousness is more complex than expected. As noted by Dennis Chong and Reuel Rogers, "acquiring a group identity and a sense of common fate is therefore just the first step toward a fully developed group consciousness" (2005: 51). In the case of Hispanics, a weak sense of linked fate provides a limited basis for group consciousness despite discontent with some security-driven policies.

Finally, it seems that concerns raised by the securitization of immigration does not negatively affect national identification. According to a recent NBC Latino poll, 74 percent of Hispanic respondents said they identified more with being American, and 19 percent said they identified with both "American" and "Latino" (2012). Hispanics remain divided over how much of a common identity they share with "typical" Americans: 47 percent consider themselves to be very different and another 47 percent said they are typically Americans. This national identification increases across generations—up to 69 percent for third-generation members (Pew Hispanic Center, 2012b). In their study of first-generation Hispanics, Shaun Wiley and his colleagues confirmed that recent data does not support the rejection-identification model. Hispanic immigrants who "perceived greater ethnic-based rejection from Americans were not significantly more likely to identify with their ethnic group" while "those who identified more with Americans reported that they were also significantly more likely to engage politically on behalf of their ethnic group" (2013: 314–315).

We can also assume that national identification is driven by intra-group comparisons. Hispanics generally have positive views of their social status. The 2012 Pew Hispanic Center survey found that 55 percent of all respondents (and up to 59 percent of native born and 60 percent of second-generation respondents) believed they have been equally successful as other minority groups. About 17 percent said they have been more successful, while only 22 percent said they have been less successful. Furthermore, large majorities of Hispanics have a very positive view of intergenerational mobility. For example, 72 percent of Hispanic immigrants expect their children to be better off than they are now, and 71 percent of first-generation Hispanics say they are better off than their parents were at the same age (Pew Research Center, 2013). Social psychologists mostly analyzed this optimistic subjective sense of integration as a response to discrimination and prejudice (Kaiser et al., 2004; Bobo and Hutchings, 1996). It might be interesting in future research to test the effect of self-esteem and subjective social status on identification as a response to securitized stigmatization.

It is worth noting that the impact of religious identification is not inversely related to national identification for both Hispanics and Muslims in the United States. Hispanics are slightly more religious than most Americans. According to the 2012 Pew Hispanic survey, 83 percent claim a religious affiliation (compared to 80 percent among the general public). They are more likely to be Catholic (62 percent versus 23 percent) and less likely to be Protestant (19 percent versus 50 percent). However, there are now more Latino Protestants in the United States than either Jews, Muslims, or Episcopalians. Only small minorities of Hispanics identify with other religions such as Mormonism, Orthodox Christianity, Judaism, Buddhism, and Islam. About 14 percent are unaffiliated (compared to 19 percent among the general public). When asked how important religion is in their life, Hispanics and the general public are equally likely to say that religion is very important (61 percent and 58 percent, respectively). According to a 2005 Gallup survey, 49 percent said they attended church once a week or almost every week (compared to 44 percent among the general population), and 32 percent said they seldom or never attend church (compared to 41 percent of the general population). To put these numbers in perspective, the United States continues to be a highly religious nation. Most Americans (up to 76 percent), for example, say that prayer is an important part of their daily life. An identical percentage agrees that "we will all be called before God at the Judgment Day to answer for our sins," and 81 percent never doubt the existence of God (Pew Research Center, 2012). Hispanics are therefore as religious as most Americans, with no impact of perceived discrimination on their religiosity.

While Hispanics significantly contribute to the evolution of the religious and political US landscape, there is no evidence that their religious identification is negatively related to their national identification. Analyzing the 1996 General Social Survey, Jack Citrin and his colleagues (2001) found that ethnic differences were slight when it comes to patriotic sentiment. Hispanics, for example, expressed patriotism at levels equal to, or higher than did whites. Up to 83 percent of both whites and Hispanics said they felt very close or close to America. These findings were confirmed by another similar study conducted after 9/11 and the implementation of tougher immigration measures. Jack Citrin and his colleagues (2007) found that patriotism among Hispanics (including the foreign-born) was on average as high as among white Americans. Using a Patriotism Index based on answers to the Los Angeles County Social Surveys (LACSS), they demonstrated that native-born Hispanics had significantly higher scores than whites—after adjusting for differences in age and years of education. In 2012, a Fox News Latino poll found that 70 percent of Hispanics had a positive opinion of American fighting forces. Yet, still only 47 percent of non-Hispanics describe Hispanics as patriotic (NBC Latino, 2012).

When asked if religion is very important in their lives, Muslim Americans (69 percent) are as religious as Hispanics (61 percent), and as all Americans who identified themselves as Christians (70 percent). About 47 percent report at least weekly attendance at a mosque for prayer (up to 63 percent for African Americans). Levels of religious attendance are slightly lower among Catholics (45 percent), but significantly higher among other religious groups (up to 65 percent among Mormons). When asked to choose whether they identify themselves as "national identity" or "Muslim" first, 49 percent of respondents say they think of themselves as Muslim first, while 26 percent answer American first. Notwithstanding the bias introduced by this question, it is worth noting that 46 percent of Christians identity themselves as Christian first, and 70 percent of white Evangelicals. Conversely, only 35 percent of African American Muslims think themselves as American first, although no one would seriously suspect them of being un-American (Pew Research Center, 2011). When asked how strongly they identify with certain groups by having the option of multiple choices, Muslim respondents to a Gallup survey were equally as likely to identify with their faith (65 percent) as they do with the United States (69 percent). This survey also found that Muslim Americans' strong identification with those around the world who share their religious identity does not diminish their sense of national identity (Gallup, 2011).

Mosque attendance, often perceived as a measurement of "Islamization," has increased by 75 percent between 2000 and 2005 (Jamal, 2005). Yet, the majority of Muslims (estimated between 70 and 80 percent) are not active participants in mosques or Islamic religious institutions. As noted by Yvonne Yazbeck Haddad and Robert Stephen Ricks, "they have embraced the fact that they are part of American society...That has not spared them or their children the abuse that is often heaped on Islam and its adherents in post 9/11 America" (2009: 20). Scholars have identified various strategies framed by Muslims as responses to religious discrimination. For Muna Ali (2011), they either isolate themselves to create an Islamic community, or they erase their differences by denying their faith, or they refuse to be fixed within only one categorical identity. Ingrid Mattson (2003) studied how Muslims use Islamic paradigms to define their role in the United States. She listed four paradigms: "resistance" (used by those who believe that America is a decayed society); "embrace" (which allows Muslims to be loyal to the American culture); "selective engagement" (between resistance and embrace); and "integration" (through which Muslims are active in social engagement but without compromising their faith). Both Ali and Mattson, as well as other scholars (Inglehart and Norris, 2009; Halim, 2006), agreed that the isolationists constitute a tiny minority (such as the followers of the Nation of Islam), while the majority of US Muslims want to integrate by combining their faith and their "Americaness." Actually, 63 percent of Muslims see no conflict between being a devout Muslim and living in a modern society, and 93 percent say they are loyal to America (Gallup, 2011). Despite multiple initiatives from Muslim organizations (such as the adoption in 2011 by the Fiqh Council of North America of a resolution on "Being Faithful Muslims and Loyal Americans," or the Ahmadiyya Muslim community campaign on "Muslim for Loyalty") 32 percent of the general public still believe Muslims are less loyal to the United States than to Islam, and 40 percent believe Muslims are as loyal to the United States as they are to

Islam. A majority of Americans report being "somewhat" (38 percent) or "very worried" (16 percent) about radicals within the Muslim community. This concern about radicalism translates into support for FBI wiretapping of mosques (up to 52 percent) (Princeton Survey Research Associates International, 2012).

While sharing a strong level of national identification and sense of loyalty, Hispanics and Muslims differ widely when it comes to naturalization. As previously suggested, individuals and groups targeted by security measures should demonstrate a high motivation to become citizens in order to secure their rights and civil liberties, especially in the United States where access to naturalization remains quite open. The share of all legal foreign-born residents who have become naturalized US citizens actually rose to 56 percent in 2011—the highest level in three decades and an 18 percent point increase since 1990. When asked for the main reasons they decided to naturalize, large majorities cited practical reasons that may relate to concerns raised by the securitization of immigration. As illustrated in table 3.3, obtaining "better legal rights and protection," having "equal rights and responsibilities," as well as "the right to vote" constituted the top motivations among all immigrants groups, Mexicans, and Muslims. Furthermore, there is evidence that these motivations have become more important over time, as well as "commitment and pride of being American"—a trend consistent with the tendency of having a positive opinion of the United States despite perceived discrimination.

These findings have been confirmed by other studies. According to a survey conducted in 2010 by the National Council of La Raza, 48 percent of Hispanic respondents sought citizenship because of their desire to defend or exercise their rights (Ramirez and Medina, 2010). When asked in 2012 why they decided to naturalize, 22 percent of Mexicans gave reasons related to acquiring civil and legal rights as their main motivation for obtaining US citizenship (compared to 14 percent among non-Mexican immigrants). Muslim immigrants often mention the urgency to secure their rights against security-driven discrimination and marginalization (Chicago Council on Global Affairs, 2007). We can therefore assume that both Hispanics and Muslims have an instrumental conception of citizenship, based on practical considerations (such as rights and opportunities, costs and benefits). However, there are strong dissimilarities between Hispanics and Muslims in terms of actual naturalization rates. By 2011, 5.6 million immigrants from Latin America and the Caribbean had become naturalized—Mexico being the leading birth country of persons naturalizing (up to 14 percent). An even larger

Table 3.3 Motivations for becoming US citizens (Q: For each of the following, please tell me if it is a major reason for becoming citizens)

(%)	All immigrants	Mexicans	Muslims (*)
To have better legal rights and protection in the US	78 (2010) 70 (2003)	92 (2010) 80 (2003)	80 (2010)
Not have to worry about your immigration status	69 (2010) 58 (2003)	87 (2010) 67 (2003)	67 (2010)
To have equal rights and responsibilities (*)	80 (2010)	87 (2010)	81 (2010)
To make it easier to get certain jobs	69 (2010) 55 (2003)	86 (2010) 71 (2003)	70 (2010)
To get the right to vote	78 (2010) 76 (2003)	85 (2010) 81 (2003)	77 (2010)
To make it easier to travel in and out the United States	65 (2010) 51 (2003)	78 (2010) 61 (2003)	68 (2010)
To show a commitment and pride of being American	71 (2010) 65 (2003)	76 (2010) 63 (2003)	68 (2010)
To make it easier to bring other family members to the United States	49 (2010) 36 (2003)	69 (2010) 43 (2003)	35 (2010)
To qualify for government programs (Medicaid, food stamps, etc.)	36 (2010) 22 (2003)	48 (2010) 23 (2003)	19 (2010)

Source: Adapted for Carnegie Corporation—Public agenda (2003 and 2010). (*) not asked in 2003

number (5.8 million) who were currently eligible have not done so—Mexicans having the lowest rate of naturalization (36 percent) compared with other immigrants from the region (49 percent) and all other immigrants (72 percent). By contrast, 81 percent of Muslim Americans are US citizens, including 70 percent of those born abroad who have been naturalized. It is not just that a record number of Muslims are naturalizing, they are also naturalizing quickly. Of those who arrived after 2000, 42 percent already have become naturalized (Pew Research Center, 2011) despite facing challenges on the road to naturalization, such as the covert government program called Controlled Application Review and Resolution Program (CARRP) created in 2008. This program was meant to "ensure that immigration benefits are not granted to individuals and organizations that pose a threat to national security" by blacklisting some Muslims (mostly from Arab and Middle Eastern countries), and putting their applications on hold for years (ACLU, 2013).

There are several possible explanations for these variations between Hispanics and Muslims in terms of naturalization. According to the

Pew Hispanic Center, 94 percent of Hispanic respondents who had not naturalized so far (despite being eligible) mentioned administrative barriers, such as the cost of the naturalization application. Other key factors are the lack of English proficiency (for 65 percent of the respondents), with 23 percent finding the citizenship test too difficult (Pew Hispanic Center, 2012a). According to Alejandro Portes and Ruben Rumbaut, "immigrants of low human capital not only may take longer to grasp the advantages of citizenship, but also find the process of naturalization much more difficult" (2006: 146). The 2007 Pew survey, by contrast, found that Muslim Americans generally mirror the US public in education and income levels, with Muslim immigrants slightly more affluent and better educated than native-born Muslims. About 29 percent of Muslim immigrants have college degrees (compared to 25 percent for the general US population). They are also well represented among higher-income earners, with 19 percent claiming annual household income of $100,000 (compared to 16 percent for the Muslim population as a whole, and 17 percent for the US average). Thus, they enjoy a higher social capital than Hispanics, which in turn makes access to citizenship easier—in addition to their strong motivation to secure their status in the current contentious political climate triggered by anti-Muslim measures and negative stereotypes.

Other factors relate to the role of origin countries in civic and political participation (Zapata-Barrero and Gropas, 2012). According to Catherine Simpson Bueker (2005), the "source country effect" involves a "reversibility hypothesis" by which the participation of immigrants is affected by the possibility (or lack of) to reverse their migratory course and return home. One assumption is that Mexicans are more likely than other immigrants to maintain close ties with their home country because of the geographical proximity of Mexico. Furthermore, a large number of Mexicans are not aware that they can hold both US and Mexican citizenship at the same time (18 percent still believe that dual citizenship is not allowed, and 11 percent said they "don't know") (Pew Hispanic Center, 2012a). Existence of transnational ties (as illustrated by remittance practices, ease of travel and communication, and hometown associations) is thus often invoked as a factor precluding civic integration. Moreover, studies of Mexican hometown associations show that their members "tend to have less education and lower English proficiency than those who participate in other civic associations" (Ramakrishnan and Viramontes, 2010: 156)—two characteristics that discourage application for naturalization.

The opposite trend is predicted in the case of Muslims for two reasons. First, Muslims have come from at least 77 different countries, the largest subgroup (41 percent) from Arab countries in the Middle East and North Africa. Muslims thus constitute the most diverse group in the United States, and contrary to Hispanics, no single subgroup constitutes a majority. Among Middle Eastern immigrants, 81 percent consider the United States as their "permanent home" (compared to 68 percent of Mexican immigrants), while only 15 percent envision returning to their country of origin. Furthermore, some Muslims, such as refugees, do not have the option of returning home. Since 1975, nearly 300,000 refugees from Near Eastern and South Asian countries have been resettled in the United States, most from Iraq (110,000), Iran (90,000), Bhutan (60,000), and Afghanistan (26,000). In 2013, more than 50 percent of the 70,000 refugees admitted came from these countries (State Government, 2013). Second, Muslims are less engaged in transnational activities than Mexicans. According to the Carnegie Foundation of New York (2010), only 28 percent of Middle Eastern immigrants telephoned family and friends at least once a week (compared to 53 percent of Mexican respondents), and only 1 percent send money regularly to relatives (compared to 23 percent of Mexican respondents). This can be partly explained by the impact of the securitization of the integration governance that has fuelled concerns about a potential linkage between transnationalism and terrorism. Transnational organizations (such as Muslim relief groups and charities) have been scrutinized by federal authorities since 9/11—leading to the closure of the Holy Land Foundation and the Global Relief Foundation.

Security, Identity, and Loyalty in Europe

Compared to US Muslims, Muslims in Europe have to deal with a more adverse context of integration. The "retreat from multiculturalism" and fears expressed by the general public and politicians that a growing "Islamic identification" might lead to "Islamic extremism" illustrate these effects. Existing attempts to evaluate Islamic identification often confound ethnic identification and self-assessment of religiosity. Yet, as noted by Peter Mandaville, "many who fall within the 'Muslim in Europe' label do not regard their religion as a primary component of their self-identity, and do not necessarily make choices and decisions driven by 'Islamic' motivations" (2009: 493). Immigrants, for example, may actually prefer to define themselves in terms of their country of origin while sharing a Muslim transnational identity based on an ummah-oriented solidarity. Muslims for whom religion is not a primary source of identity, and "who define themselves as Muslim because they are born into a Muslim family and are proud of this Islamic heritage but do not actively follow Islamic principles" can also express a sense of "Muslimness" (Akbarzadeh and Roose, 2011: 320). "Cultural Muslims" can refer to Islam as an identity marker for both religious and nonreligious reasons. Islamic identification may thus appear as "a strong personal marker rather than a sign of communal or group identity," and/or be mixed with other social markers (Cesari, 2013: 33).

Furthermore, secularism is generally a much stronger force in Europe than in the United States. The greater religious visibility of Muslims may thus be explained by the fact that majorities of the general population in many European states do not identify with any religion at all (up to 56.6 percent in the Netherlands, 52 percent in the United Kingdom, and 51.5 percent in France). Muslims therefore tend to express higher levels of religiosity when measured against secular society (Irving Jackson and Doerschler, 2012). In Great Britain, for example, 86 percent of Muslims declare that religion is "the most important thing in my life," compared to only 11 percent among the general population. However, according to a report about religion published in 2006 by the National Office of Statistics, more than 50 percent of Jewish, Sikh, and Hindu adults also said that their religion was comparably important to their self-identification (Mirza et al., 2007). In France, 22 percent of African and Turkish Muslim respondents said that they attend mosque at least once a month, compared with 18 percent of their Catholic counterparts (Klausen, 2005). It should thus be more appropriate to compare religious groups instead of contrasting Muslims with the general population—an option limited by the lack of reliable data in most European countries.

It is extremely difficult to discern broad trends at the European level due to the diversity of national situations. Yet, it is possible to categorize the variegated "Muslim experience" according to few criteria, such as nativity, legal status, and age. The distinction between foreign-born and native-born Muslims, as the previous chapter on discrimination demonstrates, remains crucial in trying to explain ethnic/religious identification processes and their impact on national identification, as well as on social and political behaviors. Variations among citizenship regimes delineate a further distinction between Muslims who are citizens (whether naturalized foreign-born or native-born when jus soli is applied) and those who remain excluded from citizenship (whether foreign-born who do not qualify for naturalization or native born when jus sanguinis is applied). Furthermore, evidence suggests that the Muslim population across Europe tends to be younger than of the average for the countries in which they have settled. Young Muslims (who are either foreign-born, or underage for naturalization and/or registration) represent a growing proportion of the European population. In Great Britain, for example, 78 percent of Muslims were under the age of 40 in 2008 compared with a national average of 45 percent (Field, 2011).

At first blush it appears that Muslims in Europe, like their US counterparts, combine a strong sense of ethnic/religious identification with a high level of national belonging. Findings from the study conducted by the Open Society Institute conflict with the common assumption that Muslims are reluctant to identify with their country of residence—allegedly as a result of a growing Islamic identification. As table 3.4 illustrates, a majority of both Muslim (about 62 percent) and non-Muslim (about 72 percent) respondents share a "very" or "fairly" strong sense of national belonging. Predictably, Muslims born in the EU (66.45 percent) are more likely than those born outside the EU (58.65 percent) to express such feelings. Non-Muslim respondents born outside the EU (36 percent) are more likely to have a very strong sense of belonging than Muslim respondents (24.8 percent). However,

Table 3.4 Major national identification trends among Muslims in Europe

(%)	How strongly do you feel you belong to the country?	Do you see yourself as (British, French, etc.)?
Muslims born in the EU	- Very strongly: 25.8 - Fairly strongly: 40.65 - Not very strongly: 22.8 - Not at all strongly: 6.9 - Don't know: 3.8	- Yes: 67.4 - No: 32.6
Muslims born outside the EU	- Very strongly: 23.8 - Fairly strongly: 34.85 - Not very strongly: 26.25 - Not at all strongly: 11.85 - Don't know: 3.25	- Yes: 39.8 - No: 60.2
Non-Muslims	- Very strongly: 35.9 - Fairly strongly: 35.6 - Not very strongly: 20.4 - Not at all strongly: 6.4 - Don't know:	- Yes: 77.1 - No: 22.9

Source: Adapted from OSI (2010)

27 percent of non-Muslim respondents say their sense of belonging is not very strong or nonexistent—compared to 29.7 among Muslims born in the EU. When asked if they feel themselves to be "nationals" (British, German, French, etc.), a majority of Muslims expressed a sense of cultural identification with the state (up to 67.4 percent among those born in the EU). Muslims born outside the EU are more likely than Muslim EU nationals to express a low level of cultural identification. Only 40 percent see themselves as nationals. Yet, it is worth noting that being Muslim is a less important variable than the country of birth because only 47 percent of non-Muslims born outside the EU describe themselves as nationals.

Other studies found no significant correlation between religiosity and sense of national identity. In their survey conducted on behalf of Gallup, Dalia Mogahed and Zsolt Nyiri (2007) found that Muslims in Paris, London, and Berlin identified strongly with their religion (46 percent, 69 percent, and 56 percent respectively). Muslims were also at least as likely as the general public to identify strongly with their country of residence (46 percent being the same figure for Muslims and the general French public, and 35 percent compared to 36 percent among the German public). In London, Muslims were more attached to their country than the general population (57 percent compared to 48 percent respectively). They also expressed a high degree of confidence in the British democratic institutions (64 percent compared to 36 percent among the general population) (Nyiri, 2007). According to a National Office for Statistics report about religion in the United Kingdom, 86 percent of Muslims considered that their religion was the most important thing in their life. Yet, 93 percent of Muslims born in the United Kingdom described themselves as British, English, Scottish, or Welsh—compared to 94 percent of Buddhists, 90 percent of Sikhs, and 91 percent of Hindus (Mirza et al., 2007). The 2007–2008 Citizenship Survey asked British Muslims to what extent they agreed that they personally felt part of British society. This survey included a new question on national identity (with a list of six options: English, Scottish, Welsh, Irish, British, and "other"). Muslims respondents were less likely than the general population in England to choose English as one of their national identities (12 versus 60 percent, respectively), but more likely than the general population to choose British (65 versus 44 percent respectively). Furthermore, although religion was designated as an important element of their identity (31 percent compared to 4 percent among the general population), 48 percent of Muslims selected their family as their most important identity marker (Communities and Local Government, 2010). In their study of the 2008 wave of the European Values Study in 12 European countries, Tim Reeskens and Matthew Wright found that mosque attendance negatively moderates national pride among Muslims, but only among nonimmigrants. For the first generation, in contrast, attendance was unrelated to national identification (2013). As Pamela Irving Jackson and Peter Doerschler argued, the level of religiosity among Muslims does not appear to influence their sense of national identification, their support for democracy, and their trust in the political system. "These attitudes," they concluded, "reflect (Muslim) integration into Europe, not self-segregation into parallel societies" (2012: 136).

A majority of Muslims perceive political participation as a necessary means for societal integration. Dalia Mogahed and Zsolt Myiri found than 68 percent of Muslims in Paris supported this view (compared to 54 percent among the broader French public). Yet, it is important to make a distinction between Muslims' desire to be involved (as de facto citizens) and their recognition by the state (as de jure citizens) when evaluating their political engagement in the European context. Like other non-EU immigrants, Muslims indeed face a "complicated matrix of legal alienation" (Klausen, 2008). This explains many of the differences between them and their US counterparts. According to the Immigrant Citizens Survey (ICS), most temporary residents in Europe want to become long-term residents and/or citizens in the countries where they live in order to obtain a more secure status. Immigrants from Muslim countries constitute the largest group to naturalize in many European countries (such as Moroccans in Belgium and the Netherlands, and Turks in Germany and Denmark). Yet, large numbers of Muslims feel excluded from applying for citizenship as a result of legal requirements. Half of those Muslims living in French cities who do not apply for naturalization argue that the procedure is too complex. In German cities, the same percentage do not apply because they may need to renounce their current citizenship—dual citizenship being granted in Germany only by exception (ICS, 2012). As a result, 68 percent of Muslims are not citizens in Germany and 31 percent in France (Irving Jackson and Doerschler, 2012). In the Netherlands, citizenship tests include questions about gay marriage and church-state relations, which, according to Jaap Dronkers and Maarten Peter Vink, "raise the suggestion of being a litmus test for immigrants with a specific religious background" (2012: 396).

In addition to legal requirements, a number of eclectic, psychological factors apply. Using a pooled data set in 15 European countries,

Dronkers and Vink found that second-generation Muslims were less likely to naturalize than their non-Muslim counterparts (including members of other religious groups). Yet, adherence to Islam had no significant effect on the likelihood of having host country citizenship. Motivation to become a citizen was instead affected by social stratification factors—which confirms the pessimistic conclusions of segmented assimilation theories. In the United States, by contrast, a majority of Muslims enjoy a high level of social capital, both objectively and subjectively. Some 64 percent of them in 2011 reported their standard of living got better, compared with 46 percent in 2008 (Gallup, 2011). The case of most Muslims in Europe thus symmetrically contrasts to those in the United States. They are at sharp socioeconomic disadvantage compared to non-Muslim groups and they interpret the high discrimination they experience as indicating that they have a low degree of social capital. In turn, their relatively high degree of socioeconomic deprivation decreases allegiance to the host country—especially among members of the second and third generation who faced difficult integration trajectories (Khattab, 2009; Hussain and Bagguley, 2005). Saffron Karlsen and James Nazroo found evidence that religion, religious practices, and strength of religious identity were unrelated to variations in national identification (as measured by "to feel at home in their country of origin" and to "think as British/German/Spaniard"). Their findings suggested instead that, "the drivers of any variations in these sentiments are associated more with experiences and perceptions of social exclusion than any lack of integration caused by the insularity, religious affiliation or religious practices of Muslims" (2013: 703). Furthermore, less welcoming contexts are often associated with a higher degree of religious commitment among some minorities. In a study of Muslim immigrants in 16 countries, Philipp Connor found that contexts of immigrant receptivity alter the religious adaptation of foreign residents stating an Islamic affiliation. Findings from the ESS demonstrated that "immigrant Muslims have higher religious attendance than their Western counterparts, with the highest level of religious attendance deviation found in the least welcoming areas" (such as France) (2010: 394).

Furthermore, both national identification and interest in politics are affected by the difference between how Muslims perceive themselves and how they feel others perceive them. As Zsolt Nyiri (2010) noted, more than 70 percent of Muslims in Paris, London, and Berlin said they were loyal citizens. Yet, the majority of the French, British, and German general public did not believe Muslims were loyal to their respective countries. Only 35 percent of German respondents, for example, thought that Muslims were loyal citizens. An OSI survey also found a significant relation between national identification among Muslims and their feeling that they are not perceived as nationals. Few Muslim respondents in Hamburg and Berlin, for example, saw themselves as nationals (22 percent and 25 percent respectively). Even fewer said that Germans consider them to be nationals (11 percent in both cities). By contrast, 82 percent of Muslims in Leicester and 72 percent in London expressed a strong sense of national identification, as well as the feeling of being perceived as nationals by the general public (up to 40 percent in both cities). The perception of being excluded increases with the "culture distance" between value systems. According to Borja Martinovic and Maykel Verkuyten, perceived discrimination enhances a sense of religious identity, although the effect of this process on national identification is not always negative. These authors noted that, "the association between Muslim identification and host national identification was clearly negative for participants who perceived a relatively high degree of value incompatibility but not for those who felt little value incompatibility" (2012: 900). Unsurprisingly, Muslims feel less attached to a country in which they feel "symbolic boundaries" are erected against them (Shrobanek, 2009).

Being identified as the prototypical "other," if not "the enemy within" particularly affects young Muslims. Existing studies reveal complex patterns of identification and behavior. There is evidence that most young Muslims are integrated into mainstream society. The majority expresses a strong sense of cultural belonging, as well as openness to interethnic contact. The FRA study of Muslim youths in France, Spain, and the United Kingdom measured the strength of cultural identity by asking respondents to describe their cultural background. Two-thirds of Muslim youths in the United Kingdom, for example, identified with the dominant cultural identity (i.e., Scottish, English, or British), and 50 percent of Muslims in Spain described themselves as Spanish (2010). A study of young Turks in Germany revealed that the proportion of those who wish to have friends among the German community was extremely high (up to 95 percent)—although only 29 percent actually had a friend of German origin (DIK, 2008).

Yet, other studies of young Muslims emphasize their sense of socio-economic and political alienation, as well as their subsequent dis-identification with national values and politics (Valentine and Sporton, 2009; Hopkins, 2007; Lewis, 2007; Barnes, 2006). Second-generation Muslims often face significant and persistent disadvantages in education and in the labor market; hence, their status of religious minority overlaps with low socioeconomic status due to their immigrant background (Fleischmann et al., 2011). As Jeffrey Reitz (2005) noted in his study of the French riots, the education system teaches them about the entitlements of citizenship. Yet, unlike their parents, they are unable to rationalize and accept their second-class status. Similarly, Yasmin Hussain and Paul Bagguley demonstrated, in their study of British Pakistani youth after the 2001 riots, that their mobilization was a response to their sense of frustration at being denied the rights associated with their strong British identity (2005).

Experiencing a sense of exclusion may conflict with a sense of national belonging—with variations according to the national context. Joachim Bruess (2008), for example, analyzed the effect of perceived victimization and disrespect among Muslims groups in Great Britain, Spain, and Germany. He found a perception of "separation and marginalization" among younger Bangladeshi Muslims in Great Britain that was not apparent among Moroccan Muslims in Spain—where they felt less marginalized by the general population. Saffron Karlsen and James Y. Nazroo found that less than a fifth of Turkish Muslims living in Germany said they thought of themselves as German, compared with a third of Moroccan Muslims who thought of themselves as Spanish, and over nine in ten Bangladeshi Muslims who thought of themselves as British. They argued that "citizenship, reported experiences of victimization and strength of religious identities are shown to have important influences on forms of national identity in Europe among these groups...In contrast, measures of cultural identity and practice, such as the importance of religion, religious practices and strength of religious identity were not related to these outcomes" (2013: 702–703). Beyond variations among countries, there is a large consensus among scholars about the effect of marginalization experienced by many young Muslims. In her study of Muslim youth in Europe, Barbara Franz provided evidence that experiences of social exclusion may conflict with a sense of access to national identities and undermine a sense of "being at home." Relative deprivation, as defined in this context by the realization that one will remain a second-class citizen with clear limits to one's socioeconomic mobility, "might entice individuals who seem perfectly integrated to find elucidation for their resentment within other realms of existence. Extremist Islam is one such way" (2007: 103).

CHAPTER 4

Securitization and Conventional Mobilization

A September 2012 *Newsweek* cover featured a photograph of a mob of yelling men accompanied by a headline proclaiming "Muslim Rage." The unspecified photograph was presumably taken during one of the anti-US protests in a Muslim country. *Newsweek* invited readers to comment on the photo by using the hashtag #MuslimRage. This generated a storm of tweets, some offensive (from non-Muslims), but most of them satirical (from Muslims), such as "there is no payer room in this nightclub," and "my hijab does not match my outfit." The most popular ironical tweet, purportedly expressing *true* "Muslim Rage" was: "Lost your kid named Jihad at the airport and can't yell for him."

A group of undocumented immigrants occupied the church of Saint Joseph Artisan in Paris in 1991 as a way to protest against different forms of exclusion in their daily lives. Subsequently, groups or networks of undocumented immigrants have mushroomed in France and other European countries, including the Collectif des Sans-Papiers (in Paris and other French cities), the Voice Refugee Forum (in Germany), the Sin-Papeles (in Spain), and the Strangers into Citizens movement (in the United Kingdom). These groups have varied characteristics but share a common set of mobilization strategies (mostly demonstrations, marches, occupations, public meetings, and hunger strikes) and common goals (legal regularization, access to labor market and health care, and eligibility for citizenship). Furthermore, the collective actions of undocumented migrants' have intensified since the mid-2000s as a result of the introduction of further restrictive immigration and integration policies. In France, for example, "the demand for the regularization of families with children attending school emerged when new police practices allowing for the identification of undocumented migrants' children in schools came into force" (Monforte and Dufour, 2011: 217).

During the 2009 local elections in the German state of North Rhine Westphalia, the Bündnis für Frieden und Fairness (Confederation for Peace and Fairness, BFF) won two seats on the city council. The two elected candidates were Haluz Yildiz, chairman of both the BFF and the Muslim Council, and Hülya Dogan, the first veiled women to hold office in a German parliament. As Maike Didero noted, "this fact triggered attention by media far beyond the local scope" because the BFF has been founded exclusively by Muslim citizens—as a result of the decision of the Muslim Council to create Muslim voter associations instead of relying on local mainstream politicians (2013: 34). The BFF did not mention religious issues in its platform, focusing instead on social, cultural, and environmental issues. Elsewhere, other Muslim organizations, by contrast, support religious mobilization (such as the Muslim Council of Britain), or Islamic sociopolitical mobilization (such as the French Union of Young Muslims whose members were active in the demonstrations against the 2004 law banning the hijab in schools). A third group of organizations openly criticize Islam and support secular mobilization—such as the Central Committee for Ex-Muslims present in Germany, Great Britain, Scandinavia, and the Netherlands. The founder of the Dutch section published an article in September 11, 2007, that compared the supposed Islamization of the country with the rise of Nazism (Frégosi, 2013).

Hispanics in the United States will account for 40 percent of the growth in the eligible electorate in the United States by 2030 (up to 40 million). They now constitute a swing vote in several competitive states (including Florida). More importantly, Hispanic voters support candidates based on their records, not simply party affiliation. While campaigning, candidate Barrack Obama named comprehensive immigration reform as a priority for his first year in office if elected. But the lack of legislative progress had an impact on the Hispanic vote during the 2010 midterm elections. Hispanic support for Democratic candidates decreased to 60 percent, while support for Republicans comparably increased (up to 38 percent). The political leadership in the Hispanic community clearly recognizes their constituents' importance, and the signs are that it intends to use this electoral empowerment to obtain concessions from both political parties. The National Council of La Raza (NCLR)—the largest national Hispanic civil rights and advocacy organization in the United States —has warned the Obama administration of possible sanctions against its extensive deportation policy. In March 2014, NCLR president Janet Murguia declared President Obama "the deporter-in-chief" and announced a series of mass demonstrations to stop deportations, as well as to force Congress to pass immigration reform (Epstein, 2014).

These examples illustrate the diversity of the mobilization agenda of immigrants and minorities on both sides of the Atlantic. Their involvement can be electoral or nonelectoral, take place at different levels (local, national, transnational), use different tools (including new communication technologies), and with differing objectives. The strategies they opt for involve either potentially conflictive forms of mobilization (such as protests) or more institutionalized forms of political lobbying. Mobilization may relate to ethnic organization membership, to a general associational involvement, or to individual motivations only. Mobilization can also be based on identity politics—ethnicity or religion, or both. In order to explain the increasing diversity of mobilization, we thus need to identify a range of factors that explain immigrant choices. Any framework should include their subjective perception of the political and social arena, their form and degree of group membership, and their views of their own capacity for mobilization (or lack thereof). As my prior discussion demonstrated, both perceived discrimination and subjective integration play a key role in migrant and minority perceptions of their host country's environment, on the evolution of intergroup relations, as well as on their individual and group identification process and sense of national belonging. This raises two sets of questions: First, does security governance change the scope, content and forms of mobilization of targeted groups? If it does, to what extent and in which fields (conventional electoral participation, unconventional politics, nonpolitical involvement)?

How to Analyze the Responses of Immigrants and Minorities to Security Governance?

Answering these questions requires us to first identify and clarify two common assumptions. One relates to the perception of immigrants and minorities as "passive agents" whose actions are mechanically determined by their ethnicity, their position in the class structure, and other traditional socioeconomic status (SES) variables. It is often assumed that minority members who have a high degree of social capital (in terms of education, language proficiency, legal status, and knowledge of the political system) are more likely to be engaged in conventional political participation than more recent immigrants who have a correspondingly lower degree. Yet, despite this purported variance, the fact is that many immigrants remain "the objects of politics, not political subjects" (Mollenkopf, 2013: 111). Clearly, the relationship between objective measures of integration and modes of political action is not straightforward, as illustrated by studies that have evaluated the impact of perceived discrimination and ethnic identification. Among Hispanic students enrolled in elite private universities (and thus, presumably successfully integrated), for example, only those who perceived limited degrees of discrimination against their group were more likely to engage with politics through conventional electoral participation. By contrast, those who perceived a lot of discrimination were more likely to participate in protests or be members of advocacy groups (Hochschild and Mollenkopf, 2009; Deaux, 2006; Sears et al., 2003). Whether degrees or forms of political socialization and socioeconomic integration affect the chosen modes of participation needs to be treated as empirical question instead of being assumed.

A second assumption, advocated by proponents of the political opportunity structure (POS) approach, is that structural conditions can either hinder or facilitate mobilization. Opportunity structures available to immigrants and minorities markedly differ from one country to another, depending on a series of factors (such as the labor market conditions, citizenship laws, housing and health care policies, local government policies, and the presence or absence of coethnic communities). According to Ruud Koopmans, "the central tenet of the political opportunity approach to collective action is that mobilization is not a direct reflection of social structural tensions, problems, and grievances, but is mediated by the available opportunities and constraints set by the political environments in which mobilizing groups, in the case at hand migrants, operate" (2004: 541). Opportunity structures, whether institutional or discursive, thus vary by policy area, group, or venue (national, regional, or local). Current scholarship from this perspective, in attempting to understand differences in behavior and mobilization outcomes, focuses on the degree of centralization of the decision-making and policy-implementation processes; the characteristics of citizenship and integration regimes; the extent to which migrants have been granted cultural group rights; and the role of civil society and network resources (Pilati, 2012; Odmalm, 2004; Penninx et al.; 2004).

The POS approach has its undoubted virtues, which have grown as the field has expanded. The question of changing forms of immigrant politics and mobilization in contemporary societies has received a lot of attention in the last decade from scholars who have refined the POS approach (Però and Solomos, 2010; Ramakrishnan and Bloemraad, 2008; Lee et al., 2006; Jacobs and Tillie, 2004). The main aspects commonly explored include the dimensions of political incorporation (Mollenkopf, 2013; Hochschild, 2013); the effects of structural conditions, such as public policies, political institutions, social context, symbolic resources, and antiimmigrant actors (McDermott, 2013; Dancygier, 2013; Andersen and Cohen, 2005; Ireland, 2000); the role of race and/or ethnicity in electoral mobilization (Sandovici and Listhaug, 2010; Frymer, 2005; Leighley, 2005); the influence of religion in political affiliation and participation (Foley and Hoge, 2007; Cesari and McLoughlin, 2005); the impact of social capital on political participation (Morales and Giugni, 2011); the levels of "ethnic civic community" (Jacobs et al., 2004; Fennema and Tillie, 2001); and vectors of mobilization such as immigrant organizations and civic institutions at the national and transnational levels (Takle, 2013; Pilati, 2012; Kugelberg, 2011; Martinez, 2011; Eggert and Giugni, 2010; Lahav, 2009; Predelli, 2008; Wong, 2006; Schrover and Vermeulen, 2005).

Yet, this approach only addresses one slice of the factors that shape immigrant mobilization. As Davide Però and John Solomos note, other key subjective explanatory factors should be analyzed in order to complement the rational choice assumptions that underpins POS studies on mobilization. Furthermore, Però and Solomos argued that "migrants, like the rest of the population, may at time mobilize in partial or total disregard of the chances of success and the achievement of concrete goals and material rewards, and be substantially driven by their values, affection, sense of group membership, need to feel well and realize themselves, and so forth" (2010: 10). In this respect, we may expect that the feeling of being a "threat," while not displacing more traditional forms of mobilization, may itself generate new forms. It may also actively encourage nonparticipation in "politics as usual" (Hochschild and Mollenkopf, 2009:26).

This emerging literature suggests three trends that provide useful insights for a better understanding of the impact of security governance on political mobilization. The first relates to the distinction between political interest (the attitudinal dimension) and political participation (the behavioral dimension). Political interest is often operationalized through proxies such as political trust, talking about politics in the host country, and an interest in homeland politics (Berger et al., 2004; Fennema and Tillie, 2001 and 1999). Young Muslims, for example, express a great deal of interest in national politics. In France (50 percent) and Great Britain (45 percent), they are slightly more likely than non-Muslim youth to express this interest (48 and 38 percent, respectively) (Irving Jackson and Doerschler, 2012). Levels of political participation are measured by registration, turnout rates, and running for office (conventional electoral participation), as well as nonelectoral forms of politics (such as attending a public meeting, contacting an elected official, or being a member of civic organizations). An increase in the degree of political interest and confidence in the political system does not in itself automatically translate into a higher degree of political activity. In Germany, for example, Maria Berger et al. (2004) found that 43 percent of Turks expressed an interest in German politics. Yet, 53 percent of ethnic Turks and 62 percent of German Turks were uninvolved in political activities. We should not assume a linear relationship between political interest and political participation; nor should we assume a bifurcated one between electoral and nonelectoral participation. However, identifying the ingredients that influence the relationship between securitization and choices of forms of political mobilization is a key concern.

A second trend is evident among scholars who examine how processes of social movement politics, networks, collective action, and contentious politics create new resources in order to incorporate excluded or marginalized groups into the polity (Costain, 2005; Diani and McAdam, 2003; Imig and Tarrow, 2001). Such an approach focuses on the varied relationship between mobilization, collective action, and exclusion, as illustrated by the alternative modes of participation during the fight of African Americans for civil rights. A process of exclusion can fuel what Jane Mansbridge and Aldon Morris (2001) labeled "oppositional consciousness," an empowering mental state that prepares members of an oppressed group to undermine, reform, or indeed overthrow a dominant system. Oppositional consciousness can in turn trigger contentious politics through collective action and politics. Charles Tilly and Sidney Tarrow argued that, "most forms of contentious politics are not social movements." Yet, social movement politics and contentious politics "often co-occur and intersect in the same places" (2007: 9). Such an approach begs the question of whether new security governance measures have generated a new "cycle of contention" by creating a new "repertoire" of claims. Further, Tilly and Tarrow appropriately pointed out that "the creation of a new boundary or the crystallization of an existing one between challenging groups and their targets" plays a key role in contentious politics" (Ibid: 34), as illustrated by the activation after 9/11 of boundaries separating "patriots from terrorists" by the US government (Ibid: 80).

A third trend relates to the emergence of new political subjectivities or "grammars" of action expressed within social movements (O'Toole and Gale, 2010; McDonald, 2006). This is illustrated by the changing nature of identity politics among ethnic groups who prefer to engage in unconventional forms of participation. Low levels of electoral participation should not be interpreted as evidence of political apathy but rather as a preference for alternative empowerment strategies. These strategies are connected with questions of identity, especially among young people who distance themselves from the religious/ethnic heritage of their parents' generation. Catarina Kinnvall and Paul Nesbitt-Larking (2011 a, 2011 b) identified three responses: retreatism (to stay under the definitional radar by distancing from the modern polity); essentialism (to establish clear boundaries between oneself and the other as a response to existential anxiety); and engagement (to promote dialogue, mutual recognition, and respect as a way of overcoming negative stereotypes). Kinnvall and Nesbitt-Larking noted that these three strategies overlap with Rashmi Singla's categories of response toward discrimination, "constructive, destructive, and passive" (2005). From this cognitive perspective, political mobilization moves beyond "cost-benefit calculations" to include struggles for recognition rather than only the "classic" struggles for redistribution (Simon, 2011).

Taking into account these varied contributions, we may wonder if the advocates of security governance pay attention to the relationship between their measures and countervailing forms of engagement by the communities they target. It may be assumed that being targeted as a "threat" will provide incentives for some immigrants and minorities to increase their participation and representation in order to secure their right and civil liberties, as well as to press specific claims. Yet, there is no line of agreement among scholars about the nature of the relationship between discrimination and participation. Indeed, a number of studies specifically conclude that there is no reliable positive correlation between discrimination, identification, and participation (Leighley and Vedlitz, 1999; Verba et al., 1993). Some scholars argue that ethnic identification based on rejection decreases political engagement (Simon, 2011), while others conclude that stronger ethnic identification is associated with stronger political engagement (Cronin et al., 2012; Wiley et al., 2012). A few studies reconcile these seemingly contradictory results by making a distinction between political engagement and ethnic political engagement—defined as a "willingness to give political voice to concerns related to one's ethnic group" (Wiley et al., 2013: 310); between political participation and other forms of civic engagement such as nonelectoral activities (Marshall, 2001); or between attitudinal and behavioral components of political engagement as being jointly shaped by perceptions of discrimination and self-identification (Schildkraut, 2005).

I respond to this quandary by analyzing the mobilization agenda of the most targeted migrants and minorities from a broader perspective: by combining mobilization theories with the findings analyzed in the previous chapters on discrimination (both objective and subjective), social identity, intergroup relations, relative deprivation, and group-based emotion. This approach is inspired by the "dynamic dual pathway model of approach coping with collective disadvantage" designed by Stürmer and Simon (2004) and refined by Martijn van Zomeren et al. (2012; see also van Zomeren et al., 2004). Their model integrates many common explanations of collective action (such as cost-benefit calculation, and group efficacy beliefs) in the context of collective disadvantage (both objective and subjective). It also includes social psychological predictors of collective action such as anger, perceived group injustice, and subjective feelings of deprivation, as well as an appraisal of blame for unfairness. Based on the assumption that collective action is the outcome of two processes (emotion-focused and problem-focused approach coping), this model assumes not only that cognitive appraisal feeds into coping strategies but also that coping feeds back into reappraisal—by increasing the belief that social change is possible, as well as strengthening a collective sense of empowerment. Another coping strategy lies in the appraisal of a situation as threatening, when coping challenges outweigh material and symbolic resources. Although not included in this model, we may assume that a threatening situation fuels either apathy (an avoidance coping strategy), or a more destructive response (such as violent protest and rioting).

I apply this model to the analysis of the two main forms of mobilization, conventional and unconventional. The former includes electoral participation (e.g., naturalization, voting registration, political representation at the local and national levels). The latter, analyzed in chapter five, relates to various types of nonelectoral activities such as making political donations, signing petitions, writing to officials, lobbying, membership of an organization (ethnic, mainstream, or mixed), and participating in demonstrations or protests.

Conventional Mobilization in the United States

As the prior chapters demonstrate, both Hispanics and Muslims express strong concerns about the excesses of security policies and restrictive immigration measures. Both also share an instrumental conception of citizenship based on practical considerations, such as a greater protection of their civil rights. Yet, contrary to the common assumption that discrimination may increase traditional participation (registration and voting), Hispanics combine low naturalization rates with relatively low civic participation rates. Their share of the electorate is increasing (from 13.2 million in 2000 to 21.3 million in 2010). Yet, their proportion of the electorate remains below their percentage of the general population. They represent 16.3 percent of the total population, but only 10.1 percent of eligible voters (Lopez, 2011). In 2010, their voter registration rate (62 percent) was much lower than the rate for native-born citizens (72 percent), or for other naturalized immigrants (up to 82 percent for naturalized Canadian citizens). Only 56 percent of registered Hispanic voters actually voted (compared to 64 percent of native-born citizens and 76 percent of Canadian naturalized citizens). In 2012, 11.2 million Hispanic adults were eligible to vote but chose not to. As a result, the estimated 44 to 53 percent turnout rate of eligible Hispanic voters lagged significantly below the turnout of whites (66 percent) and blacks (65 percent) (Pew Hispanic Center, 2012a). According to the US Census Bureau, post-second-generation Hispanics tend to vote less. While first- and second-generation Hispanics voted at the same rate (52 percent), less than 47 percent of third-plus-generation Hispanics did so in 2008. As Chris Garcia and Gabriel Sanchez note, "the most accurate generalization one can make about Hispanics' rate of electoral is that it has been and remain strikingly lower than other demographic segments of the US population" (2008: 121).

Unlike Hispanics, Muslims have a very high naturalization rate. Yet, like Hispanics, they continue to be relatively less engaged in the political process than the general US population. While a majority of Muslim Americans (64 percent) said they were registered to vote, this was lower than the general population (81 percent) according to a 2009 Gallup survey—and constituted the lowest percentage among religious groups in the United States (compared to 90 percent of Protestants, 90 percent of Jews, 82 percent of Mormons, and 76 percent of Catholics). A 2011 Pew survey found that 66 percent of Muslim US citizens said they were registered to vote (compared to 79 percent of all US residents), with no significant difference in registration rates between native-born and foreign-born respondents. Approximately 64 percent said they did vote in the 2008 elections (compared to 76 percent of all US residents).

These results can be partially explained by the younger average age of the Hispanic and Muslim community members. The Muslim American population is much younger on average than the non-Muslim population. About 59 percent of adult Muslims are between the ages of 18 and 39, including 36 percent who are between the ages of 18 and 29 (compared respectively with 40 percent, and 22 percent of adults in the general population) (Pew Research Center, 2011). Young people (55 percent) are the least likely to be registered to vote among US Muslim citizens (66 percent). More than 35 percent of Hispanics are younger than the voting age of 18 (and an additional 23 percent are of voting age but not US citizens). In 2010, 31 percent of Hispanic eligible voters were between the ages of 18 and 29 (compared to 19 percent of white, and 25.6 percent of black eligible voters). Among this group, only 18 percent voted in the 2010 elections (Lopez, 2011).

In addition to these distinct demographic characteristics, Hispanics and Muslims share a greater sense of relative political disaffection than the broader population. Muslim Americans are slightly less attentive to government and politics than the general public, with 37 percent following "what is going on in government and public affairs" compared to 50 percent among the general public (Pew Research Center, 2011). When asked in 2010 "what was the main reason you did not vote?" 26 percent of Hispanic respondents said they were "too busy or facing a conflicting work/school schedule," and 15.6 percent said they were not interested (Lopez, 2011). These findings fuel "debates about how attached immigrants really are to the United States" (Fraga et al., 2010: 118). However, it is worth noting that registered US citizens offer similar responses when asked why they do not vote (with 25.5 percent being too busy, and 15.6 percent not interested).

Yet the behavior of Hispanics and Muslims may thus be part of a broader cultural syndrome: according to the US Census Bureau, turnout rates for presidential elections stagnated at 55.7 percent in 2000 and 57.5 percent in 2012. Low turnout rates among Hispanics and Muslims may thus be a product of a growing American disaffection toward voting rather than an "un-American" attitude. This raises the question of whether there is anything distinctive about immigrants' political incorporation compared to the native-born population. One possible answer has been provided by Christian Joppke: "Of course there is, but it depends" (2013: 65)—an effective, if frustrating, way to summarize the huge diversity of findings.

I thus emphasize three specific aspects related to the impact of security governance on various political mobilizations of Muslims and Hispanics: their attitudinal engagement; their political affiliation; and their organizational influence. First, there is evidence that perceptions of discrimination and self-identification has affected the forms and degree of political engagement since 9/11. Yet, there is no simple direct relationship between them. Findings from the studies discussed so far indicate that Hispanics perceive a high level of group discrimination (which could decrease their political participation), and a low level of personal discrimination (which should not affect their engagement). To get a better sense of how discrimination affects behavioral engagement, it is therefore essential to examine the role of self-identification. As I analyzed in chapter three, Hispanics tend to identify themselves mostly in terms of their country of origin, while—less obviously—concerns over securitization have not increased their use of a pan-ethnic label nor decreased their self-identification as Americans. Many scholars agree that self-identification alone has no consequential effect on political engagement (Citrin and Sears, 2009; Pearson and Citrin, 2007; de la Garza et al., 1996). According to Deborah Schildkraut, there are "relatively small group-based differences in registration and voting absent perceptions of discrimination, with American identifiers being the most likely to register and vote." This tendency, however, "drops dramatically as the perception of individual-level discrimination increases, and large differences in registration and voting emerge across the different types of identifiers" (2005: 297–298). She found that American identifiers were the most affected by individual discrimination, both in terms of their registration and voting.

These findings are consistent with the "integration paradox" analyzed in chapter two: Hispanics who are relatively well integrated are more sensitive to discrimination, more critical of the "American dream," and thus less likely to be engaged in conventional politics. By contrast, the political engagement of national origin and Hispanic identifiers increases in response to individual-level discrimination. Yet this trend does not balance the relative electoral apathy of Hispanic voters because the perception of individual-level discrimination increases the likelihood of engaging in nonelectoral forms of political activity rather than conventional participation.

Muslims combine a low level of perceived discrimination (both collective and individual) and a strong degree of group consciousness. They are more likely than Hispanics to naturalize, and enjoy a higher degree of both objective and subjective social capital. They should therefore be more politically active in terms of registering and voting. Yet, they are less likely to register and vote than other ethnic and religious groups. Matt Baretto and Karam Dana argued that "for Muslim Americans, our traditional models of the American voter are far less appropriate...because the political system in place post 9/11 does not afford an opportunity for full inclusion to the American Muslim voter" (2010: 158). Barreto and Dana demonstrated that Muslim Americans reflect many of the same relationships between resources (such as age, education, income) and turnout as the general public. They also found that both perceived discrimination and religiosity increase their propensity to vote. However, neither Democrats nor Republicans target Muslim voters as political allies—which explains their low voter mobilization and, in turn, their low level of "politicized group consciousness." Muslim voters, as the 2008 presidential campaign illustrates, "were a target of a different kind—as political scapegoats that were seen as a liability rather than coalition partners" (Ibid: 157).

We should not assume that Muslims are indifferent about the impact of security governance. John Ayers and Richard Hofstetter (2008), for example, found that Muslims' concern about the discriminatory aspects of counterterrorism has increased their political participation since 9/11. The war on terror, the Iraq intervention, and military conflicts against Muslims around the world caused a shift in partisanship, which led to the creation of the American Muslim Task Force on Civil Rights and Elections by a coalition of ten Muslim organizations that endorsed John Kerry. According to Farida Jalalzai, "this was coupled with successful mobilization efforts, resulting in a 20 percent increase in Muslim American voters" (2009: 172). US Muslim political involvement sustained a greater degree of visibility during the 2006 Congressional elections, which were characterized by a higher turnout of US Muslim voters and the election of the first Muslim member to the US Congress, Minnesota Democrat Keith Ellison. A second Muslim, André Carson, was elected in a special election in 2008.

However, the underrepresentation of American Muslims in electoral politics remains striking, and cannot be completely explained by traditional voting variables. There is evidence, for example, that the small size of the Muslim community may explain why US Muslims do not capture the interest of political leaders. The attractiveness of courting their ethnic vote is rather limited since the potential pool of voters remains extremely limited. Conversely, US Muslim political candidates cannot win by strictly relying on the Muslim American vote. Yet, this "size effect" explanation does not address the puzzling underrepresentation issue. In their study of the composition of the 110th Congress elected in 2006, Eileen Braman and Abdulkader Sinno found that comparably sized groups to the Muslim community (such as the Methodists, Presbyterians, and Jews) were overrepresented. Despite the small size of the Asian community (about 5 percent of the total population, and less than 1 percent of eligible voters), Asians were relatively less underrepresented in electoral positions than American Muslims. According to Morrison Wong (2010), about 190 Asian American candidates ran in 2002 at the national, state, and local levels. In 2004, the number of Asian Americans running for office reached 230—an increase of 21 percent in two years. In 2005, there were about 555 Asian American elected officials nation-wide, including 64 state senators, 97 state representatives, 3 state governors, 19 mayors, 123 city or county council members, and 236 judges. In the 2006 Congress, there were nine Asian American legislators (six representatives and one delegate in the House, and two senators). In contrast, Braman and Sinno pointed out that there were no Muslim governors or lieutenant governors, and that only five state legislators were Muslims in 2006. After testing different explanatory variables, Sinno concluded that the low degree of Muslim political representation was mainly due to hostility toward Muslim candidates from large sections of the American voting public, one "that deters Muslims from running for elected office and discourages the two large parties from recruiting them" (2009: 90). Manochehr Dorraj (2010) reached a similar conclusion in noting the tenacity and resilience of anti-Muslim sentiments.

The second identifiable effect of security governance relates to political affiliation. There is evidence that concerns about security policies and restrictive immigration measures influence policy preferences and political partisanship. When Hispanics and Muslims cast their vote, the context of anti-immigrant sentiment and the effects of security policies directly affect their choice. According to a Zogby poll, 42 percent of Muslims supported George W. Bush in 2000 and 31 percent supported Al Gore (Jalazai, 2009). Candidate Bush's foreign policy promises (especially regarding the Arab-Israeli conflict), largely explained this distribution. President Bush, however, quickly departed from those pledges. A majority of Muslim organizations perceived his attitude toward Palestinians in Gaza and the West Bank as overwhelmingly favoring Israeli interests. Additionally, the post-9/11 policies of the Bush administration perpetuated a feeling of betrayal among those Muslims who had voted for Bush. In 2004, an exit poll conducted by Council on American Islamic Relations (CAIR) indicated that more than 90 percent of Muslim voters cast their votes for John Kerry. This trend was sustained in 2008. Nearly 90 percent of US Muslims supported Democrat Barack Obama and only 3 percent voted for the Republican candidate, John McCain. On balance, 63 percent of all US Muslims identified as Democrats in 2007, or were inclined to support the Democratic Party. By 2011, that figure had grown to 70 percent. Only 6 percent identified themselves as Republicans. Maintaining that trend, 85.7 percent of Muslims voted for President Obama (compared to the 4.4 percent who voted for Mitt Romney) in 2012.

Similar trends (the influence of the securitization of immigration issues and a majority support for Democratic candidates) are noticeable among Hispanic voters. During the 2000 presidential campaign, both Bush and Gore actively courted the vote of ethnic minorities. The states with the largest Hispanic populations (California, Texas, New York, and Florida) collectively accounted for 144 of the 270 electoral votes needed to win the election. In California, for example, the Republican Party invested $10 million dollars in campaign commercials in Spanish. George Bush reminded Hispanic voters that he opposed the "spirit of Proposition 187" and all "English only" proposals. Yet, the 2000 Republican Party platform remained quite restrictionist, with a focus on limiting family reunification. Al Gore, for his part, advocated restoring welfare benefits (stripped away by a Republican Congress in 1996), supported expansive legal immigration, and called for "amnesty" for undocumented immigrants, while endorsing the family reunification status quo.

Voter survey exit polls taken in November 2000 found that 60.3 percent of Hispanic voters in the United States were Democrats, while only 25.8 percent were Republicans. The partisan gap was even greater for presidential voting: 67.6 percent of Hispanic voters cast their ballots for Al Gore, while only 27.7 percent voted for George W. Bush. These results convinced Republicans that the best way to attract more Hispanic votes was to amend their immigration proposals by introducing more liberal measures. Congress subsequently approved a measure allowing the legalization of immigrants who entered the country before 1982. About 200,000 "green card" applicants would also be allowed to reside in the United States pending their visas being approved upon payment of a fine. Negotiations began with labor unions and farmers' organizations about opportunities for guest workers to gradually earn their legal residence. President Bush actively pursued a rapprochement with the Hispanic community. It took various forms, from the celebration of Cinco de Mayo at the White House to meetings with US Hispanic leaders and Vicente Fox, Mexico's president. Bush's strategy proved successful. His support among Hispanic male voters grew from 35 percent in 2000 to 41 percent in the 2004 presidential elections.

The 2006 midterm elections did demonstrate the importance of the Hispanic vote, contributing to a sweeping victory for the Democratic

Party. It captured the House of Representatives, the Senate, and a majority of governorships and state legislatures. Large segments of the broader electorate prioritized the war in Iraq as their most important electoral issue. Opposition to security and restrictive immigration measures, however, played a key role in the mobilization of Hispanic voters at a cost to the Republican Party: National exit polls showed that in elections for the US House of Representatives, 69 percent of Hispanics voted for Democrats and only 30 percent for Republicans. Fifty-seven percent of Hispanic registered voters called themselves Democrats or said they lean toward the Democratic Party in 2007, while just 23 percent then aligned themselves with the Republican Party. A Pew Hispanic Center national survey conducted that year revealed that many more Hispanics (41 percent) believed that the policies of the Bush administration had been harmful to Hispanics than had been helpful (16 percent). Some 79 percent of Hispanic registered voters prioritized immigration as an "extremely" or "very" important issue in the upcoming presidential race (compared to 63 percent in 2004).

In the 2008 presidential election, Hispanics voted for Democrat Barack Obama over Republican John McCain by a margin of more than two-to-one (67 percent versus 31 percent). Obama even won 57 percent of Florida's traditionally more conservative Hispanic vote, including large support from the Cuban community. He also gained 78 percent of the Hispanic vote in New Jersey, 76 percent in Nevada, and 74 percent in California, three other important electoral states. While campaigning, Obama said that comprehensive immigration legislation would be a priority in his first year in office. In May 2009, while acknowledging that the economic crisis has made this goal more difficult to achieve, he reaffirmed his intention to convene working groups and to begin discussing possible legislation. Obama followed up with his first major speech on immigration in July 2010, urging the Congress to fix the "broken" immigration system. Yet, as a result of a lack of legislative progress, Hispanic support for Democratic candidates decreased from 69 percent in the 2006 midterm elections to 60 percent in those held in 2010, while support for Republicans correspondingly increased (to 38 percent, compared to 30 percent in 2006). The antimigrant rhetoric of Mitt Romney during the last presidential election, for example, helped the Democrats to secure a strong Hispanic electoral basis (only 27 percent of Hispanics voted for Romney, compared to 71 percent for Obama). On the eve of the next midterm elections, some Republicans have tried to manage a rapprochement with the Hispanic community. Their incentive is evident: settling for a quarter or less of the Hispanic vote nationally will damage the prospects of Republican candidates in presidential elections.

The third identifiable effect of security governance relates to the evolution of organizational influence. As previously mentioned, shifts in partisanship are largely the result of the mobilization efforts of Hispanic and Muslim organizations. Dating back to the 1967 Arab-Israeli war, Arab Americans have created a number of organizations and interest groups that actively encourage political participation (such as the Arab American Institute—AAI), while the civil rights movement boosted the political activism of many African American Muslim groups. In the 1980s and early 1990s, Arab Americans and new Muslim immigrants focused on US foreign policy issues affecting the Islamic world, such as the Israeli-Palestinian conflict, US sanctions against Iraq, and the conflicts in Afghanistan and Chechnya. Arab Americans waver in terms of their political allegiance: It is dependent on a party or candidate's position on these issues. African American Muslims, by contrast, tend to focus on domestic issues, and consistently support the Democratic Party. Formulating a united political platform between the two groups has not been easy, as illustrated by the recurrent tensions between African American organizations and immigrant Muslim organizations, such as the Islamic Society of North America (ISNA). Despite these tensions, US Muslims have increased their political visibility, mainly as the result of the activism of the Muslim Public Affairs Council (MPAC) and the American Muslim Council (AMC). Other influential organizations include the American Muslim Alliance and the Muslim American Society. In addition, evidence suggests that mosque participation is correlated with higher levels of political activities, especially among Arab Muslims (Stockton, 2006; Jamal, 2005; Bakalian and Bozorgmehr, 2005).

"Chicano militancy" began after the Second World War, as illustrated by the creation in 1923 of the League of United Latin American Citizens (LULAC), which focused on issues of ethnicity and discrimination. This trend was sustained after the Second World War, when Mexican American veterans organized the GI Forum and campaigned against ethnoracial exclusion. The civil rights movement during the 1960s and early 1970s, as well as the rapidly growing Hispanic population, stimulated the multiplication of Hispanic organizations. These included the Mexican American Political Association, La Raza Unida Party, and the Mexican American Legal Defense and Education Fund. As a result, "the doors of high political office opened for the first time to Mexican Americans; citizens of Mexican ancestry finally began registering and voting in high numbers" (Portes and Rambaut, 2006: 149). This trend was consolidated during the 1980s and 1990s, as illustrated by the multiplication of political, social, and religious organizations (Espinosa et al., 2005). Transnational organizations often also serve as important sources of empowerment for Hispanic immigrant residents by providing them with opportunities for the development of civic skills (Dovidio et al., 2010; Fraga et al., 2010; Waldinger, 2006; Guarnizo et al., 2003).

Concerns about immigration and security policies have had a significant impact of the agendas of Hispanic and Muslim organizations. Most Hispanic organizations mobilize at the federal level around issues related to the reform of the immigration system, and focus on "Hispanic issues" in various fields (such as education, access to job market, and citizenship). Yet controversial initiatives, such as the HR 4437 and the Secure Communities Program, have not translated into a higher sense of ethnic identification—as analyzed in chapter three. Hispanics do not feel more "Hispanic" when they are discriminated against. Indeed, electoral data show that both national origin and education continue to strongly influence political affiliation (Manzano and Sanchez, 2010; Sanchez, 2006). Cubans, for example, are more likely to be Republican than Democratic. Yet, such initiatives have provided strong incentives to Hispanic organization to promote a pan-ethnic political consciousness based on shared interests and "civic-linked fate" among diverse Hispanic communities. According to Cristina Beltrán, "the unifying logic of *Latinidad* means that both liberals and conservatives can invoke the 'Latino vote' to mean almost anything" (2010: 126). Hispanic organizations, such as the NCLR, thus use the threat of a "swing vote" against both Democrats and Republicans as a way of reforming an immigration agenda that has been built on the perception of Hispanics as a threat.

Muslim organizations obviously don't benefit from a "critical mass" effect in national or regional terms. However, like their Hispanics counterparts, they have responded to the post 9/11 policies in varied ways. Increased concerns about threats to their civil liberties have resulted in the growth of public affairs groups, such as CAIR and MPAC. Together with the American-Arab Anti-Discrimination Committee (ADC), these organizations fight against anti-Muslim discrimination and express their concerns about the treatment of Muslims by the government, the media, and local authorities. Their main objectives are to make stereotyping of Muslims a matter of public debate, and to publicize government initiatives that target Muslims. Meanwhile, the AMC has led the way in developing relations with the various branches of the government, as well as coordinating meetings between local Islamic centers and elected officials. Since the reelection of President Bush in 2004, Muslims have become more active in electoral politics. Local election organizers developed state-wide voter lists in order to mobilize Muslim voters. Financial contributions to political candidates have increased, including political action committees (PACS) organized by Muslim and Arab Americans. As Mohamed Nimer noted, "politicization was clearly the Muslim response to post 9/11 grievances" (2005: 14). Most organizations are keen to place Islam squarely in mainstream political spaces by promoting a distinctly "American Muslim" identity, combining the essential elements of Islam and the values of American democracy (Bakalian and Bozorgmehr, 2005; Chishti et al., 2003). According to Caroline Nagel and Lynn Staehli, this implicitly, "gives Muslims a legitimate place at America's multicultural table and to secure for Muslims a voice in the country's pluralistic political system" (2011: 442).

Conventional Mobilization in Europe

Muslims in Europe have to deal with a relatively more adverse context than their US counterparts. In addition to the obstacles analyzed in chapter three (such as the consequences of assimilationist policies and the intricacies of many citizenship regimes), we need to add another layer of factors specifically related to political mobilization. In the United States, ethnic politics constitute one of the many options in consolidating the presence of minorities in the political arena. In European countries, ethnic solidarity and ethnic politics are rarely considered part of the political integration process. Rather, the politics of identity assertiveness is viewed as posing a threat to liberal democracy—either characterized as opportunistic strategies designed to make claims based on sectarian interests, or, worse, used to fuel ethnic conflicts. During the last French presidential election, for example, some Muslim organizations (such as the Union of Muslim Families) publicly supported the socialist candidate François Hollande as a way of protesting against the anti-immigrant and anti-Islam agenda of the conservative incumbent, Nicolas Sarkozy. There is no "Muslim voting bloc" in France, and only a tiny minority of French Muslims describe themselves as practicing Muslims. This initiative was nevertheless described in the media and by some mainstream politicians as a step toward the "Islamization" of the country (although 57 percent of the electorate is Roman Catholic and only 5 percent is Muslim)—or at least the birth of a "Muslim lobby" mobilizing a communitarian vote around Islamic issues (what the far right called a "green fascism" in reference to the color of Islam).

In some European countries, state policies did actually invite ethnic mobilization, converting latent ethnic sentiments into activist organizations at the national and/or local levels. British ethnic relations, for example, have been characterized by a significant immigrant political assertiveness and an increasing level of political mobilization among immigrants who easily converted into official ethnic minorities (such as South Asians and Sikhs). Yet the ideal of a plural state, supported by multiculturalists, has eroded during the last two decades. According to Tariq Modood, "it would be no exaggeration to say that many multiculturalists are dismayed by the emergence of Muslim consciousness... They never intended the recognition of difference to be extended to Muslims" (2009b: 243).

Respect—The Unity Coalition, for example, has been largely criticized for being "communalist," only campaigning for British Muslim interests, and flirting with radicalism through its relationship with the Islamic Forum Europe (IFE, which was inspired by the Islamist party Jama'at-i-Islami). Created in 2003, this party grew out of the antiwar movement and the Stop the War Coalition. It attracted former Labour leaders, such as the MP George Galloway, and stood 26 candidates in the 2005 general election. As Timothy Peace explained, "Respect never aimed to base itself exclusively on Muslim voters, even though its support was disproportionately from the Muslim communities" (2013: 308)—especially in East London and the Bradford West constituency. Nevertheless, the party was criticized for only using Muslim candidates and promoting a "Muslim voting bloc." As in other European countries, politicized group identity among Muslims is currently often associated with Islamic mobilization, if not with radical Islamism. In Germany, the BFF faced criticisms similar to those leveled at Respect, despite its claims of not being a Muslim party.

Furthermore, concerns about identity politics involve Muslims who run for office and/or are elected, although only a few in Europe identify themselves as Muslims whereas the majority are openly secular or explicitly do not want to be defined by their religion. Moroccan-born Ahmed Aboutaleb, a Labour Party politician, was elected mayor of Rotterdam in 2008. Some Dutch media and politicians heatedly criticized his election and contested his loyalty (he possesses dual Dutch-Moroccan citizenship). Geert Wilders, leader of the far right Party for Freedom, declared that "appointing a Moroccan as mayor of the second largest Dutch city is just as ridiculous as appointing a Dutchman as mayor of Mecca. Soon we may even have an imam serving as arch-bishop." In 2012, Lutfur Ralman, who was born in Bangladesh, was elected mayor of the London borough of Tower Hamlets. Suspected of supporting the IFE's agenda, he has been accused of stocking the public libraries with books and DVDs containing extremist propaganda from banned Islamist preachers.

European suspicions about ethnic politics are combined with ambivalence about Muslim political participation. On the one hand, there are concerns that Muslims would feel too alienated to engage in conventional activities, opting instead for retreatism in their enclaves, protest, or violent radicalization. On the other hand, there is some disquietude about the prospect that Muslims would be too actively engaged, becoming a "swing bloc" (at least at the local level), and putting pressure on mainstream parties to reform their agenda. According to Carolyn Warner and Manfred Wenner, "there are fears in Europe that Muslims have the potential for mass mobilization and to undertake large-scale political action" (2006: 457). In the 2010 British election, for example, Muslim voting proved decisive in 82 constituencies. The key objective of European policymakers is therefore to ensure that Muslim minorities do not feel excluded from the political process, while simultaneously trying to discourage Muslims from representing themselves—and subsequently disturbing the traditional conventions of electoral competition. This ambivalent strategy was illustrated by the Labour Party's attempts in 2010 to secure its dominance in constituencies with large numbers of Muslims by standing only Muslim candidates while simultaneously accusing Respect of encouraging a "Muslim vote." In Germany, concerns about the "electorate muscle of the Turkish-origin electorate" (up to 800,000 voters) prompted mainstream parties to devise strategies for capturing the "ethnic vote" during the 2005 general elections. *Bild*, the country's most widely circulated daily, captured the latent fear among politicians and the general population when it asked: "Will Turks Decide the Election?" (Dancygier and Saunders, 2006: 963). French media echoed a similar concern during the 2012 presidential election. In the front page of many newspapers, the main question was: "Did Muslims decide the presidential election?"

A similar tension between concerns about underrepresentation of Muslims and fears of their potential mass mobilization is palpable when European governments seek to create a single, broad-based Muslim organization with which to negotiate, while simultaneously fearing that Muslims would collectively organize and assert their interests in the political arena. Yet attempts to turn "Islam in Europe" into a "European

Islam" have met with little success, both at the EU and national levels. Muslim representation in Europe has slightly increased through,
for example, the European Council for Fatwa and Research (ECFR),
the Federation of European Muslim Youth and Student organizations
(FEMYSO), the Federation of Islamic Organizations in Europe, and
the Union of the Islamic Organizations in Europe. These organizations
have affiliates in various European countries but their actions produce
meager results at the grassroots level. Attempts to unify the Muslims
under a single umbrella organization at the national level have also been
unsuccessful. The Conseil français du culte musulman (CFCM), for
example, was created in 2003 by the French government with the goal
of the organization being the main interlocutor with the state. Since
then, its role has been undermined by internal tensions, conflicts with
other Muslim organizations, and criticism that it does not adequately
represent the diverse make up of French Muslims. In Germany, there are
at least a hundred different Muslim organizations, in addition to several
umbrella organizations (such as the Islam Council and the Coordination
Council of Muslims). Efforts made by the Central Council of Muslims
to embody a "German Islam" have been undermined by the fact that
it represents less than 25 percent of the Muslim community, despite its
strong support from German officials. The Muslim Council of Britain
(MCB) is the primary representative of Muslims, with a network of at
least 380 smaller organizations. Questions have been raised in recent
years about the extent to which the MCB is actually representative of
the extremely diverse Muslim community. For example, 75 percent
of British Muslims believe there is more diversity and disagreements
within the Muslim population than people realize (Mirza et al., 2007).

Many factors can explain the fragmentation of Muslims in Europe,
such as the lack of centralized structure of the Islamic faith; the resilience of religious and ethnic cleavages among Muslims; and a low
level of religiosity that leads a vast majority of Muslims to organize
instead on the basis of class, ethnicity and national origin. As a result,
"in no Western European country has a dominant Islamic organization emerged that speaks with authority for the Muslim community,
nor is there any successful pan-European Islamic organization" (Warner
and Wenner, 2006: 458). Interestingly, concerns about security governance do not arrest this fragmentation process. Muslim organizations,
in the aftermath of 9/11, have framed their concerns in terms of feelings
of vulnerability and a backlash against Muslims. Like their American
counterparts, British organizations (such as the Islamic Human Rights
Commission, and the Forum against Islamophobia and Racism) actively

lobby against negative stereotypes and anti-Muslim practices. Muslim organizations also actively argue about "what they are not" in a context in which Islam is often portrayed as a religion of violence and terrorism. According to Ali Aslan Yildiz and Maykel Verkuyten, "these organizations sometimes face accusations that they condone or support terrorist acts targeting the Western world, or that they at least are indirectly responsible because they propagate an orthodox or fundamentalist interpretation of Islam that hampers the integration of Muslims into the host societies" (2012: 360). Some organizations, such as Milli Görüş in Germany and Fethullah Gülen in the Netherlands, have, in response, become "entrepreneurs of identity" by redrawing identity boundaries in order to define a "morally acceptable" position of Islam. They strongly argue that Islam does not propagate terrorism, and exclude Muslim terrorists from their own moral community of "socially responsible" Muslims. This discursive strategy construes acts of terrorism as "un-Islamic," contrastingly emphasizing the integrative role of Islam into European societies. Another example is provided by a declaration of the Austrian Iman Conference, which held its first meeting in 2005. This declaration stressed the rejection of all kinds of extremism, as well as the participant's loyalty to the Federal Constitution and attachment to freedom of opinion and of religion (Abid, 2006). Yet, Muslim organizations are still unable to overcome internal divisions among Muslims despite their members strong concerns about Islamophobia and issues related to the accommodation of Islam in secular societies. In response to the question "will a million Muslims march?" in Europe, Steven Pfaff and Anthony Gill (2006) responded negatively.

Furthermore, governmental efforts to connect with a so-called Muslim electorate and to negotiate with Muslim organizations are undermined by the temptation to attract the anti-Muslim vote. Mainstream politicians, Abdulkader Sinno noted, "now find it acceptable and even advantageous to denigrate Muslim minorities in traditionally liberal countries such as Italy, France, the Netherlands, and Germany" (2009: 3). Furthermore, overtly anti-Muslim political parties (such as French Front National, and the Belgian Vlaams Belang) have multiplied since 9/11, and flourished in the aftermath of the terrorist attacks in the United States in September 2001, Madrid in 2004, and London in 2005. Mainstream politicians have adopted some components of the far-right propaganda in their own platforms. The specter of "homegrown terrorist" was also added to the existing list of negative stereotypes fueled by a series of previous "affairs" related to Islam (such as the Rushdie affair in the United Kingdom, and the headscarves affair in France), and have been revived by new controversies across Europe (about the building of mosques, halal food in school, wearing of hijab in public places, and ritual slaughtering).

What motivates Muslims to vote, and more substantially, to stand for election—locally, nationally, and for which party in this polarized environment? Muslims represent about 3 percent of the total population in the United Kingdom and about 7 percent in France. They constitute a minority group everywhere in Europe, ranging from 12 percent in Bulgaria to 1 to 2 percent in other countries. They constitute a small pool of potential voters because even fewer are citizens. According to Jytte Klausen, about one million Muslims were eligible to vote in the May 2005 British parliamentary elections, and 70–76 percent went to the polls—compared to an average turnout of 62 percent of nonminority voters. However, Muslim participation is significantly lower in other countries, mostly due to a lack of eligibility. Only 50 percent of adult Muslims can vote in the Netherlands, (Klausen, 2008) while an OSI survey found that only 41 percent of Muslim respondents in Paris and 51 percent in Berlin were eligible to vote in national elections (OSI 2010). These low figures are partially explained by demographic factors. In Germany, for example, about one million naturalized Muslims are too young to vote. Among the remaining 2.4 million adult Muslims, the number of naturalizations has dropped since 2001 as a result of the introduction of citizenship tests requiring greater cultural assimilation.

Among those who have acquired the right to vote, turnout rates remain lower compared to the general population. There are, however, significant variations from one country to another, depending on the type of elections; the nature of the electoral system (whether there is a proportional representation system); the influence of mainstream political parties (as advocates or opponents of diversity); and the socioeconomic characteristics of Muslim voters, as well as their degree of geographical concentration. Each of these factors produces different outcomes. For example, having the right to vote in local elections significantly increases the political representation of minorities in some countries, but not in others. In both England and Belgium, where some categories of resident nonnationals are entitled to vote at the local level, many studies find that Muslims are underrepresented—as well as other minorities. In Denmark, by contrast, the number of elected candidates with a foreign background almost corresponds to their percentage in the general population—as a result of the 1981 reform of the electoral system, which allows foreign permanent resident to vote and stand for local elections (Togeby, 2004).

The interaction of institutional factors and economic and demographic characteristics of minorities also varies. In their study of three localities where British Muslims are highly concentrated (Newham in London, Birmingham and Bradford), Hiranthi Jayaweera and Tufyal Choudhury found that Muslim minorities were more likely to vote than were non-Muslims in the 2005 general election. The likelihood of voting was positively related to the economic status and level of religiosity, but not the level of education: respondents with lower levels of education demonstrated a greater propensity to participate in both national and local elections. More importantly, Muslims living in neighborhoods with people of similar backgrounds were more likely to vote, suggesting "the importance of the mobilizing rather than segregating effects of community networks" (2008: 78). In France, where ethnic representation is more limited and where non-EU nationals cannot vote, Fareen Parvez (2013) argued that political participation differs across class. Middle-class Muslims tend to participate in a politics of recognition with the objective of being politically integrated into the mainstream. Lower-class Muslims, by contrast, tend to practice a form of antipolitics by retreating into parallel communities or by using violence. Geographical segregation in the *banlieues*, directly related to class inequalities, has a detrimental effect on political participation.

Notwithstanding these variations, the overall pattern of Muslim political motivation varies little from that exhibited by non-Muslim voters. Like other citizens, they focus on socioeconomic issues, such as employment, access to social welfare, and medical care. An Open Society Institute survey (2010) found that 50 percent of non-Muslim respondents felt they could influence decisions affecting their cities in the 11 cities included in the study, compared to 46 percent of Muslims born in Europe. More importantly, there was no significant influence of religious identity on various forms of political participation. Jørgen Nielsen noted in *Muslim Political Participation in Europe* that, "being a Muslim does not necessary mean having a life centered on religion; therefore Muslims do not only mobilize to achieve religious goals" (2013: 8). According to Pamela Irving Jackson and Peter Doerschler, "the mounting evidence that Muslims do not vote in a bloc, but rather, like the other Europeans, on the basis of their own individual concerns should not be surprising... Their voting record, based as it appears to be on their situation as individual citizens, provides one more piece of evidence of their integration" (2012: 86). Furthermore, although Muslim voter turnout generally lags behind national rates, Jackson and Doerschler found that Muslim voters in the Netherlands were only about

6 percent less likely to vote than non-Muslims in 2008 (80 percent and 86 percent respectively). In the United Kingdom, eligible Muslims were about 4 percent less likely than eligible non-Muslims were to vote in 2008 (66 percent and 70 percent, respectively).

Other scholars have confirmed the absence of any Muslim *exceptionalism*. For example, David Sanders et al. found that ethnic minority engagement in Great Britain was motivated by the same general factors that influence the political disposition of whites. Citizens of Indian, Pakistani, and Bangladeshi origin displayed the same political attitudes and dispositions as whites. For example, very few people (of all national background) believed they have "any real influence on political decisions or the political process." Similarly, in deciding which political party to vote for, most people emphasized "their evaluations of party leaders and their assessments of the problem-solving capabilities of rival political parties" regardless of their ethnic origin (2014: 123). The level of identification with mainstream parties was similar among various groups (78 percent for whites, 76 percent for Bangladeshis, 79 percent for Indians, and 80 percent for Pakistanis). According to Quintan Wiktorowicz's study of Muslims in Great Britain (2005), a majority of respondents expressed their optimism about politics although they felt inadequately represented by political parties. About 87 percent of Muslims said that it was "very" or "somewhat" important for them to work through the British political system to address issues of concern to Muslims.

Attitudes of young Muslims have received a lot of attention, mostly due to the fact that some have embraced their religious identity more strongly than their foreign-born parents (Voas and Fleichmann, 2012). In Great Britain, where one-third of Muslims are much younger than the general population, the majority of 16–24 year olds feel that "religion is the most important thing in my life"; about 74 percent prefer that Muslim women choose to wear a veil; and 37 percent would prefer to live under Sharia law (compared to 17 percent among those 55 and older). Yet, as M. Mirza et al. noted, their religiosity is not motivated by the sentiment that they should follow their parents' traditions. Their interest in religion is more politicized, not always resulting in participating in conventional prayers at mosques. Rather, "many young Muslims who have become interested in Islam feel that it offers answers to existential questions. For these youngsters, the attraction of religion is that it satisfies their quest for meaning" (2007: 40). In France, 63 percent of those 18–24 year olds declare that they have "no religion" but 93 percent say they observe the requisites of Ramadan (INED, 2013). Their religiosity is therefore unrelated to a political "Islamic identification"—to the exception of some radicals for whom this identification is both the result and the vector of alienation.

Actually, the vast majority of young Muslims in Europe have a lot in common with their non-Muslim counterparts. According to the 2010 FRA survey, Muslim and non-Muslim youth prioritized similar issues "affecting the world today," such as poverty, nuclear weapons, socioeconomic inequalities, and climate change. Muslims are only more likely to prioritize some issues that affect them more than non-Muslims (such as racism, and the conflict between different cultures). The survey's findings about potential involvement in "active citizenship" (including writing a letter of complaint to the local authority, signing a petition, or joining a demonstration) showed little or no difference between the Muslim and non-Muslim respondents in France and in Great Britain in terms of their levels of activity. Muslims were more likely to participate in almost all forms of civic participation in Spain—except contacting a religious leader. Only in France did being from a Muslim background and being a victim of discrimination correspond with having a positive attitude toward violence. Furthermore, there was no evidence in any of the three countries that the religious background of a respondent was an indicator of any actual engagement in physical violence.

The absence of any Muslim political exceptionalism is consistent with the findings presented in chapter three that most Muslims in Europe choose an integrative acculturation strategy, and do not perceive any insurmountable obstacle between their beliefs and national values. They maintain a resulting dual identity: they possess a national or civic identity, which they share with the dominant group; simultaneously they often maintain a strong sense of belonging to their ethnic/religious group. From a social psychology perspective, this dual identification encourages minorities to become politically engaged (Simon and Klandermans, 2001), a process that is critical for their societal integration. Many studies have confirmed that a dual identification is positively related to participation in mainstream politics, and generates more harmonious intergroup relations (Berry et al., 2006; Gonzales and Brown, 2006). Other studies have demonstrated that civic identification was as important, if not more, than dual identification in terms of political engagement, especially in a context where dual identities are rejected by the majority population. This civic identification is illustrated by the high level of trust in institutions expressed by a large majority of Muslims in Europe—despite evidence of discrimination and socioeconomic alienation.

There are, however, distinctive factors specific to Muslims citizens that derive from their experience of being a targeted minority group. As in the United States, the impact of security governance is noticeable at three levels: attitudinal engagement, political affiliation, and effective participation. The major difference, as previously noted, relates to the relative weakness of European Muslim organizations compared to US Muslim organizations. To the factors already listed (such as the fragmentation of Muslim communities in Europe), we can add the absence of pro-Muslim groups that would be able to promote the particular interests of Muslims. Pro-migrant groups have emerged in Europe, both at the national and EU levels—as illustrated by the Sans Papiers movement that has subsequently expanded its representation and forms of activism across Europe. National pro-migrant groups have also transformed their organizational structures to better accommodate the Europeanization of migration and asylum issues (Guiraudon, 2001). A key lobbying opportunity for pro-migrant groups, according to some scholars, is generated by the fact that the "EU offers new institutional venues and access points for representatives of electoral popular diffuse interests, such as women's groups, environmentalists and consumers" (Mazey, 2000: 633). However, pro-migrant lobbying faces serious obstacles in Europe. In contrast to the American situation, there are no significant groups advocating the expansion of immigration (with the marginal exception of some business groups who support recruiting high skilled immigration), especially when it comes to advocate increased flows from Muslim countries. Furthermore, efforts to promote a more migrant-friendly agenda remain rather limited, especially in the field of social and political rights. Finally, pro-migrant groups do not deal specifically with "Muslim issues" (such as Islamophobia), while anti-racist organizations are torn between protecting Muslims against discrimination and condemning anti-Semitic opinions expressed by some Muslims. As a result, the opportunities for Muslims to strengthen their organizational influence remain rather limited.

In terms of attitudinal reaction to security governance, widespread majority views of Muslims as second-class citizens leads, in turn, to the dual identification of Muslims and decreases their civic trust, especially among the second generation. Fenella Fleischmann et al. therefore argue that, "as a source of identity threat for dual identifiers, perceived discrimination may have direct implications for their political engagement" (2013: 215). These implications are, however, more complicated than is commonly assumed. They found in their study of second-generation Turks and Moroccans living in Belgium that perceived incompatibility (between Muslim and non-Muslim values and lifestyles) encourages political apathy. Yet the second generation's perception that they are discriminated against fuels political participation and democratic protest among the second generation. Interestingly, Fleischmann et al. found that, in Belgium, "especially the highly educated (i.e., those who are best equipped to turn their grievances into effective political action) among the second generation perceive discrimination and are politically engaged in (ethno-religious as well as mainstream) organizations" (Ibid: 220). Yet David Sanders et al. (2014) found that the combined effect of the level of education with generational status produced a different outcome among British Bangladeshis. The "migrant optimism" hypothesis, was confirmed by their findings in relation to trust in national institutions (with 67 percent of Bangladeshi expressing a high level of trust compared to 51 percent of whites) and satisfaction with democracy (76 percent and 62 percent, respectively). Their findings also confirmed the "integration paradox": Members of the second generation were less engaged than their parents, more aware and sensitive to discrimination, less trustful in institutions, and less likely to report voting in the 2010 general elections.

Another factor specific to Muslim political mobilization relates to the increasing convergence of leftist and rightist agendas on security and immigration issues. Leftist parties have been assumed to be more open to marginalized groups and more active in enhancing their political representation. Rightist parties, by contrast, have been assumed to be less sympathetic to ethnic minorities in general, and thus less open to their political representation. Most minorities thus support mainstream parties located at the left of the political spectrum (such as the Labour Party in the United Kingdom, the Socialist Party in France, and the Social Democrats in Germany). In 2001, for example, there were an estimated 160 Muslim local councilors in Britain. The party breakdown reflected these assumptions: 153 represented Labour, 6 the Liberals, and 1 the Conservatives. Since 9/11, however, the left across Europe is virtually indistinguishable from the right when it comes to policies that focus on domestic Muslim minorities and foreign policy positions toward the Muslim world. Subsequently, Muslims have gradually diversified their partisan support along a wider political spectrum. Like other minorities, Muslims are still more inclined to vote for leftist parties (Ajala, 2011). In Great Britain, for example, 47 percent of Muslims said they had affinity with the Labour Party in 2010, while only 5 percent said they identified with the Conservatives. In Denmark, about 89 percent of Muslims said they voted for Socialist or leftists parties in 2011.

Yet, Muslims are increasingly dissatisfied with leftist parties because of their use of anti-Muslim rhetoric, and support for assimilationist policies, security policies, and liberal social reforms (such as same-sex marriage). In France, the Socialist Party lost the support of part of the Muslim electorate between the 2012 presidential and 2014 local elections. According to Gilles Kepel (2014), the loss of historical bastions of the left (such as Aulnay-sous-Bois and Bobigny) to the right was partly due to Muslim voter absenteeism—an electoral choice at least partially reflective of dissatisfaction with governmental policies. Rightist parties however remain unattractive. Like some Republicans in the United States, some Conservatives in Great Britain are alarmed by their party's huge disparity in support among ethnic voters. According to Lord Ashcroft, former deputy chairman of the Conservative Party, "bluntly, the party's problem with ethnic minority voters is costing it seats" (2012: 8). Findings from a poll Lord Ashcroft commissioned showed that 83 percent of Muslim respondents (compared to 35 percent of white voters) said they would never vote for the Tories. Their main reason was that they perceived the Conservative Party as unfair and actively hostile to people of different ethnic and religious backgrounds. Muslim respondents also complained that they were portrayed unfairly by the media, and stereotyped as terrorists. However, Muslims in Great Britain and other European countries do share some conservative values with rightist parties while, Jonathan Laurence noted, "the left appears both opposed to Muslims' collective identity and unwilling to defend them against affronts to their religious freedom" (2013). It is worth noting that the center-right has been more likely than the left to take conciliatory positions on issues relating to practical aspects of Islamic life in Europe. For example, it was the left (Christian Democratic governments) that created the Italian Consulta Islamica in 2004, and the Deutsche Islam Konferenz in 2006. Both Muslim voters and candidates therefore have more diverse political affiliations than a decade ago, with a propensity toward membership of social democratic, conservative and Green parties.

Dissatisfaction with mainstream parties tends to fuel support for ethnic politics among some voters. In their study of people of Turkish origin in Mannheim, Germany, Claudia Diehl and Michael Blohm (2001) found that half of the respondents claimed that their interests might be advocated more effectively if they voted for special "immigrant" parties than by voting for mainstream parties. Fenella Fleischmann et al. studied politicization as a response to discrimination among the Turkish and Moroccan second generation in five European cities. Combining the rejection-identification and identification-politicization hypotheses, they showed that discrimination fueled a politicized religious identification, which in turn increased support for political Islam, especially among the second generation (2011). Yet, attempts to create Islam-based political parties have proved relatively unsuccessful at the national level in all European countries. In Denmark, for example, the Liberal Alliance created by Naser Khader won five parliamentary seats in 2007, but the party crumbled shortly after. Khader established a new movement, Democratic Muslims, which attracted few members and was relatively inactive. He joined the Conservative Party in 2009, but lost his mandate in the 2011 parliamentary elections. Representation of Muslims at the local level has fared slightly better, as illustrated by the creation of PRUNE in Andalusia (Spain) in 2010 and the election of two representatives of the Islam Party in Brussels in 2012.

Dissatisfaction with mainstream parties sometimes produces perverse outcomes, as illustrated by Muslims voting for the Front National during the 2014 local election in Fréjus (South of France). A journalist judiciously noted, "it was previously unthinkable that French Muslims with roots in the Maghreb, other than the families of Harkis, who fought with France in the Algerian war of independence, would dream of supporting it. Equivalents would arguably be African Americans voting for the Ku Klux Klan or British miners supporting Margaret Thatcher" (Randall, 2014). It is worth noting, however, that the Front National has used token ethnic representatives since the 1980s (such as Mourad Kaouah, unsuccessful Front National candidate for the 1984 European election). A similar small-scale tendency is noticeable in other countries. The right-wing Freedom Party of Austria (FPÖ), for example, listed Muslim candidates in the 2008 national elections. In Italy, almost all parties listed a Muslim candidate in 2008, including the right-wing Northern League.

Similar to the United States, the political representation of Muslims in Europe remains limited. A series of explanatory factors relate to the character of electoral regimes, as well as the role of party system and intraparty dynamics. Proportional systems are generally regarded as promoting higher degrees of representation. Yet, ethnic minorities can also obtain representation in majority systems if they are geographically concentrated within constituency boundaries (Alonso and Ruiz-Rufino, 2007). In both cases, parties may attempt to restrict minority representation to ethnic-minority districts, limiting the national representation of such groups (Sobolewska, 2013; Bloemraad and Schönwälder, 2013). As a result, Muslims are consistently underrepresented in national parliaments. They enjoy more opportunities at the local level for at least two reasons. First, geographical concentration in some areas provides a pool of voters. Muslims in Austria, for example, constitute 4.2 percent of the total population, but account for about 8 percent of Vienna's inhabitants. In Belgium, Muslims make up one-quarter of Brussels' population. Second, political interest and political participation are still spurred by local issues, and framed by local politics—as confirmed by studies at the local level, such as in Zurich (Eggert and Giugni, 2010), Brussels (Jacobs et al., 2004), Berlin (Berger et al., 2004), and various French and British cities (Garbaye, 2005).

Yet, as in the United States, Muslims who run for office at the local level face serious challenges. Colin Copus notes that, in Great Britain, "local representation has been reduced from broad ideals of citizen empowerment and involvement to a narrow focus on party loyalty and party interest" (2004: 10). Eren Tatari (2010) has identified several obstacles to Muslim political representation in Great Britain, such as a lack of political skills, discrimination from other party members, and power struggles among Muslim councilors and community leaders. More importantly, strong party whips limited the ability of Muslim councilors to contribute to the agenda of party politics or adequately serving their communities. Karen Celis et al. (2013) examined the issue of underrepresentation of minorities in two cities in Belgium. They found that all parties included ethnic minority candidates on their electoral lists in order to promote their own electoral competitiveness. Yet, the representation of minorities was not the priority of political leaders: they neither included minority claims in their platform, nor provided them with opportunities for inclusion in the party organization.

Studies conducted in other countries have strengthened the claim that mainstream political parties do little to enhance the degree of political representation of minorities. They are only interested in ethnic minority candidates if doing so will substantially contribute to the party's prospects for electoral success (Ruedin, 2013; Bird et al., 2011; Caul and Tate, 2004). In his study of 16 German regions and cities, Ruud Koopmans (2004) found significant intralocal differences in migrant mobilization. His findings demonstrate a strong and consistent positive relation between the inclusiveness of local incorporation regimes, and the degree to which immigrants participate proactively in public debates on issues that concern them. There was significant local variation, ranging from Frankfurt (the most multicultural and inclusive city) to Munich (the most exclusive one). Lise Jamila Abid (2006) found a similar positive correlation in Austria between Muslim participation and a "soft" pragmatic policy approach at the local level.

Furthermore, the degree of Muslim political representation is affected by anti-Muslim sentiments. In the United Kingdom, for example, tensions have increased in the last two decades between Muslim and non-Muslim Labour Party members at both the local and parliamentary levels. Non-Muslims have accused Muslims of illegal practices of recruitment and of using council funds to bribe Labour Party members to facilitate the election of Muslim candidates. Jim Fitzpatrick (the Environment Minister at that time) went further in 2010 in stating "Islamic radicals infiltrate the Labour Party to create an Islamic social and political order" in Britain (Gilligan, 2010). Muslims, in response, have accused the Labour Party of discrimination, prejudice in candidate selection, and being excluded from meetings. Critics of European mainstream parties tend to view political representation of minorities as tokenism. In France, for example, mainstream parties on both the left and the right select the most "republicanized" of minorities who are the least connected with their ethnic community. This dualism is problematic because Muslim politicians who are secular usually wish not to be defined by their ethnic or religious background. Those who do define themselves as Muslims either accept their symbolic role as a member of a minority group (which affects their capacity to represent their community), or play the "ethnic card" (which may further antagonize anti-Muslim groups).

CHAPTER 5

Securitization and Unconventional Mobilization

The main objective of immigrant mobilization is political empowerment that involves various activities—not only voting but also donating, signing a petition, writing to officials, lobbying, and demonstrating. Research over the last decade has emphasized the importance of exploring all these avenues of ethnic and immigrant mobilization (Martiniello, 2009; Ramakrishnan and Bloemraad, 2008; Martinez, 2005; Ramakrishnan, 2005). "There is more to participation than simply formal politics," Michael Jones-Correra pointed out, and therefore the "definition of political incorporation should be expanded to include both participation in electoral and non-electoral forms of politics, and indeed in forms of organizational life that might not be overtly considered political at all" (2005: 75–76).

There is a vast literature on how different types of participation interact, generating conflicting results. As Ronald Stockton summarized it, "strong correlations show that people who are more active in one organization tend to be more active in another. They also show that people not active in one organization tend not to be active in another" (2006: 60). Furthermore, different kinds of participation can operate independently from each other—depending on the type of the organization (such as community-wide organizations, ethnic associations, religious congregations, class-based associations, advocacy groups, sport clubs, PTO, or PTA), the nature of their activities (either bridging or bonding, issue-specific or group-specific), and the level at which they operate. "Participation in national political processes such as voting," Stockton adds, "would be different from participation in localized organizations such as social clubs" (Ibid: 55).

These variations are interpreted in different ways by scholarly experts. Proponents of ethnicity theories, for instance, argue that racial and ethnic identities play a dominant role in the integration process (Constant et al., 2009; Constant and Zimmermann, 2008; Foner and Fredrickson, 2004; Solomos, 2000). Marxist and neo-Marxist scholars, by contrast, argue that immigrants share common class interests determining their integration patterns and the nature of their mobilization (Rex, 2001). Most studies, however, combine class and racial factors by studying the interactions of various systems of discrimination. Proponents of intersectionalism thus examine how immigrants have to deal with being members of both a sub-proletariat and a minority group (Alberti et al., 2013; Kraal et al., 2009; Wrench, 2007). Participation of immigrants into the organizations of the working classes as part of the integration process has been studied in various countries such as the United Kingdom (Gilroy, 1987), France (Grillo, 1985), and Italy (Però, 2007)—as well as from a comparative perspective (Penninx and Roosblad, 2002; Castles and Kosack, 1973). These contributions highlighted immigrant mobilizations about issues of material justice, especially during the "era of collective action." "The retreat from class" (Meiksins Wood, 1998) during the postindustrial era has then lead to the "demise of class politics" characterized by the decline of traditional working-class organizations. As a result, Davide Però and John Solomos argued, "a political discourse centered on ethnicity and ethnocultural recognition" has been established "as the master political discourse through which to address questions of integration of migrants and minorities" (2010: 4).

What is missing in most studies is the perspective of immigrants and minorities when facing different modes of participation. Jan. E Leighley has pointed out that "most empirical analyses focus on *who* participates in each type of activity, rather than *why individuals participate in one mode rather than* another" (italics in original) (1995: 183). Studies based on a rational choice approach either focus primarily on electoral participation, or on unconventional mobilization. They are rarely considered simultaneously (for an overview, see McVeigh and Smith, 1999). Other studies question the effects of emotions (such as a sense of alienation, fear, or anger) and grievances on unconventional mobilization (mostly protest movement participation) from a social psychology perspective, (for an overview, see Van Stekelenburg and Klandermans, 2007) without specifically addressing the political context that fuel grievances. Still other studies indicate immigrant civic participation is shaped by political opportunities at the national or local levels, although the forms and goals of this participation remain understudied.

As for unconventional mobilization, we may wonder if security governance has affected the unconventional mobilization of discriminated immigrants and minorities. Does security governance hinder nonelectoral participation or does it provide new incentives to lobby and demonstrate? Do obstacles to traditional political involvement lead to an increased interest in other forms of mobilization, or do they fuel civic apathy? Is unconventional mobilization actually providing mechanisms for the democratic inclusion of targeted groups? Or, does it reflect the emergence of new forms of collective behavior? If so, what is the main goal: becoming part of the political community, or avoiding incorporation into "politics as usual"?

Unconventional Mobilization in the United States

There is evidence that nonelectoral political participation is increasing as a result of security governance. This trend is difficult to measure because of a lack of empirical data about a possible trade-off between different forms of political activities because of security governance. Despite this limitation, we can assume that nonelectoral participation plays a key role in the mobilization of Hispanics and Muslims as a response to security governance for at least three substantive reasons: First, studies of social capital suggest that low status individuals are less likely to participate in electoral activities, and may correspondingly participate in protest politics more than dominant group members. According to Lisa Martinez, "historically, minorities and the poor have turned to protest politics after encountering institutional and extra-institutional barriers that blocked their ability to exercise political influence through more legitimate channels" (2005: 137). Participation in nonelectoral activities helps individuals overcome the disadvantages associated with their lower socioeconomic status and, in the case of immigrants, their legal status. According to Rodolfo de la Garza (2004), nonelectoral activities are crucial for noncitizens who want to express their claims and preferences. These activities are the only option available to illegal immigrants—allowing for the fact that, in the case of protest politics, they are more fearful about participating in demonstrations and other activities that might draw attention to them.

Second, although protest politics provides a resource for all minorities, the relationship between resources and unconventional politics is not straightforward. Lisa Martinez found significant variations in behavior among disenfranchised minority populations—Hispanics being less likely to protest than other ethnic/racial groups. Yet, generational status and citizenship had a much more significant effect on the propensity to protest than race or ethnicity. This relates to the effects of the "integration paradox" previously identified: It is assumed that members of the second generation are more integrated and politically sophisticated than their parents—characteristics that increase their likelihood to vote. They also have higher expectations, are more aware of the limitations of traditional politics, and are more sensitive to discrimination—which increases their likelihood to engage in nonconventional politics (including protests) and join voluntary organizations (Somma, 2010; Norris, 2002). Furthermore, resource-rich individuals (in terms of education, income, civic skills) are more likely to engage in high-cost activities (in terms of time, energy, and personal commitment) such as making donations, contacting politicians, working in community groups, or demonstrating. In contrast, voting or signing a petition is a relatively low-cost activity. As a result, nonelectoral activities are a tool for individuals with both low and high social capital—for different, and often, opposing reasons—as illustrated by the breadth of participation in the 2006 protests against the HR 4437. These protests were intergenerational (Bloemraad and Trost, 2008), transcending socioeconomic boundaries, and gathering Hispanics of varied national origins, Catholics and non-Catholics, immigrants and native born. Interestingly, second-generation and third-generation Hispanics were as likely to participate in these protests as foreign-born ones (Barreto et al., 2009).

Third, security policies provide new political stimulus for targeted groups to engage in nonelectoral activities. Not only has Hispanic protest participation focused on immigration reform and pathways to citizenship for immigrants, but HR 4437 was perceived as a specific political threat that activated multiple communities to act in solidarity in opposing its provisions. Many scholars (Bloemraad et al., 2011; Martinez, 2011; Barreto et al., 2009) have argued that HR 4437 was such a threat that it activated multiple constituencies, as well as various "mobilizing structures" (such as hometown associations, church groups, unions, student associations, and ethnic media). Furthermore, the 2006 protests fostered stronger partnership between immigrants and civic organizations, as well as the emergence of new migrant-led organizations and new modes of immigrant civic organizing at the local level (Benjamin-Alvaro et al., 2009). Scholars vary in their optimism about the long-term impact of the 2006 demonstrations in terms of political engagement, electoral politics, and collective identity of Hispanics. Exit poll data from the 2008 presidential election found a slight increase in Hispanic turnout nationally. In states with higher electoral participation, Hispanic mobilization was often counterbalanced by the mobilization of anti-immigrant groups. Furthermore, the subsequent erosion of group solidarity led to a significant demobilization. In 2010, only 15 percent of all Hispanics said that they have participated "in immigration rights protest in the past year" (Pew Hispanic Center, 2010). It thus remains open to question whether the 2006 protests were a short-term response to a specific policy, or the beginning of new Hispanic forms of social engagement. Yet, as the dynamic dual model of coping would predict, there were psychological "feedback loops" (van Zomeren et al., 2012) in terms of a higher sense of empowerment and a greater belief that Hispanics are able to address their collective disadvantage through collective effort. According to Roberto Suro, the 2006 marches "offer a window into the Latino psyche" (2011:258). Hispanics "made an existential statement, powerful for its simplicity: 'We are here. We are human, flesh and blood, parents and children.' And then there was the other message: 'We are many'" (Ibid: 251).

As a result, Hispanics actively participate in politics besides voting, such as attending a public meeting or demonstration in the community where they live (26 percent); contacted an elected official (22 percent); volunteered their time to religious groups (42 percent), school or tutoring program (31 percent), or any organization representing their particular nationality/ethnic group (16 percent) (Pew Hispanic Center, 2004). As Alejandro Portes and his colleagues demonstrated (2009), large pluralities of Hispanics are politically engaged despite a lack of formal legal membership. The particular contribution of ethnic and religious organizations to Hispanic civic life has been largely documented (Lichterman and Potts, 2009; Foley and Hodge, 2007; Bada et al., 2006). In their study of civic engagement among Mexicans, Elaine Howard Ecklund and her colleagues (2013) found that religious and nonreligious organizations provide different rationales for services—the former promoting bridging capital and the later enhancing bounding capital.

In the same vein, evidence suggests that Muslims in the United States participate actively in civic activities. According to a 2004 survey by Georgetown University and Zogby International on Muslims in the American Public Square (Project MAPS), 95 percent of Muslim respondents said that Muslims should participate in the American political process. Despite their evident disillusionment with the current political system, 77 percent reported that they were involved with organizations designed to help the poor, the sick, and the elderly. More than two-thirds reported involvement in a school or youth program, and 51 percent said they had either petitioned or written to the media or a politician on a given issue. The survey also reported that 97 percent believed that Muslims should donate to non-Muslim service programs (such as aid for the homeless) and 90 percent agreed that Muslims should participate in interfaith activities. Other surveys demonstrated complementary trends. The 2009 Gallup survey, for example, found that Muslims had similar or higher rates of civic engagement than both the general population and other religious groups. About 70 percent reported giving money to a charity (compared to 64 percent among the general population, and 65 percent among Catholics). As for Hispanics, most studies focus on the role played by religious and secular organizations in the process of civic education and enhancement of civic skills (Haddad et al., 2003; Leonard, 2003; Bagby et al., 2001).

For most scholars, skills gained through civic engagement play either a direct or an indirect role in increasing the propensity for political participation. This role, however, varies according to the specific features of Muslim groups. Amaney Jamal, for example, demonstrated that mosque participation among Arabs and South Asians was highly correlated with involvement in civic organizations, while it has no effect on the level of civic involvement among African American Muslims. The underlying causal mechanism that explains these variations relate to group consciousness and its relationship with both perceived discrimination and political distrust. For Arabs, "the mosque is highly associated with greater political activity, civic involvement and group consciousness . . . For African Americans, mosque involvement is not directly linked to either political participation or civic involvement." The latter express a strong sense of collective identity but are the least supportive of political participation among the various Muslim subgroups. Finally, "for Asian Muslims, mosque activity is not directly linked to political activity" although it is "associated with higher levels of civic participation"—Asian Muslims expressing a lower level of perceived discrimination and a weaker sense of group consciousness than Arabs and African Americans (2005: 535).

What motivates US Muslims to engage in unconventional forms of politics in the current context of securitization remains unclear. The current literature is attuned to the potential trade-off between electoral and nonelectoral participation. Yet do forms of civic engagement constitute a strategy to overcome obstacles hindering conventional political participation? Do these types of mobilization represent a form of Muslim political activism or only political activism used by Muslims and others? Does unconventional politics involve active non-incorporation or resistance to the political system fueled by perceived discrimination and political disillusionment? Or should it be understood as a "transition moment" (Però, 2010) or "movement contention" (Tilly, 2004) in the political mobilization of Muslims? Data are in short supply in attempting to explore the differences between diverse forms of Muslim engagement.

Nevertheless, there are two notable trends. First, Muslim concerns about the US Patriot Act and other security measures have fostered the emergence of Muslim organizations that promote civil liberties (Peña, 2007). Proactive initiatives that have been developed by the American-Arab Anti-Discrimination Committee (ADC) and other civil rights organizations include initiating legal actions, petitioning state and federal politicians, engaging in lobbying activities, and organizing educational outreach programs for the general public (Chebel d'Appollonia, 2012b). Some activities have proved successful, such as the mobilization led by the Muslim American Civil Liberties Coalition in 2013 against the NYPD's surveillance program of Muslims in mosques and other public places. Unlike their Hispanic counterparts, however, American Muslims have been unable (to date) to mobilize other communities in solidarity in opposing the excesses of security governance. American Muslims collectively share a sense of a "linked fate," as analyzed in chapter three, primarily based on their experience of being perceived as a "threat."

Their attempts to coalesce around the issue of discrimination and civil liberties have nevertheless failed, as illustrated by the controversy surrounding the Million American March against Fear in September 2013 (originally named the Million Muslim March in reference to the Million Man March organized in 1995 by the Nation of Islam). The Missouri-based American Muslim Political Action Committee (AMPAC) scheduled the event to coincide with commemorations of 9/11, while simultaneously refusing to attribute the terrorist attacks to Islamic extremists. AMPAC suggested, instead, that the US government orchestrated the attacks to make Americans fearful of Muslims, as well as to justify discriminatory policies. The march was condemned by other Muslim organizations (such as the American Islamic Congress), and gathered only hundreds of supporters—who were opposed by Christian and Muslims protestors, and thousands of bikers roared into Washington DC to pay tribute to all the victims of 9/11.

Second, US Muslims have engaged in protests, motivated by US foreign policy. Survey data suggests that American Muslims, much like the American public in general, are more concerned with domestic than foreign policy and with the economy in particular. Yet, when it comes to American policy in the Middle East and the war on terror, Muslims differ from the general population. There is broad opposition to the use of force in Iraq and Afghanistan across all groups of Muslims (up to 75 and 48 percent respectively in 2007 and 2011), although native-born Muslims were more likely than foreign-born ones to express the view that it was the "wrong decision" in both cases (Pew Research Center, 2011). Dissatisfaction with US foreign policy has generated protests— although varied Muslim communities were torn between supporting and opposing the war in Iraq. In his study of the reactions to conflicts in the Middle East among Arab-Muslims living in Detroit, Juris Pupcenoks (2012) found that the relatively low level of political protest about the Iraq war was due to cleavages along ethnic and sectarian lines (with Shi'a Iraqi Americans and Chaldean Christian Arab Americans, for example, supporting the war). In contrast, anti-Israel protests during the Israeli-Hezbollah war (summer 2006) and during the Israeli incursion into the Gaza strip (winter 2009) united and mobilized the entire Arab Muslim community in nonviolent protest.

Muslims, however, remain reluctant taking part in controversies involving Muslims abroad, as illustrated by the lack of direct involvement in the political debate over the video *Innocence of Muslims* in 2012. The major Muslim organizations have condemned the violence abroad, including the killing of Ambassador Chris Stevens and three other Americans in Benghazi, Libya. According to Reema Khrais, "aside from that, Muslims in American have stayed on the peripheries, not wanting to be drawn into a burning fire overseas" (2012). Actually, one response has been to engage in activism on the Internet, as illustrated by the "Muslim rage" campaign. Another response has been the use of political satire as Muslim comedians have begun to participate in US mainstream entertainment, as illustrated by "The Muslims are Coming" tour founded in 2011, and the creation of the New York Arab American Comedy Festival. As the Muslim organizers of these initiatives explained, they have launched a "cultural jihad, a jihad for truth, justice and the American way." "But don't be fooled," they added caustically, "it may be a way of trying to impose Sharia law, one joke at a time" (TAM, 2013).

Unconventional Mobilization in Europe

In Europe, the engagement of Muslims in nonelectoral activities is diverse. Franck Frégosi, for example, identified three ideal types of mobilization in terms of type of social involvement (conflicted or consensual mobilization), whether it is related to religious claims, and if there is a partnership with other social and political forces. First, religious mobilization includes ceremonial mobilization (intended to get people to be more observant and to obtain accommodation for religious practices from the state), associative mobilization (to create a community consciousness), and sectarian mobilization (as illustrated by the Salafist movement). Second, sociopolitical mobilization aims to promote either civic mobilization (a goal supported by integrationists groups) or radical mobilization (as illustrated by the Jihadist movement). Third, secular mobilization focuses on cultural identity and leads to varied forms of mobilization. One is centered on republican ideology (as illustrated by French Movement of Secular Muslims), another on radical secularism (involving Muslims who publicly recommend leaving Islam and are involved in the Committee for Ex-Muslims). "Throughout their daily mobilizations," Frégosi argued, "Muslims show that when it comes to coordinated collective actions, heterogeneity is the norm, whereas uniformity is the exception" (2013: 138).

The demands of Muslim groups also vary. Ruud Koopmans et al. (2005), for example, analyzed minority group demands in Great Britain, France, and the Netherlands. They found a strong relationship between the level of cultural pluralism in these countries and two types of group demands—either "exceptional" (when Muslims demand rights that are not granted to other groups) or "parity" claims (when Muslims request the same rights already granted to other groups). In the Netherlands, the majority of demands were for parity—and Dutch politicians were receptive. In Great Britain, Muslim group demands were more confrontational, with a higher number of exceptional demands and a greater propensity for protest. The main reason for the exceptional nature of these demands is the character of the United Kingdom's "race relations" framework, whereby Muslims are not officially recognized as a religious minority group. In France, where there is no traditional framework for the expression of cultural group differences, most demands were reactive in response to state actions (such as the expulsion of pupils from state schools for wearing a headscarf). The common challenge in these three countries was the fact that there was heated discussion about whether Islam should be more accommodated than other religions. According to Koopmans et al., the Islam's unique situation was due to its more visible and public nature, as well as the failure by public institutions in many European countries to specifically recognize the needs of Muslims.

Little is known about what factors influence the choice of one type of mobilization over another by Muslims in Europe, and under which circumstances a trade-off between conventional and unconventional activities is made. Studies that have analyzed migrant and minority mobilization have identified different trends (De Rooij, 2012; Van Deth et al., 2007) that can be applied to Muslims. What is most pertinent at that stage is how Muslims relate to civil society, and how their degree of "social embeddedness" is shaped by their suspect status as posing a threat. For example, can they voice their concerns like other citizens? Moreover, do they engage more in ethnic civic mobilization than do other groups? There is no clear answer to these questions, because of the variety of factors (both institutional and noninstitutional) that influence the propensity toward civic engagement among Muslims across Europe. Findings from the 2010 European Social Survey (ESS) conducted in France, Spain, and Great Britain demonstrated that levels of informal political participation vary by country. For instance, Muslims tend to participate less than the general public in signing petitions or working with associations in Germany, France, the United Kingdom, and the Netherlands. Yet, Muslims were more likely to boycott certain products than the general public in the Netherlands and the United Kingdom, while in Germany and France they were more likely to participate in a demonstration.

The Open Society Institute (OSI) report showed variations depending on the type of activities and the composition of organizations. About 47 percent of Muslims were involved in associational activities (compared to 56 percent of non-Muslims). Conversely, Muslims were more likely to be engaged in religious activities than non-Muslims (24 percent and 16 percent, respectively). Muslims were also less likely to be involved in ethnically mixed civic organizations than non-Muslims (52 percent and 62 percent respectively). Muslims involved in their own ethnic/religious organizations, however, were more likely to trust their city councils than those involved in mixed organizations. There was one uniform aspect: activities connected to children's education or schools were the most popular form of engagement among both Muslims and non-Muslims (OSI, 2010).

Other studies emphasize variations at the national level determined by generational cleavages, national origin, and immigration status. Hiranthi Jayaweera and Tufyal Choudhury (2008) found that overall levels of active organizational involvement among Muslims were far lower than those of electoral participation in the United Kingdom. Muslims, especially recent immigrants, were less likely than non-Muslims to be involved in heterogeneous organizations. The most common barriers to voluntary participation among established residents were a lack of time because of work commitments, and a sense of powerlessness about their influence on national decision-making. In their comprehensive study of the relationship between religion and political action in Western Europe, Aida Just et al. found that second-generation Muslims are not only more religious and more dissatisfied with their host countries than foreign-born Muslims, but also that religiosity contributed to stimulating their political engagement. Using data from the ESS collected between 2002 and 2010, Just et al. demonstrated that religiosity has a specifically positive effect on mobilization among second-generation members—but only for uninstitutionalized forms of political engagement. Furthermore, although political engagement (both conventional and nonconventional) increases with religiosity among young Muslims, "heightened religiosity merely brings their political activism to the same level as the one observed in the secular public" (2014: 138).

Lise Togeby (2004) found variations among members of the second generation from different groups in Denmark. For Pakistanis, membership in ethnic organizations had a positive and very strong effect on political participation. Other forms of membership had no effect (such as in cross-ethnic sport clubs or unions). For Turks, participation in both ethnic organizations and cross-ethnic sport clubs had some effect, but a weaker one than among Pakistanis. For both groups, education was significantly related to participation in informal activities and for higher levels of social trust, but not for voter turnout. In Belgium, Fenella Fleischmann et al. argued that "in line with a European tradition of trade unionism and street protests for worker's rights, the second generation looks beyond conventional politics and is aware of such tried and tested political means to challenge inequality and to bring about social change" (2013: 220). Their study pointed to the importance of voluntary organizations (both ethnoreligious and mainstream) as a route to collective action.

These studies provide useful insights, but they do not directly address the question of the effect of securitization on the motivations and objectives of unconventional political mobilization. We can only deduce from them that Muslims are responding to their societal situation by engaging in different nonelectoral activities. Their behavioral patterns vary to such an extent that it is impossible (as it is for political participation) to identify a "Muslim profile." Yet what Muslims perceive as being a threat to them (discrimination, negative stereotyping, and the depiction of Islam as incompatible with Western lifestyles) tends to have a consistent effect. A series of studies about perceived incompatibility of values and discrimination in different European countries supports the proposition that Muslims use a wide range of forms of nonelectoral mobilization: apathy (when they face a "clash of expectations" between their preference for integration and the assimilationist constraints imposed by host society); organizational membership (either ethnoreligious or mainstream, or both—depending on opportunity structures and generational status); or democratic protest (when unfair treatment becomes a motivator to actively strive for a more equal society).

Muslims who engage in protest politics occupy a delicate situation in their host country. According to Bert Klandermans et al., their "loyalty to the country of residence is placed under even more doubt if they engage in protest" (2008: 993), potentially explaining why Muslims are sometimes reluctant to do so. Some episodes have received significant attention, such as protests in Denmark and elsewhere after the publication of offensive cartoons of the Prophet Muhammad in the Danish newspaper *Jyllands-Posten* in 2005. In France, several demonstrations took place against the 2004 law on the banning of the wearing of "conspicuous" religious symbols in state schools. Many Muslims characterized this law as "a form of government-sponsored religious persecution against Islam and its adherents" (Croucher, 2009: 10). Intense media coverage and heated political debates have generated a distorted image of angry Muslims taking to the streets on a routine basis.

However, there is evidence that Muslims in Europe are less likely than non-Muslims to demonstrate. In his analysis of the relationship between religious denomination and conflict styles in France, Germany, and the United Kingdom, Stephen Croucher (2011) developed a fourfold typology of conflict management. The integrating style attempts to best fill the needs of all parties involved in the conflict. The avoiding style does not address the conflict. The dominating style is when individuals pursue their own interests at the cost of others. Finally, the compromising style attempts to resolve conflict rapidly, attempting to find a compromise. Noting national variations, Croucher found that Muslims overall prefer the integrating, avoiding, and compromising conflict styles more than Christians—who would prefer the dominating style. One factor that explains why Muslims would prefer conflict styles that are less confrontational relates, according to Croucher, to the nature of Islam—notably its collectivist values (such as peace, patience, and a preference for mediation). Another factor is provided by the status of being a religious minority in societies where Islam is characterized as in conflict with the dominant Judeo-Christian culture. Church-state regimes, in this regard, are crucial because they define the institutional opportunity structures that shape the mobilization patterns of Muslims

(Laurence and Vaïsse, 2006; Koopmans et al., 2005; Statham et al., 2005).

In their comprehensive study of the dynamics of contestation over Islamic religious rights in six European countries, Sarah Carol and Ruud Koopmans (2013) have emphasized the varying degrees of accommodation of Muslim religious rights in order to explain why some issues (such as mosque construction, religious education, and the right to wear headscarves) were highly controversial in some countries, but entirely without debate in others. Their findings confirmed the relationship between national settings and the level of "obstructiveness," which measures the degree to which claims about rights challenge the institutions and the dominant culture in a host society. The two most contrasting cases were France (which has an unfavorable setting), and the Netherlands (which offers a favorable one), with other countries (Germany, Belgium, Switzerland, and the United Kingdom) occupying mediating positions.

Notwithstanding these cross-national variations—and in line with a "dynamic dual pathway model"—some aspects of security governance (such as racial profiling, and police harassment) fuel fear and anger, the two main emotions conducive to prompting protest. In their study of Turkish and Moroccan minorities in four European countries, Fleischmann et al. (2011) found that perceived discrimination was significantly related to an increased propensity for collective actions, fuelling contentious forms of political engagement. Bert Klandermans et al. argued that we could anticipate that "immigrants will constitute some of the major protest movements in the future in many European countries" (2008: 1009). Their prognostic is based on the resilient combination of discriminatory practices against minorities across Europe, which fuels anger (especially among young people) and grievances that they define as "a sense of indignation about the way authorities are treating a social or political problem" (Ibid: 993).

The 2005 riots in France provided a striking illustration of this process. They began with a confrontation between the police and teens in Clichy-sous-Bois that provoked the accidental death of two boys. Not all the rioters were Muslims and those who were did not riot for religious reasons. Their two central grievances were resentment toward a French state that young Muslims and non-Muslims alike believe perpetuates socioeconomic and political inequalities, and a distrust of the police and political parties. The reaction of French officials to the riots was symptomatic of the blinkered approach generated by excessive security concerns. A state of emergency was declared, followed by tightened controls on immigration—although most of the rioters were born in France—and the introduction of additional assimilationist policies. From the state's perspective, violent protests spread across the country due to the inadequate integration of youths who are unwilling to adjust to the requisites of living within the cultural norms of French society. Yet, in fact, these young members of the second generation were culturally integrated but socioeconomically excluded. They strove toward being treated in a equitable manner rather than what they perceive as second-class citizens. The same is true of youth who rioted in other countries such as Great Britain, Belgium, Sweden, and Germany. Unlike in France, protests did have a religious component in some cases, as illustrated by the involvement of young Muslims in the Danish cartoon controversy of 2005–2006. Lasse Lindekilde demonstrated that the level of political participation of Danish Muslims increased during the controversy, and that this increased propensity to make political demands should be interpreted as active citizenship, rather than as a "cultural backlash" (2013: 186). Instead of being the product of uncontrolled political frustration, evidence suggests that most protests have been motivated by considerable trust in democratic institutions, and an adherence to democratic values such as freedom of speech and freedom of religion.

What should We actually Fear?

Most of the studies and surveys analyzed in this chapter, as well as in chapter four, confirm that Hispanics and Muslims in the United States are as committed to democratic values, and are as engaged in electoral and nonelectoral participation as members of the dominant group. They also strongly reject the use of violence in politics, and of extremism. Large majorities of US Muslims, for example, say that suicide bombing and other forms of violence against civilians are never justified (81 percent in 2011, up from 78 percent in 2007). US Muslims express extremely negative views of al Qaeda (70 percent in 2011, an increase of 12 percent since 2007)—foreign-born respondents being more critical than native-born ones (75 percent and 62 percent, respectively). Finally, US Muslims are very/somewhat worried about the possible rise of extremism in the United States (60 percent in 2011) (Pew Research Center, 2011). There are common trends in all the reports and surveys that explore Muslim attitudes to terrorism in Europe reviewed for this study (e.g., BIS, 2011; FRA 2010b; Mirza et al., 2007; The 1990 Trust, 2006; Appleton, 2005; FOSIS, 2005): First, the majority of young Muslims are unequivocal in their condemnation of terrorism. For example, 85 percent of Muslim students surveyed by FOSIS condemned the London bombings, and 93 percent of those surveyed by Michael Appleton did not support the 9/11 attacks in the United States. Second, negative political attitudes expressed by some Muslims in many European countries should not be regarded as "evidence of disloyal and dangerous immigrants" but rather a sign of their frustration of not being accepted as part of the mainstream society (Maxwell, 2013: 284).

There are however three potential attitudinal and behavioral responses to security governance that would generate concerns about the adverse long-term effects of security governance on the democratic inclusion of some migrant and minority groups. The first one relates to retreatism, a form of active nonincorporation by which people react to both objective and subjective discrimination. Various groups, with differing motivations, select this option. Some young Muslims born and raised in Europe, for example, prefer to isolate themselves from society at large although this decision is not always related to religious ideology. Rather, it is the result of a reactive identity in response to social marginalization (Ysseldyk et al., 2010). This reactive identity can relate to religious symbols. It should not, however, be only interpreted as a sign of extreme religiosity. Many second-generation women in France, for example, have chosen to wear the veil in France mostly as a reaction to the controversies about headscarves in public spaces (Just et al., 2014; OSI, 2011). Another group consists of Muslims who deliberately refrain from political action because they consider it as forbidden (Haram) for believers by their religious teachings (Hopkins and Kahani-Hopkins, 2004). According to Aida Just et al., "some Muslims perceive political participation in Western democracies as a challenge to the Quran's teaching that believers are forbidden to accept the authority of the disbelievers over them. The act of voting in secular societies is seen as particularly subversive to Muslim identity because it signals direct engagement with the political system of nonbelievers" (2014: 129). Often improperly clustered together by observers under the heading "Salafi," these Muslims do not constitute an organized group, but are nonetheless quite active in informal networks. For instance, in Great Britain, some Islamist organizations (such as Hizb u-Tahir and Al-Muhajiroun) have denounced democratic politics and consider voting as un-Islamic (Hopkins and Kahani-Hopkins, 2004). In Germany, there are separatist organizations (such as the Avrupa Millî Görüs Teskilât-lari, and the Federation of Islamic Organizations and Communities) that do not accept the institutions of the German state, and "attempt either to segregate themselves into Islamic enclaves or to promote the Islamization of Europe in general, and Germany in particular" (Warner and Wenner, 2006: 465).

A second type of response to security governance—the radicalization process—raises serious concerns about societal cohesion and security in Western democracies. There are various degrees of radicalization, as F. M. Moghaddam (2005) delineates using his "multi-story building" metaphor. On the ground floor, the most important factors influencing behavior are subjective interpretations of material conditions, perceptions of discrimination, and the identification process. Few individuals from this group move up to the first floor, searching for ways to improve their personal situation. A subgroup of those who then recognize they have no voice become more politicized and dissatisfied and move up to the second floor (the floor of polarization). A further fragment then reaches the third floor, becoming separated from the dominant values of their society while those reaching the fourth floor adopt a Manichean view of the world ("good against evil"). Finally, a tiny minority reaches the fifth floor—and they participate in terrorist activities. In Europe, young Muslims who feel alienated from wider society occupy the (second) floor of polarization. As the authors of the 2010 FRA report note, excluded and thus vulnerable, Muslims may become sympathetic toward the use of violence. The report showed that these young Muslims who have been the victims of emotional or physical violence are—in turn—more likely to support and employ use of violence. Other studies confirm this strong relationship between victimization and a propensity to offend. According to Kees van den Bos et al., for example, "when people experience injustice this can easily lead to anger against society, as a result of which intentions to and actually engaging in violent and rude behavior can occur. This effect is particularly likely when people are predisposed to react in strong ways to experiences of personal *uncertainty* and when they experience that their own groups is *threatened by other groups*" (2009: 132).

Other studies focusing on Muslim youth and young adults—especially those born and raised in Europe—confirm this trend (Bos et al., 2009; Verkuyten, 2008; Vedder et al., 2006). Young Muslims who have experienced social marginalization and discrimination are more likely to distance themselves from society, and are more inclined to physical or emotional violence. Peter Hopkins' study of young Muslim men in Scotland (2007) revealed that they were skeptical about the political system, political parties, and politicians. As a result, they expressed low trust in institutions. A similar picture is evident in other European

countries: young Muslims are more likely than their non-Muslim counterparts to distrust the domestic governments, national parliaments, the
legal system, and EU institutions. Elanor Kamans et al.'s study of Dutch
Moroccan teenagers, for example, showed that they tend to distance
themselves from Dutch society when confronted with negative attitudes
from the general population. This could "eventually make them more
open to criminal behavior, less critical toward terrorism and also more
open to recognize the far reaching reasoning behind terrorism" (2009:
850).

Several studies reinforce Moghaddam's formulation. A segment of
these "angry young men" becomes radicalized, moving from the third
floor (separatism coupled with sporadic use of violence) to the fourth
floor. They express their support for terrorist organizations and praise
a systematic politics of violence. Radicalization at this stage involves
increasing justification of the use of extreme violence (including terrorist violence) (Thomas et al., 2014; van Stekelenburg and Klandermans,
2012). Support for radical groups sometimes leads to the identification
with members of extremist groups located abroad, or direct membership in local groups pursuing radical actions. As David Wright-Neville
and Debra Smith explained, "alienation is replaced by identification
with the group, powerlessness is replaced by potency derived from being
involved in group operations, while humiliation is mitigated by participation in actions" (2009:95). This trend is often fueled by perceived
injustices taking place against Muslims around the world (such as in
Iraq, Afghanistan, Chechnya, Somalia, and the Palestinian territories)
to the point, Alex Wilner and Claire-Jehanne Dubouloz argue, that some
Western Muslims "feel justified to take revenge against the citizens and
states that condone and participate in these perceived injustices" (2010:
42). The supporters of militant jihadism invoke the concept of "victim-
hood in the Islamic world" (Ibid: 44) to manipulate believers, turning
them into fanatics and zealots. Furthermore, as the political violence
literature emphasizes, proponents of radicalization increasingly justify
intergroup violence as the preferred solution to (actual or perceived)
social marginalization (Hogg and Blaylock, 2012; Hogg et al., 2010;
Thomas et al., 2010; Moskalenko and McCauley, 2009).

This has been exemplified by the pro-Gaza demonstrations that
took place in Europe in July 2014. In France, in the largely immigrant Parisian neighborhood of Barbès and in the northern suburb of
Sarcelles, demonstrations degenerated into street battles between protesters hurling stones and police firing tear gas. In Barbès, an Israeli
flag was burned. In Sarcelles, a kosher market was looted, cars set on

fire, shop windows smashed, and a funeral home attacked. Not only do rioters have a limited religious education—"nothing but cherry-picked Koranic statements laced with poisonous jihadist messages" (Wilner and Dubouloz, 2010:41), but they are also poorly informed about geopolitical realities. They would rather adopt a Manichean conception of the world, thus strengthening a sense of "who they are" by engaging in intergroup violence.

The third and most problematic attitudinal response to security governance is terrorist engagement. This, of course, constitutes the ultimate stage of radicalization. Scholars and analysts have identified a plethora of contributory factors that lead to terrorist activities. These include sociopolitical alienation, political distrust, cultural and religious factors, geopolitical crises, and individual psychological patterns (such as emotional vulnerability, identity crisis, and attraction for martyrdom). Yet, a "terrorist profile" remains elusive, and few generalizable rules can be applied (Chebel d'Appollonia, 2010). According to the literature on terrorism, the causal relationship between behavioral intentions and the actual triggers of terrorist acts behavior remains obscure and elusive. As Jytte Klausen argued, "sufficient evidence exists to conclude that the social anger expressed in riots and that expressed in Islamist political extremism have very different sources... anger and terrorism are different matters" (2009: 31). Radicalization and violent protest does not automatically result in homegrown terrorism. A further catalyst is required, such as a process of "double marginalization" of eventual terrorists—both from society and from fellow activists (van Stekelenburg and Klandermans, 2011). Yet, terrorist activity does not develop in a vacuum. Western governments have used the actual threat of radicalized minorities to justify discriminatory measures against the majority of Muslims. This process has obfuscated rather than clarified the distinction between moderate Muslims and terrorists. It has increased the number of Muslims who feel alienated, while fueling the anti-Western propaganda of terrorist organizations.

Conclusion

The preceding chapters have linked the main targets of security governance to three sets of issues: economic and social welfare, national identity, and homeland security. I have illustrated how varied immigration policies and integration policies shape immigrants' responses to securitization by raising new obstacles to their incorporation into their host societies.

Federal agencies have been given "unprecedented authority" to target immigrants, to deport newcomers, and to police minorities under the guise that they constituted threats to national security in the United States (Kubrin et al, 2012). Both Federal law and local political practices have implications for individuals and the communities of which they are members (e.g., sense of alienation, fear of reporting crime, social isolation, unwillingness to interact with authorities). These, in turn, complicate social incorporation without providing greater societal security. In Europe, further steps have included new assimilationist measures that, Jocelyn Cesari noted, go "hand in hand with states' active policies to transform the behavior and identities" of Muslims. These policies (such as value tests for would-be citizens, and restrictions on Islamic practices seen as illiberal) are designed to produce "Muslim subjects with the correct moral identity," if not to "civilize the enemy" (2013: 143).

Furthermore, building upon the work of social psychologists, I have demonstrated that a "clash of expectations" is currently damaging the relationship between immigrants and differing components of the host societies. What is currently expected from immigrants and minority groups extends beyond the socioeconomic and cultural requirements conventionally needed to comply with mainstream security-defined social norms. In this context, the traditional conception of integration has been altered to actually mean something approximating "conformity," "obedience," or "loyalty."

This securitization of integration affects the mobilization patterns of immigrants and minorities in two ways that seem paradoxical, but actually complement each other. First, it hampers the democratic inclusion of groups objectively discriminated against into the political system by erecting a series of obstacles such as limited actual citizenship rights, and overt political discrimination. As I illustrated in chapter three, these problems plague Muslims in most European countries. Comparably, albeit to a lesser extent, both Hispanics and Muslims remain largely outside the formal political system in the United States.

Second, security policies have provided new opportunities for targeted populations to mobilize. Both political and nonpolitical forms of mobilization are facilitated by new social movements and mediating institutions (such as ethnic/religious organizations, and interest groups) that have emerged as a response to concerns about discrimination, and the subsequent potential radicalization of ostracized minorities. As a result, all the groups studied in this book are simultaneously marginalized and mobilized—recognizing the significant variations among ethnic groups and socioeconomic subgroups in their form and degree. These variations, I argued, can be partly explained by the traditional SES variables, objective discrimination, and the formal rules and practices of integration that together facilitate or hinder mobilization. While understanding the general conditions under which "outsiders can begin to become political insiders" (Mollenkopf, 2013: 108) is important, it is insufficient to address the complex relationship between integration, attitudes toward the host society, sense of group consciousness, and various forms of mobilization. A key lesson drawn from the studies analyzed in this book is that the less integrated groups can have a positive perception of their host society (the "migrant optimism" phenomenon), while the more integrated groups are more critical, feel more alienated, and are more likely to engage in protests politics (the "integration paradox"). Factors explaining these dynamics, I have argued, include perceived discrimination, as well as a series of factors that contribute to subjective integration outlined in chapter three.

Both American Hispanics and Muslims, as well as Muslims in Europe, are subsequently engaged in various forms of mobilization, either conventional or unconventional. I provided evidence that the relationship between integration and mobilization is complex. A "successful" socioeconomic integration can lead to active conventional political participation; it can also result in a strong involvement in protest politics, especially among members of the second generation who expect to be treated in ways comparable to their nonminority peers.

Their disillusionment renders them less likely to be supportive to conventional democratic politics, and in turn, more likely to participate in acts of political protest.

Yet, most of the studies and surveys analyzed in this book tend to confirm an optimistic scenario. The central question of this book is "how does it feel to be a threat?" The response of the targeted groups in the United States and Europe is it feels traumatic, unstable, and alienating. This book's first major finding is that the vast majority of migrants, however, do not translate their sense of alienation into social isolation, cultural estrangement, a heightened sense of political distrust, negative feelings toward the host society, and ultimately, separatism or radicalization.

This book's second major finding is that immigrants and minorities are able to shape policy outcomes through processes of mobilization and substantive representation. As Maria Lorena Cook has argued, "collective mobilization and protest—marches, occupations, strikes, hunger strikes, and the like—may constitute political actions that can lead to changes in policy and even to legalization ... Even absent policy outcomes, collective action and individual cases of protest can expand issue visibility and increase protestors' resources and networks" (2013: 59). Responsiveness to security governance thus involves a series of feedback loops that affect the mobilization strategy of immigrants as well as the opportunity structures in the host societies. One plausible effect is a "desecuritization move," which should be understood as a distinct outcome, not simply the reversal of a securitization process.

A successful desecuritization strategy includes political activity by the targeted population themselves (from protest to political participation), one that shifts the board conception of them from victims to citizens. It involves a process of agency, one in which the excluded explicitly identify with their excluded position in order to claim the "right to have rights." As Rens van Munster has noted, "the desecuritization move exists in turning the excluded, securitized illegal migrant to the place of the political figure per se, that is, as a constitutive force that can move the institutional scheme of belonging beyond the status quo" (2004: 148). A proactive visibility can counteract a negative one, providing a platform from which targeted populations formulate their demands—as illustrated by those DREAMers willing to "come out" as an identifiable subgroup of illegal immigrants in the United States.

Furthermore, the desecuritization process has to generate a significant pressure "from below" that may force policymakers to reconsider their advocacy and implementation of security policies. Effective collective action strategies by migrants and minorities can have an impact on the evolution of security governance, prompting a reassessment of security measures by Western governments. Pressure from below may thus provide an important counterweight to the current process of securitization, as illustrated by significant changes introduced in 2011 by the British government to the Prevent program. This program, initially set up after the 2005 London bombing, was designed to fight radicalization among Muslim communities. It involved gathering intelligence about the thoughts and beliefs of Muslims who were not engaged in criminal activity, as well as trying to turn religious and community groups into intelligence providers in exchange of public funding. Serious concerns about this program have been voiced, not only by Muslim organizations but also by youth workers, teachers, and members of the House of Commons Select Committee for Communities and Local Government. The British government finally admitted that the program was "flawed," damaging "community cohesion" instead of improving it, and fuelling resentment among Muslims who have been victims of "state snooping" (Secretary of State for the Home Department, 2011: 10). The new agenda now includes the limitation of "disproportionate and in some cases unnecessary" counterterrorism powers (such as "stop and search" powers used by the police), as a way to restore cooperation with local communities. Another important change relates to the recent acquiescence that the government should not "securitise its integration strategy" (Ibid: 13). Prevent "depends on a successful cohesion and integration strategy," but, as a general rule, integration policy and counterterrorism "must not be merged together" (Ibid: 35).

This book's third major finding is that there is no guarantee, however, that democratic inclusion will take place everywhere and for all groups. The main obstacles are either a lack of responsiveness of access points within the political system, a refusal of policymakers or politicians to respond, or resistance to incorporation by some immigrants and minorities who "refuse to permit the political system to influence them" (Hochschild and Mollenkopf, 2009: 27).

I conclude on a sobering point: radicalization is a complex phenomenon that cannot be addressed only with indiscriminate "security packages." Socioeconomic exclusion can facilitate radicalization, yet socioeconomic integration is an insufficient means to address the root causes of terrorism. How to encourage a variety of nonviolent means of participation among immigrants and minorities remains an unanswered question—one that poses a significant challenge to our foundational understanding of integration policy.

Alternative policy initiatives to security governance must therefore address a series of interrelated issues: racial and religious discrimination, poor and segmented urban planning, inadequate educational services, and limited, discriminatory welfare provisions. Yet, fighting socioeconomic inequality is insufficient. What also matters is the "well-being" of immigrants and minorities—a multidimensional concept that includes enhancing subjective integration and increasing perceived social capital. Equally important is to introduce measures that help restore the public image of those groups suspected of posing a threat. "Hard repression" (such as police brutality), as well as "soft" forms of repression—"such as ridicule of individuals, stigmatization of groups, and public statements that distance specific actors" (Lindekilde, 2010: 454)—have been found to have counterproductive consequences that lead to increased dissent and alienation among immigrants and minorities. This situation increases the propensity toward a "backfire" response from individuals prone to political and social violence that, in turn, encourages law enforcement authorities to intensify repression. A reassertion of democratic principles, such as the respect for civil liberties and civil rights, is thus crucial in order to stop the "dynamics of contention" (McAdam et al., 2001) and limit the self-reinforcing effect of scapegoating.

Furthermore, the civic integration of targeted populations should be improved as a means to arrest their sense of political impotence. Effective political representation and new opportunities for organizational incorporation of minorities are equally important. These goals can be achieved through policy changes from a top-down perspective. "Responsiveness of the political system" includes policies designed to "satisfy interests and promote the recognition of native-born disadvantaged minorities," as well as immigrants (Hochschild and Mollenkopf, 2009: 23). The array of potential policy changes is extensive, ranging from religious accommodation to enfranchisement in nonnational elections.

Predictably, I conclude with a discussion of the research questions generated in this book. A future research agenda could focus on the question of the means by which migrants and minorities are incorporated, and simultaneously arrest the propensity toward radicalization in favor of greater democratic engagement. First, scholars might consider the conditions under which immigrants and their descendants become involved in various forms of mobilization, and, second, how these forms of mobilization affect the context of their integration. The history of previous immigrants' mobilization has provided various patterns, such as "coalition of faith," "linked fate," and pan-ethnic "coalition of power."

Research efforts should thus address the current relationship between empowerment strategies and collective identities, notably by inquiring the emergence of new commonalities and new modalities of incorporation. Several important questions related to the scope and goals of mobilization have received little attention to date: Does security governance imply a trade-off between political and nonpolitical activities? What are the factors explaining how and why some individuals or groups are more likely to engage in violent protest, or conversely to become more politically apathetic? What are the most effective strategies in terms of collective identification to respond to objective discrimination?

In order to address these questions, scholars will require an in-depth analysis of self-perceptions of the polity by targeted groups based on their self-identification. They will need to be able to evaluate objectively the sense of belonging of individuals in the targeted group, their degree of sociability and organizational membership, and their amount of in-group/out-group trust.

National sample survey data, despite providing useful insights, fails to capture all the dynamics involved in the mobilization processes for two major reasons. First, local practices significantly vary among countries and across groups. One issue that deserves to be examined further concerns the differential impact of security governance in large urban settings (such as New York City and London), versus in small localities (where immigrants are more fearful of security measures but have less opportunities for grassroots mobilization), and rural areas. We therefore need to supplement national surveys with interviews at the regional and local levels. Second, some national surveys tend to implicitly reproduce the binaries framed by the dominant discourse of security governance, such as religiosity versus loyalty, and ethnic identification versus national belonging. This reinforces a perspective that treats migrants as passive receptors. We need to refine key concepts (such as ethnicity, religion, or identity) by examining them from the immigrants' perspective in order to better understand the immigrants' perspective. Furthermore, scholars can use this approach to investigate if other, often neglected identity markers matter as much—if not more—to immigrants and their descendants, such as their occupation, residential location, political affiliation, family role, gender, and sexual orientation.

Finally, and critically, scholars might better conceptualize the feedback effects of immigrants' mobilization on political opportunity structures and integration policies. There is a vast literature on how immigrants influence the policies and the politics of their host country.

Yet, we still have little information about their capacities to desecuritize the context of their integration. How can groups currently targeted more effectively form alliances with other excluded categories? What kind of material and symbolic resources are available to those suspected of posing a "threat"? These are questions I hope to address in future work.

Bibliography

Abbas, Tahir. 2011. *Islamic Radicalism and Multicultural Politics: The British Experience.* London, New York: Routledge.

———. 2007. *Islamic Political Radicalism: A European Perspective.* Edinburgh: Edinburgh University Press.

Abid, Lise Jamila. 2006. "Muslims in Austria: Integration through participation in Austrian society," *Journal of Muslim Minority Affairs*, 26 (2): 263–278.

Abramson, P., Aldrich, J., Rickershauer, J., and Rohode, D. 2007. "Fear in the voting booth: The 2004 presidential election," *Political Behavior*, 29 (2): 197–220.

Adamson, Fiona. 2006. "Crossing borders: International migration and national security," *International Organizations*, 31 (1): 165–199.

Adler, R. H. 2006. "But they claimed to be the police, not la migra! The interaction of residency status, class, and ethnicity in a (post-PATRIOT Act) New Jersey neighborhood," *American Behavioral Scientist*, 50 (48): 48–69.

Afshar, Haleh. 2013. "The politics of fear: What does it mean to those who are otherized and feared?" *Ethnic and Racial Studies*, 36 (1): 9–27.

Agamben, Giorgio. 1998. *Homo Sacer: Sovereign Power and Bare Life.* Stanford: Stanford University Press.

AIVD (Dutch Intelligence Service). 2007. *The Radical Dawn in Transition: The Rise of Islamic Neo-Radicalism in the Netherlands.* The Hague.

Ajala, I. 2011. "The Muslim vote and Muslim lobby in France: Myths and realities," *Journal of Islamic Law and Culture*, 12 (2): 77–91.

Akbarzadeh, S., and Roose, J. M. 2011. "Muslims, multiculturalism and the question of the silent majority," *Journal of Muslim Minority Affairs*, 31 (3): 309–325.

Alba, R., and Foner, N. 2009. "Entering the precincts of power: Do national differences matter for immigrant minority political representation" (pp. 277–293) in J. L. Hochschild and J. H. Mollenkopf (eds.), *Bringing Outsiders In: Transatlantic Perspective on Immigrant Political Incorporation.* Ithaca and London: Cornell University Press.

Alba, R., and Nee, V. 2003. *Remaking the American Mainstream: Assimilation and Contemporary Immigration.* Cambridge and London: Harvard University Press.

Alberti, G., Holgate, J., and Tapia, M. 2013. "Organizing migrants as workers or as migrant workers? Intersectionality, trade unions and precarious work," *The International Journal of Human Resource Management*, 24 (22): 4132–4148.

Alden, Edward. 2008. *The Closing of the American Border: Terrorism, Immigration and Security since 9/11.* New York: Harper.

Alexseev, Mikhail. 2006. *Immigration Phobia and the Security Dilemma.* New York: Cambridge University Press.

Ali, Muna. 2011. "Muslim American/American Muslim identity: Authoring self in post 9/11 America," *Journal of Muslim Minority Affairs,* 31 (3): 355–381.

Allen, Christopher. 2010. *Islamophobia.* Farnham: Asghate.

Allport, Gordon Willard. 1954. *The Nature of Prejudice.* New York: Addison-Wesley.

Almeida, Paul. 2003. "Opportunity organizations and threat-induced contention," *American Journal of Sociology,* 109 (2): 345–400.

Alonso, S., and Ruiz-Rufino, R. 2007. "Political representation and ethnic conflict in new democracies," *European Journal of Political Research,* 46 (2): 237–267.

Altheide, David. 2002. *Creating Fears: News and the Construction of Crisis.* Hawthorne, NY: Walter de Gruyter.

American Civil Liberties Union (ACLU). 2013. *Muslims Need Not Apply: How USCIS Secretly Mandates the Discriminatory Delay and Denial of Citizenship and Immigration Benefits to Aspiring Americans.* ACLUsoCal/LCCR/SF Bay. Available at http://www.aclusocal.org/CARRP/. Accessed February 5, 2014.

American Religious Identification Survey (ARIS). 2008. *Summary Report.* Hartford, CT: Trinity College.

Amnesty International. 2012. *Choice and Prejudice: Discrimination against Muslims in Europe.* London: Amnesty International.

Amnesty International. 2004. "US Domestic Human Rights Report." *Threat and Humiliation: Racial Profiling, Domestic Security and Human Rights in the United States.* New York: Amnesty International USA Publications.

Andersen, K., and Cohen, E. F. 2005. "Political institutions and incorporation of immigrants" (pp. 186–205) in C. Wolbrecht and R. E. Hero (eds.), *The Politics of Democratic Inclusion.* Philadelphia: Temple University Press.

André, S., Dronkers, J., and Fleischmann, F. 2010. "Perceptions of in-group discrimination by first and second generation immigrants from different countries of origin in EU member states," Working Paper. Firenze: European University Institute. Available at http://www.eui.eu/Personal/Dronkers/English/Andre.pdf. Accessed September 10, 2013.

Appleton, Michael. 2005. "The political attitudes of Muslims studying at British Universities in the post 9/11 world," *Journal of Muslim Minority Affairs,* 25 (2): 171–191.

Arends-Tóth, J., and Van de Vijver, F. J. R. 2003. "Multiculturalism and acculturation: View of Dutch and Turkish-Dutch," *European Journal of Social Psychology,* 33 (2): 249–266.

Armenta, B. E., and Hunt, J. S. 2009. "Responding to societal devaluation: Effects of perceived personal group and group discrimination on the ethnic identification and personal self-esteem of Latino/Latina adolescents," *Group Process and Intergroup Relations,* 12 (1): 23–39.

Ashcroft (Lord), KCMG. 2012. *Degrees of Separation. Ethnic Minority Voters and the Conservative Party.* Available at http://lordashcroftpolls.com/wp-content/uploads/2012/04/DEGREES-OF-SEPARATION.pdf. Accessed June 5, 2014.

Ayers, J. W., and Hofstetter, R. C. 2008. "American Muslim political participation following 9/11: Religious beliefs, political resources, social structure and political awareness," *Politics and Religion*, 1 (1): 3–26.

Azzi, A. E., Chryssochoou, X., Klandermans, B., and Simons, B. (eds.). 2011. *Identity and Participation in a Culturally Diverse Society: A Multidisciplinary Perspective.* New York: Wiley-Blackwell.

Bada, X., Fox, J., and Selee, A. 2006. *Invisible No more: Mexican Migrant Participation in the United States.* Washington, DC: Woodrow Wilson International Center for Scholars.

Badaccini, A., Guilg, E. and Toner, H. (eds.). 2007. *Whose Freedom, Security, and Justice? EU Immigration and Asylum Law and Policy.* Oxford: Hart Publishing.

Bagby, Ihsan. 2009. "The American mosque in transition: Assimilation, acculturation and isolation," *Journal of Ethnic and Migration Studies*, 35 (3): 473–490.

Bagby, I., Perl, P., and Froehle, B. 2001. *The Mosque in America: A National Portrait—A Report from the Mosque Study Project.* Washington, DC: Council of American Islamic Relations.

Bagguley, P., and Hussain, T. 2006. "Conflict and cohesion: official constructions of 'community' around the 2001 'riots' in Britain," *Critical Studies*, 28: 347–365.

Bagley, C., Verma, G., Mallick, K., and Young, L. 1979. *Personality, Self-Esteem and Prejudice.* Brookfield: Avebury.

Bakalian, A., and Bozorgmehr, M. 2005. "Muslim American mobilization," *Diaparo*, 14 (1): 7–43.

Balzacq, Thierry. 2005. "The three faces of securitization: Political agency, audience, and context," *European Journal of International relations*, 11 (2): 171–201.

Balzacq, T., and Carrera, S. (eds.). 2006. *Security Versus Freedom? A Challenge for Europe's Future.* Aldershot: Ashgate.

Banting, K., Johnston, R., Kymlickz, W., and Soroka, S. 2006. "Do multiculturalism policies erode the welfare state?" (pp. 49–91) in K. Banting and W. Kymlicka (eds.), *Multiculturalism and the Welfare State.* Oxford: Oxford University Press.

Barnes, Hugh. 2006. *Born in the UK: Young Muslims in Britain.* London: Foreign Policy Center.

Barreto, M., and Dana, K. 2010. "The American Muslim voter: What explains voting when nobody cares?," Paper presented at the APSA conference, Washington, DC, September 4: 156–178.

Barreto, M., Manzano, S., Ramírez, R., and Rim, K. 2009. "Mobilization, participation, and *solidaridad*: Latino Participation in the 2006 immigration protest rallies," *Urban Affairs Review*, 44 (5): 736–764.

Barreto, M., Masuoka, N., and Sanchez, G. 2008. "Religiosity, discrimination and group identity among Muslim Americans," Paper presented at the WPSA annual conference (March): 1–37. Available at http://www.muslimamericansurvey.org/papers/wpsa2008.pdf. Accessed December 18, 2014.

Barry, D. T., and Grillo, C. 2003. "Cultural, self-esteem, and demographic correlates of perception of personal and group discrimination among East Asian immigrants," *American Journal of Ortho-Psychiatry*, 73 (2): 223–229.

Beaman, Jean. 2012. "But Madame, we are French also," *Context*, 11 (36): 46–51.

Beltràn, Cristina. 2010. *The Trouble with Unity*. Oxford: Oxford University Press.

Benet-Martinez, V., and Haritatos, J. 2005. "Bicultural identity integration: Components and psychological antecedents," *Journal of Personality*, 73 (4): 1015–1049.

Benhabib, Seyla. 2004. *The Rights of Others: Aliens, Residents and Citizens*. Cambridge: Cambridge University Press.

Benjamin-Alvarado, J., DeSipio, L., Montoya, C. 2009. "Latino mobilization in new immigrant destinations: The anti-HR 4437 protest in Nebraska's cities," *Urban Affairs Review*, 44 (5): 718–735.

Berger, M., Galonska, C., and Koopmans, R. 2004. "Political integration by a detour? Ethnic communities and social capital of migrants in Berlin," *Journal of Ethnic and Migration Studies*, 30: 491–507.

Berry, J. W. 2001. "A psychology of immigration," *Journal of Social Issues*, 57 (3): 615–631.

———. 1997. "Immigration, acculturation and adaptation," *Applied Psychology: An International Review*, 46 (1): 5–34

Berry, J. W., Phinney, J. S., Sam, D. L., and Vedder, P. (eds). 2006. *Immigrant Youth in Cultural Transition: Acculturation, Identity, and Adaptation across National Contexts*. Mahwah, NJ: Lawrence Erlbaum Associates.

Bertrand, M., and Mullainathan, S. 2004. "Are Emily and Brendan more employable than Lakisha and Jamal? A field experiment on labor market discrimination," *American Economic Review*, 94 (4): 991–1013.

Bird, K., Saalfeld, T., and Wüst, A. M. 2010. *The Political Representation of Immigrants and Minorities: Voters, Parties and Parliaments in Liberal Democracies*. London: Taylor and Francis.

BIS (Department for Business Innovation and Skills). 2011. "Amplifying the voice of Muslim students: Findings from literature review," *BIS Research Paper*, 55: 1–36.

Bjørnskvo, Christian. 2006. "The multiple facets of social capital," *European Journal of Political Economy*, 22: 22–40.

Blick, A., Choudhoury, T., Weir, S. 2006. *The Rule of the Game: Terrorism, Community and Human Rights*. York: Joseph Rowntree Trust.

Bloemraad, Irene. 2011. "'We the people' in an age of migration: Multiculturalism and immigrants—political integration in comparative perspective" (pp. 250–272) in R. Smith (ed.), *Citizenship, Borders and Human Needs*. Philadelphia: University of Philadelphia Press.

Bloemarrad, I., and Schönwälder, K. 2013. "Immigrant and ethnic minority representation in Europe: Conceptual challenges and theoretical approaches," *West European Politics*, 36 (3): 564–579.

Bloemraad, I., and Trost, C. 2008. "It's a family affair: Intergenerational mobilization in the spring 2006 protests," *American Behaviorial Scientist*, 52 (4): 507–532.

Bloemraad, I., Voss, K., and Lee, T. 2011. "The protests of 2006: What were they, how do we understand them, where do we go?" (pp. 3–43) in K.Voss and I. Bloemraad, *Rallying for Immigrant Rights. The Fight for Inclusion in 21st Century America.* Berkeley: University of California Press.

Bobo, L., and Hutchings, V. L. 1996. "Perceptions of racial group competition: Extending Blumer's theory of group position to a multiracial context," *American Sociology Review,* 61 (6): 951–972.

Bodemann, Y. M, and Yurdakul, G. (eds.). 2006. *Migration, Citizenship, Ethnos.* New York: Palgrave Macmillan.

Booth, Ken. 2007. *Theory of World Security.* Cambridge: Cambridge University Press.

Bos, K. van den, Loseman, A., and Doosje, B. 2009. *Why Young People Engage in Radical Behavior and Sympathize with Terrorism: Injustice, Uncertainty, and Threatened Groups. Utrecht/Amsterdam:* University Utrecht (Faculty of Social Science) and University of Amsterdam, WODC.

Bosniak, Linda 2006. *The Citizen and the Alien: Dilemmas of Contemporary Membership.* Princeton: Princeton University Press.

Boswell, Christina. 2003. *European Migration Policies in Flux: Changing Patterns of Inclusion and Exclusion.* London: Chatham House Papers, The Royal Institute of International Affairs, Blackwell.

Bourguignon, D., Seron, E., Yerbyt, V., and Herman, G. 2006. "Perceived group and personal discrimination: Differential effects on personal self-esteem," *European Journal of Social Psychology,* 36 (5): 773–789.

Bourhis, R. Y., Moïse, L. C., Perreault, S., and Senécal, S. 1997. "Towards and interactive acculturation model: A social psychology approach," *International Journal of Psychology,* 32 (6): 369–386.

Bowen, J. R, Bertossi, C., Duyvendak, J. W., and Krook, M. L. (eds.). 2014. *European States and Their Muslims Citizens.* Cambridge: Cambridge University Press.

Bowen, John. 2011. "Islamic adaptations to Western Europe and North America: The importance of contrastive analyses," *American Behavioral Scientist,* 55 (12): 1601–1615.

Brader, Ted. 2005. "Striking a responsive chord: How political ads motivate and persuade voters by appealing to emotions," *American Journal of Political Science,* 49 (2): 388–405.

Brader, T., Valentino N., and Suhay, E. 2008. "What triggers public opposition to immigration? Anxiety, group cues, and immigration threat," *American Journal of Political Science,* 52 (4): 959–978.

Braman, E., and Sinno, A. H. 2009. "An experimental investigation of causal attributions for the political behavior of Muslim candidates: Can a Muslim represent you?" *Politics and Religion,* 2: 247–276.

Brenick, A., Titzmann, P. F., Michel, A., and Silbereisen, R. K. 2012. "Perceptions of discrimination by young diaspora migrants," *European Psychologist,* 17 (2): 105–119.

Brewer, M. B. 2000. "Reducing prejudice through cross-categorization: Effects of multiple social identities" (pp. 165–183) in S. Oskamp (ed.), *Reducing Prejudice and Discrimination*. Hillsdale, NJ.: Erlbaum.

Brinton, M., and Nee, V. (eds.). 1998. *The New Institutionalism in Sociology*. New York: Russell Sage Foundation.

Brouard, S., and Tiberj, V. 2008. "The challenge to integration in France" (pp. 283–299) in A. Chebel d'Appollonia and S. Reich (eds.), *Immigration, Integration and Security: America and Europe in Comparative perspective*. Pittsburgh: University of Pittsburgh Press.

Brown, R., and Hewstone, M. 2005. "An integrative theory of intergroup contact," *Advances in Experimental Social Psychology*, 37: 255–343.

Brubacker, Rogers. 2001. "The return of assimilation? Changing perspective on immigration and its sequels in France, Germany and the United States," *Ethnic and Racial Studies*, 24 (4): 531–548.

———. 1992. *Citizenship and Nationhood in France and Germany*. Cambridge: Cambridge University Press.

Brubaker, Rogers (ed.). 1989. *Immigration and the Politics of Citizenship in Europe and North America*. Lanham, MD: German Marshall Fund of the United States and University Press of America.

Bruess, Joachim. 2008. "Experiences of discrimination reported by Turkish, Moroccan and Bangladeshi Muslims in three European cities," *Journal of Ethnic and Migration Studies*, 34 (6): 875–894.

Bukhari, Z. H., Nyang, S. S., Ahmad, M., and Esposito, J. L. (eds.). 2004. *Muslims' Place in the American Public Square*. Walnut Creek, CA: Alta Mira Press.

Bulmer, M., and Solomos, J. (eds.). 2012. *Migration: Policies, Practices, Activism*. London, New York: Routledge.

Buonfino, Alessandra. 2004. "Between unity and plurality: The politicization and securitization of the discourse of immigration in Europe," *New Political Science*, 26 (1): 23–49.

Buzan, B., Waever, O., de Wilde, J. 1998. *Security: A New Framework for Analysis*. Boulder, CO: Lynne Rienner Publishers.

Cainkar, Louise. 2009. *Homeland Insecurity: The Arab American and Muslim American Experience after 9/11*. New York: Russell Sage Foundation.

Cameron, David. 2013. Speech on immigration and welfare reform, University Campus Suffolk, March 25. Available at https://www.gov.uk/government/speeches/david-camerons-immigration-speech. Accessed August 29, 2013.

Cameron, J. E., and Lalonde, R. N. 2001. "Social identification and gender-related ideology in women and men," *British Journal of Social Psychology*, 40 (1): 59–77.

Cantle, Ted. 2001. *Community Cohesion: A Report of the Independent Review Team*. London: Home Office.

Canoy, M., Beutin, R., Horvath, A., Lerais, F., Smith, P., and Sochacki, M. 2006. *Migration and Public Perception*. Brussels: Bureau of European Policy Advisers (BEPA), European Commission. Available at http://ec.europa.eu/dgs/policy_advisers/publications/docs/bepa_migration_final_09_10_006_en.pdf. Accessed September 17, 2014.

Carnegie Corporation of New York-Public Agenda.(CCNY). 2010. *A Place to Call Home: What Immigrants Say Now about Life in America.* New York: Carnegie Corporation.

———. 2003. *Now I'm here: What America's Immigrants have to Say about Their Life in the US Today.* New York: Carnegie Corporation.

Carol, S., and Koopmans, R. 2013. "Dynamics of contestation over Islamic religious rights in Western Europe," *Ethnicities,* 13 (2): 165–190.

CASE Collective. 2007. "Critical approaches to security in Europe; A networked manifesto," *Security Dialogue,* 37 (4): 443–487.

Cassidy, C., O'Connor, R. C., Howe, C., and Warden, D. 2004. "Perceived discrimination and psychological distress: The role of personal and ethnic self-esteem," *Journal of Counseling Psychology,* 51 (3): 320–339.

Castles, S., and Kosack, G. 1973. *Immigrant Workers and the Class Structure in Western Europe.* London: Oxford University Press.

Caul, M., and Tate, K. 2004. *Political Parties, Minorities and Elected Office: Comparing Opportunities for Inclusion in the US and Britain.* Irvine: Center for the Study of Democracy, University of California.

Celis, K., Eelbode, F., and Wauters, B. 2013. "Visible ethnic minorities in local political parties: A case study of two Belgian cities (Antwerp and Ghent)," *Politics,* 33 (3): 160–171.

Center for Human Rights & Global Justice (CHR&GJ). 2007. *Americans on Hold: Profiling, Citizenship and the War on Terror.* New York: NYU School of Law.

Cesari, Jocelyne. 2013. *Why the West Fears Islam: An Exploration of Muslims in Liberal Democracies.* New York: Palgrave Macmillan.

———. 2004. *When Islam and Democracy Meet: Muslims in Europe and in the United States.* New York: Palgrave Macmillan.

Cesari, J., and McLoughlin, S. 2005. *European Muslims and the Secular State.* Burlington VT: Ashgate Publishing.

Ceyhan, A., and Tsoukala, A. 2002. "The securitization of migration in Western societies: Ambivalent discourses and policies," *Alternatives,* 27: 21–39.

Chebel d'Appolonia, Ariane. 2012a. *Frontiers of Fear: Immigration and Insecurity in the United States and Europe.* Ithaca: Cornell University Press.

———. 2012b. Researching the civil rights and liberties of Western Muslims," *Review of Middle East Studies,* 46 (2): 199–214.

———. 2010. "How to make enemies: A transatlantic perspective on the radicalization process and integration issues" (pp. 113–136) in A. Chebel d'Appollonia and S. Reich (eds.), *Managing Ethnic Diversity after 9/11: Integration, Security, and Civil Liberties in Transatlantic Perspectives.* New Brunswick, NJ: Rutgers University Press.

Chicago Council on Global Affairs. 2007. *The Civic and Political Integration of Muslim Americans.* Chicago: Council on Global Affairs.

Chishti, M., Meissner, D., Papademetriou, D. G., Peterzell, J., Wishnie, M. J, and Yale-Loehr, S. W. 2003. *America's Challenge: Domestic Security, Civil Liberties, and National Unity after September 11.* Washington, DC: Migration Policy Institute.

Chong, D., and Rogers, R. 2005. "Reviving group consciousness" (pp. 45–74) in C. Wlbrecht and R. E. Hero (eds.), *The Politics of Democratic Inclusion*. Philadelphia: Temple University Press.

Choudhury, Tufyal. 2010. "Integration, security and faith identity in social policy in Britain" (pp. 79–97) in A. Chebel d"Appollonia and S. Reich (eds.), *Managing Ethnic Diversity after 9/11: Integration, Security, and Civil Liberties in Transatlantic Perspectives*. New Brunswick, NJ: Rutgers University Press.

Chryssochoou, X., and Lyons, R. 2010. "Perceptions of (in)compatibility between identities and participation in the national polity of people belonging to ethnic minorities" (pp.69–88), in A. E. Azzi, X. Chryssochoou, B. Klandermans, and B. Simon (eds.), *Identity and Participation in Culturally Diverse Societies*. Oxford, UK: Blackwell.

Cihangir, S., Barreto, M., and Ellemers, N. 2010. "The dark side of ambiguous discrimination: How self-esteem moderates emotional and behavioral responses to ambiguous and unmabiguous discrimination," *British Journal of Social Psychology*, 49 (1): 155–174.

Citrin, J., Sears, D. O. 2009. "Balancing national and ethnic identity: The psychology of E Pluribus Unuum" (pp. 145–173) in R. Abdelal, Y. M. Herrera, and A. I. Johnston (eds.), *Measuring Identity: A Guide for Social Scientists*. Cambridge: Cambridge University Press.

Citrin, J., and Sides, J. 2006. "European immigration in the people's court" (pp. 327–361) in C. A. Parsons and T. M. Smeeding (eds.), *Immigration and the Transformation of Europe*. New York: Cambridge University Press.

Citrin, J., and Wright, M. 2009. "Defining the circle of we: American identity and immigration policy," *The Forum*, 73: 1–20.

Citrin, J., Lerman, A., Murakomi, M., and Pearson, K. 2007. "Testing Huntington: Is Hispanic immigration a threat to American identity?," *Perspectives on Politics*, 5 (1): 31–48.

Citrin, J., Wong, C., and Duff, B. 2001. "The meaning of American national identity: Patterns of ethnic conflict and consensus" (pp. 71–100) in R. D. Ashmore, L. Jussim, and D. Wilder (eds.), *Social Identity, Intergroup Conflict and Conflict Reduction*. Oxford: Oxford University Press.

City Commission on Human Rights (CCHR). 2003. *Discrimination against Muslims, Arabs, and South Asians in New York City since 9/11*. New York: CCHR.

Clarke, Tony. 2001. *Burnley Speaks, Who Listens?* Burnley: Burnley Borouhg Council.

Coenders, M., Lubbers, M., and Scheepers, P. 2005. *Majority Populations' Attitudes Towards Migrants and Minorities. Report for the European Monitoring Centre on Racism and Xenophobia*. Vienna: EUMC.

Cole, David. 2003. *Enemy Aliens: Double Standards and Constitutional Freedoms in the War on Terrorism*. New York: The New Press.

Cole, D., and Lobel, J. 2007. *Less Safe, Less Free: Why America Is Losing the War on Terror*. New York: New Press.

Collyer, Michael. 2006. "Migrants, migration and the security paradigm: Constraints and Opportunities," *Mediterranean Politics*, 11 (2): 255–270.

Commission Nationale Consultative des Droits de l'Homme (CNCDH). 2012. *Le racisme, l'antisémitisme et la xénophobie en France. Rapport 2012*. Paris: La Documentation Française.

Communities and Local Government. 2010. *Attitudes, Values and perceptions: Muslims and the General Population in 2007–2008*. London: Department for Communities and Local Government.

Connor, Phillip. 2010. "Contexts of immigrant receptivity and immigrant religious outcomes: The case of Muslims in Western Europe," *Ethnic and Racial Studies*, 33 (3): 376–403.

Constant, A., and Zimmermann, K. 2008. "Measuring ethnic identity and its impact on economic behavior," *Journal of the European Eco Ass*, 6 (2–3): 424–433.

Constant, A., Roberts, R., and Zimmermann, K. 2009, "Ethnic identity and immigrant homeownership," *Urban Studies*, 46 (9): 1879–1898.

Cook, Maria Lorena. 2013. "Is incorporation of unauthorized immigrants possible?" (pp. 43–64) in J. Hochschild, J. Chattopadhyay, C. Gay, and M. Jones-Correa, *Outsiders No More? Models of Immigrant Political Incorporation*. Oxford and New York: Oxford University Press.

Copus, Colin. 2004. *Party Politics and Local Government*. Manchester: Manchester University Press.

Costain, Anne. 2005. "Social movements as mechanisms for political inclusion" (pp. 109–121) in C.Wolbrecht and R. E Hero (eds.), *The Politics of Democratic Inclusion*. Philadelphia: Temple University Press.

Council of the European Union. 2005. *The European Union Strategy for Combating Radicalisation and Recruitment to Terrorism*. Brussels: European Commission.

———. 2004. 2681st Meeting Justice and Home Affairs. Press release 14615/04. Available at http://www.consilium.europa.eu/ueDocs/cms_Data/docs/press-Data/en/jha/82745.pdf#zoom=100. Accessed October 27, 2013.

Council on American Islamic Relations (CAIR). 2010. *Islamophobia and Its Impact in the United Sates: Some Hate, New Targets*. Washington, DC: CAIR

———. 2006. "Western Muslim minorities: Integration and disenfranchisement," *Policy Bulletin*: 2–3.

Crenshaw, Martha (ed.). 2010. *The Consequences of Counterterrorism*. New York: Russell Sage Foundation.

Cronin, T. J., Levin, S., Branscombe, N. R., van Laar, C., and Tropp. L. R. 2012. "Ethnic identification in response to perceived discrimination protects well-being and promotes activism: A longitudinal study of Latino college students," *Group Processes and Intergroup Relations*, 15 (4): 393–407.

Crosby, Faye. 1984a. "The denial of personal discrimination," *American Behavioral Scientist*, 27 (3): 371–386.

———. 1984b. "Relative deprivation in organizational settings," *Research in Organizational Settings*, 6: 51–93.

Croucher, Stephen. 2011. "Muslim and Christian conflict styles in Western Europe," *International Journal of Conflict Management*, 22 (1): 60–74.

———. 2009. "French-Muslim reactions to the law banning religious symbols in schools: A mixed method analysis," *Journal of International and Intercultural Communication*, 2 (1): 1–15.

Crul, M., and Schneider, J. 2012. "Comparative integration context theory: participation and belonging in new diverse European cities" (pp. 106–125) in J. Schneider and M. Crul (eds.), *Theorising Integration and Assimilation*. London and New York: Routledge.

Crul, M., and Vermeulen, H. 2006. "Immigration, education, and the Turkish second generation in five European nations: A comparative study" (pp. 235–250) in C. A. Parsons and T. M. Smeeding (eds.), *Immigration and the Transformation of Europe*. New York: Cambridge University Press.

Dana, Karam. 2011. *Muslims in America: A Profile*. Belfert Center for Science and International Affairs: The Dubai Initiative/Harvard Kennedy School of Government.

Dancygier, Rafaela M. 2013. "Culture, context, and the political incorporation of immigrant-origin group in Europe" (pp. 119–136) in J. Hochschild, J. Chattopadhyay, C. Gay, and M. Jones-Correa, *Outsiders No More? Models of Immigrant Political Incorporation*. Oxford: Oxford University Press.

———. 2010. *Immigration and Conflict in Europe*. Cambridge, New York: Cambridge University Press.

Dancygier, R., and Saunders, E. N. 2006. "A new electorate? Comparing preferences and partisanship between immigrants and natives," *American Journal of Political Science*, 50 (4): 962–981.

Deaux, Kay, 2006. *To Be an Immigrant*. New York: Russell Sage Foundation.

De Genova, N., and Peutz, N. (eds.). 2010. *The Deportation Regime: Sovereignty, Space, and the Freedom of Movement*. Durham, NC: Duke University Press.

De la Garza, Rodolfo. 2004. "Latino Politics," *Annual Review of Political Science*, 7: 91–123.

De la Garza, R. Falcon, A., and Garcia, F. C. 1996. "Will the real Americans please stand up: Anglo and Mexican-American support for core American political values" *American Journal of Political Science*, 40: 335–351.

Denham, John. 2001. *Building Cohesive Communities: A report of the Ministerial Group on Public Order and Community Cohesion*. London: Home Office.

Department of Homeland Security (DHS). 2011. *Yearbook of Immigration Statistics*. Available at http://www.dhs.gov/sites/default/files/publications/immigration-statistics/yearbook/2011/ois_yb_2011.pdf. Accessed September 29, 2013.

De Rooij, Eline. 2012. "Patterns of immigrant political participation: Explaining differences in types of political participation between immigrants and the majority population in Western Europe," *European Sociological Review*, 28 (4): 455–481.

Deutsche Islam Konferenz (DIK). 2008. *Muslim Life in Germany*. Research report 6. Berlin: Federal Office for Migration and Refugees.

De Vroome T., Martinovic, B., and Verkuyten, M. 2013. "The integration paradox: Level of education and immigrants' attitudes towards natives and the host society," *Cultural Diversity and Ethnic Minority Psychology*, 20 (2): 166–175.

Diani, M. and McAdam, D. (eds.). 2003. *Social Movements and Networks: Relational Approaches to Collective Action*. Oxford: Oxford University Press.

Didero, Maike. 2013. "Muslim political participation in Germany: A structural approach" (pp. 34–60) in Jorgen S. Nielsen (ed.), *Muslim Political Participation in Europe*. Edinburgh: Edinburgh University Press.

Diehl, C., and Blohm, M. 2001. "Apathy, adaptation or ethnic mobilization? On the attitudes of a politically excluded group," *Journal of Ethnic and Migration Studies*, 27 (3): 401–420.

Dinham, A., Furbey, R., and Lowndes, V. (eds.). 2009. *Faith in the Public Realm: Controversies, Policies, and Practices*. Bristol: The Policy Press, University of Bristol.

Donohue, Laura. 2008. *The Cost of Terrorism: Power, Politics, and Liberty*. Cambridge: Cambridge University Press.

Döring, Jan. 2007. "Influences of discriminatory incidents on immigrants' attitudes towards German Society," *International Journal of Conflict and Violence*, 1 (1): 19–31.

Dörr, S., Faist, T. 1997. "Institutional conditions for the integration of immigrants in welfare states: A comparison of the literature in Germany, France, Great Britain and the Netherlands," *European Journal of Political Research*, 31 (4): 401–426.

Dorraj, Manochehr. 2010. "Islamophobia, the Muslim stereotype, and the Muslim American political experience" (pp. 188–203) in V. Martinez-Ebers and M. Dorraj (eds.). *Perspectives on Race, Ethnicity and Religion: Identity Politics in America*. Oxford: Oxford University Press.

Dovidio, John F. 2001. "On the nature of contemporary prejudice: The third wave," *Journal of Social Issues*, 57 (4): 829–849.

Dovidio, J. F., and Esses, V. M. 2001. "Immigrants and immigration: Advancing the psychological perspective," *Journal of Social Issues*, 57 (3): 375–387.

Dovidio, J. F., Gaertner, S. L., Kawakami, K. 2003. "Intergroup contact: The past, present, and future," *Group Processes and Intergroup Relations*, 6 (1): 5–21.

Dovidio, J. F., Gluszek, A., John, M., Diltman, R., and Lagunes, P. 2010. "Understanding bias toward Latinos: Discrimination, dimensions of difference, and experience of exclusion," *Journal of Social Issues*, 66 (1): 59–78.

Dowley, K. M., and Silver, B. D. 2011. "Support for Europe among Europe's ethnic, religious, and immigrant minorities," *International Journal of Public Opinion Research*, 23 (3): 315–337.

Dronkers, J., and Vink, M. P. 2012. "Explaining access to citizenship in Europe: How citizenship policies affect naturalization rates," *European Union Politics*, 13 (3): 390–412.

Du Bois, W. E. B. (1903), *The Souls of Black Folks*. Original edition by A. C Mc Clurg Co. Reprinted in 1989, New York: Bantam.

————. 1897. *The Conservation of Race*. Reprinted in L. Back and J. Solomos, *Theories of Race and Racism* (pp. 79–86). London, New York: Routledge.

Ecklund, E. H., Davila, C., Emerson, M. O., Kye, S., and Chan, E. 2013. "Motivating civic engagement: In-group versus out-group service orientations among Mexican Americans in religious and nonreligious organizations," *Sociology of Religion*, 74 (3): 370–391.

Eggert, N., and Giugni, M. 2010. "Does associational involvement spur political integration? Political interest and participation of three immigrant groups in Zurich," *Swiss Political Science Review*, 16 (2): 175–210.

Engbersen, Godfried. 2003. "Spheres of integration: Towards a differentiated and reflexive ethnic minority policy" (pp. 59–76) in R. Sackmann, B. Peters, and T. Fiast, *Identity and Integration: Migrants in Western Europe*. Aldershot: Asghate.

Entzinger, Han. 2000. "The dynamics of integration policies: A multidimensional model" (pp. 97–118) in R. Koopmans and P. Statham (eds.), *Challenging Immigration and Ethnic Relations Politics*. Oxford: Oxford University Press.

Epstein, Reid. 2014. "National Council of La Raza leader calls Barack Obama deporter-in-chief," *Politico*, March 4. Available at http://www.politico.com/story/2014/03/national-council-of-la-raza-janet-murguia-barack-obama-deporter-in-chief-immigration-104217.html. Accessed March 13, 2014.

Escobar, G. 2006. *The Optimistic Immigrant: Among Latinos the Recently Arrived Have to Most Hope for the Future*. Washington DC: Pew Hispanic Center.

Espinosa, G., Elizondo, V., Miranda, J. (eds.). 2005. *Latino Religions and Civic Activism in the United States*. Oxford: Oxford University Press.

EU Agency for Fundamental Rights (FRA). 2012. *Roma Migrants from Bulgaria and Romania: Migration Patterns and Integration in Italy and Spain*. Vienna: FRA.

————. 2010a. *Data in Focus Report: Police Stops and Minorities*. Vienna, FRA.

————. 2010b. *Experiences of Discrimination, Social Marginalization and Violence: A Comparative Study of Muslim and Non Muslim Youth in Three EU Member States*. Vienna: FRA.

————. 2009. *Data in Focus Report: Muslims*. Vienna: FRA.

————. 2009. *EU-MIDIS: European Union Minorities and Discrimination Survey – Main Results Report*. Vienna: FRA.

EUMC (European Monitoring Center on Racism and Xenophobia). 2006a. *The Annual Report of the Situation Regarding Racism and Xenophobia in the Member States of the EU*. Vienna: EUMC.

————. 2006b. *Muslims in the European Union: Discrimination and Islamophobia*. Vienna: EUMC.

————. 2006c. *Perceptions of Discrimination and Islamophobia: Voices from Members of Muslim Communities in the European Union*. Vienna: EUMC.

————. 2005. *Racist Violence in 15 Member States*. Vienna: EUMC

European Commission. 2013. *Using EU Indicators of Immigrant Integration*. Final Report for Directorate-General for Home Affairs. Brussels: European Commission.

Faist, Thomas. 2002. "Extension du domaine de la lute: International migration and security before and after September 11, 2001," *International Migration Review*, 36 (1): 7–14.

Favell, Adrian. 1998. *Philosophies of Integration*. London: Macmillan Press.

Federal Ministry of the Interior (FMI). 2007. *Muslims in Germany: Integration, Barriers to Integration, Religion and Attitudes towards Democracy, the Constitutional State, and Politically and Religiously Motivated Violence*. Rostock: Publikationsversand der Bundesregierung.

Fennema, M., and Tillie, J. 2001. "Civic community, political participation and political trust of ethnic groups," *Connections*, 24 (1): 26–41.

———. 1999. "Political participation and political trust in Amsterdam: Civic communities and ethnic networks," *Journal of Ethnic and Migration Studies*, 25 (4): 703–726.

Fetzer, J., and Stoper, J. C. 2004. *Muslims and the State in Britain, France, and Germany*. Cambridge: Cambridge University Press.

Field, Clive. 2011. "Young British Muslims since 9/11: A composite attitudinal profile," *Religion, State & Society*, 39 (2/3): 159–175.

Fish, Steven. 2011. *Are Muslims Distinctive? A Look at the Evidence*. New York: Oxford University Press.

Fleischmann, F., and Dronkers, J. 2010. *The Effects of Social and Labour Market Policies on EU Countries on the Socio-Economic Integration of First and Second Generation Immigrants from Different Countries of Origin*. EUIRSCAS Working Paper 2007/19.

Fleischmann, F., Phalet, K., and Klein, O. 2011. "Religious identification and politicization in the face of discrimination: Support for political Islam and political action among the Turkish and Moroccan second generation in Europe," *British Journal of Social Psychology*, 50 (4): 628–648.

Fleischmann, F., Phalet, K., and Swyngedouw, M. 2013. "Dual identity under threat: When and how do Turkish and Moroccan minorities engage in politics?" *Zeitschrift für Psychologie*, 221 (44): 214–222.

Foley, M. W., and Hoge, D. R. 2007. *Religion and the New Immigrants: How Faith Communities Form Our Newest Citizens*. Oxford: Oxford University Press.

Foner, N., and Fredrickson, G. (eds.). 2004. *Not Just Black and White: Historical and Contemporary Perspectives on Immigration, Race, and Ethnicity*. New York: Russell Sage Foundation.

FOSIS (Federation of Students Islamic Societies). 2005. *The Voice of Muslim Students: A report into the Attitudes and Perceptions of Muslim Students Following the July 7th London Attacks*. London: Federation of Students Islamic Societies.

Fox News. 2012. "Patriotism and respect for armed forces high among Latinos," *Fox News Latino*. Available at http://latino.foxnews.com/latino/politics/2012/03/09/latinos-patriotism-respect-armed-forces-high/. Accessed February 16, 2014.

Fraga, Luis R. 2009. "Building through exclusion: Anti-immigrant politics in the United States" (pp. 176–192), in J. L. Hochschild and J. H. Mollenkopf (eds.), *Bringing Outsiders In: Transatlantic Perspective on Immigrant Political Incorporation*. Ithaca and London: Cornell University Press.

Fraga, L. R., Garcia, J. A., Hero, R., Jones-Correa, M., Martinez-Ebers, V., and Segura, G. M. 2010. *Latino Lives in America: Making it Home*. Philadelphia: Temple University Press.

Fram, Alan. 2010. "Hispanics face most discrimination," *Huffington Post*. May 20. Available at http://www.huffingtonpost.com/2010/05/21/hispanics-face-most-discr_n_583538.html. Accessed August 27, 2013.

Franz, Barbara. 2007. "Europe's Muslim youth: An inquiry into the politics of discrimination, relative deprivation and identity formation," *Mediterranean Quarterly*, 18 (1): 89–112.

Freeman, Gary. P. 2006. "National models, policy types, and the politics of immigration in liberal democracies," *West European Politics*, 29 (2): 227–247.

———. 2001. "Comparative analysis of immigration politics: A retrospective," *American behavioral Scientist*, 55 (12): 1541–1560.

———. 1995. "Modes of immigration politics in liberal democratic states: Rejoinder," *International Migration Review*, 29 (4): 909–913.

Frégosi, Franck. 2013. "Muslim collective mobilisations in contemporary Europe: New issues and new types of involvement" (pp. 129–139) in Jorgen S. Nielsen (ed.), *Muslim Political Participation in Europe*. Edinburgh: Edinburgh University Press.

Frymer, Paul. 2005. "Race, parties, and democratic inclusion" (pp. 122–142) in C. Wolbrecht and R. E. Hero (eds.), 2005. *The Politics of Democratic Inclusion*. Philidalphia: Temple University Press.

Furedi, Frank. 2002. *Culture of Fear: Risk-Taking and the Morality of Low Expectation*. London: Continuum.

Gaertner, S., Dovidio, J. F. 2000. *Reducing Intergroup Bias: The Common Ingroup Identity Model*. New York: Psychology Press.

Gallup. 2011. *Muslim Americans: Faith, Freedom, and the Future*. Abu Dhabi Gallup Center. Available at http://www.gallup.com/poll:148799. Accessed April 3, 2014.

———. 2009. *Muslim Americans: A National Portrait*. Washington, DC: Gallup.

———. 2005. *Where Do Hispanic Americans Stand On Religion, Politics?* Washington, DC: Gallup.

Gans, Herbert. 2007. "Acculturation, assimilation, and mobility," *Ethnic and Racial Studies*, 30 (1): 152–164.

Garbaye, Romain. 2005. *Getting into Local Power: The Politics of Ethnic Minorities in British and French Cities*. Oxford: Blackwell.

Garcia, A. S. and D. G. Keyes. 2012. *Life as an Undocumented Immigrant*. Washington, DC: Center for American Progress.

Garcia, C., and Sanchez, G. 2008. *Moving (into) the Mainstream? Latinos in the US Political System*. Pearson, NJ: Prentice Hall.

Geddes, Andrew. 2003. *The Politics of Migration and Immigration in Europe*. London: Sage.

German Marshall Fund. 2011. *Transatlantic Trends: Immigration 2011*. Washington, DC: GMF.

Gijsberts, M., Hagendoorn, L., and Scheepers, P. (eds.). 2004. *Nationalism and Exclusion of Migrants: Cross-National Comparisons*. Aldershot: Ashgate.

Gilligan, Andrew. 2010. "Islamic radicals infiltrate the Labour Party," *The Telegraph*, February 27. Available at http://www.telegraph.co.uk/news/politics/labour/7333420/Islamic-radicals-infiltrate-the-Labour-Party.html. Accessed June 2, 2014.

Gilroy, Paul. 1987. *There Ain't No Black in the Union Jack: The Cultural Politics of Race and Nation*. London: Hutchison.

Giugni, M., and Passy, F. 2004. "Migrant mobilization between political institutions and citizenship regimes: A comparison of France and Switzerland," *European Journal of Political Research*, 43: 51–82.

Glassner, Barry. 1999. *The Culture of Fear*. New York: Basic Book.

Global Commission on International Migration (UN). 2005. Final Report. Available at http://www.gcim.org/. Accessed October 28, 2013.

Gong, Li. 2007. "Ethnic identity and identification with the majority group: Relations with national identity and self-esteem," *International Journal of Intercultural Relations*, 31 (4): 503–523.

Gonzales, R., and Brown, R. 2006. "Dual identities in intergroup contact: Group status and size moderate the generalization of positive attitude change," *Journal of Experimental Social Psychology*, 42: 753–767.

Grillo, Ralph D. 2005. *Backlash against Diversity: Identity and Cultural Politics in European Cities*. Working Paper 14. Oxford: University of Oxford (Center on Migration, Policy and Society).

———. 1985. *Ideologies and Institutions in Urban France: The Representation of Immigrants*. Cambridge: Cambridge University Press.

Guarnizo, L. E., Portes, A., and Haller, W. 2003. "Assimilation and transnationalism: Determinants of transnational political action among contemporary migrants," *American Journal of Sociology*, 108 (6): 1211–1248.

Guglielmo, Jennifer, and Salerno, S. (eds.). 2003. *Are Italians White?* New York: Routledge.

Guild, Elspeth. 2003. "International terrorism and EU immigration, asylum and border policy: The unexpected victims of 11 September 2001," *European Foreign Affairs Review*, 8 (3): 331–346.

Guiraudon, Virginie. 2006. "Immigration policy in Europe: The politics of control," *West European Politics*, 29 (2): 287–303.

———. 2001. "Weak weapons of the weak? Transnational mobilization around migration in the European Union" (pp. 163–183) in Doug Imig and Sidney Tarrow (eds.), *Contentious Europeans: Protest and Politics in an Emerging Polity*. Boston: Rowman & Littlefield Publishers.

Haddad, Yvonne Y. 2002. *Muslims in the West*. Oxford: Oxford University Press.

Haddad, Y. Y., and Esposito, J. 2000. *Muslims on the American Path?* New York: Oxford University Press.

Haddad, Y. Y., Ricks, R. S. 2009. "Claiming space in America's pluralism: Muslims enter the political maelstrom" (pp. 13–34), in A. H. Sinno (ed.), *Muslims in Western Politics*. Bloomington and Indianapolis: Indiana University Press.

Haddad, Y. Y., Smith, J. I., Esposito, J. L (eds.). 2003. *Religion and Immigration: Christian, Jewish, and Muslim Experience in the United States*. Walnut Creek: Alta Mira Press.

Hagendoorn, L., Pepels, J. 2003. "Why the Dutch maintain more social distance from some ethnic minorities than others" (pp. 41–61) in L. Hagendoorn, J. Veenman, and W. Vollebergh, *Integration of Immigrants in the Netherlands: Cultural versus Socio-Economic Integration. Aldershot:* Asghate.

Halim, Fachrizal. 2006. "Pluralism of American Muslims and the challenge of assimilation," *Journal of Muslim Minority Affairs*, 26 (2): 235–244.

Hammar, Thomas. 1985. *European Immigration Policy: A Comparative Study.* New York: Cambridge University Press.

Haubrich, Dirk. 2003. "September 11, anti-terror laws and civil liberties: Britain, France, and Germany compared," *Government and Opposition*, 38 (3): 3–28.

Hernandez, David M. 2005. *Undue Process: Immigrant Detention, Due Process and Lesser Citizenship.* UC Berkeley: Institute for the Study of Social Change.

Hirsch, E., and Lyons, C. 2010. "Perceiving discrimination on the job: legal consciousness, workplace context, and the construction of race discrimination," *Law & Society Review*, 44 (2): 269–297.

Hispanic Federation. 2010. *US Latino's Perceptions and Actions around Immigration Debate.* Study by Latino Metrics for the Hispanic Federation and Lulac (July 14).

Hochschild, Jennifer. 2013. "Moving up and in: Two dimensions of immigrant political incorporation" (pp. 288–305) in J. Hochschild, J. Chattopadhyay, C. Gay, and M. Jones-Correa, *Outsiders No More? Models of Immigrant Political Incorporation.* Oxford: Oxford University Press.

Hochschild, J. L., and Mollenkopf, J. H. (eds). 2009. *Bringing Outsiders in: Transatlantic Perspectives on Immigrant Political Incorporation.* Ithaca: Cornell University Press.

Hogg, Michael A. 2000. "Subjective uncertainty reduction through self-categorization: A motivational theory of social identity process," *European Review of Social Psychology*, 11 (1): 223–255.

Hogg, M. A., and Blaylock, D. L (eds). 2012. *Extremism and the Psychology of Uncertainty.* Oxford: Wiley-Blackwell.

Hogg, M. A., Adelman, J. R, and Blagg, R. D. 2010. "Religion in the face of uncertainty: An uncertainty identity theory account of religiousness," *Personality and Social Psychology Review*, 14 (1): 72–83.

Hogg, M. A., Meehan, C., and Farquharson, J. 2010. "The solace of radicalism: Self-uncertainty and group identification in the face of threat," *Journal of Experimental Social Psychology*, 46: 1061–1066.

Hollifield, James. 1997. *Immigration et l'Etat nation à la recherche d'un modèle national.* Paris: L'Harmattan.

Hopkins, N., and Kahani-Hopkins, V. 2004. "Identity construction and British Muslims' political activity: Beyond rational actor theory," *British Journal of Social Psychology*, 43: 339–356.

Hopkins, Peter. 2007. "Global events, local lives: Young Muslims in Scotland," *Environment and Planning*, 39 (5): 1119–1133.

Howard, Marc. 2009. *The Politics of Citizenship in Europe.* New York: Cambridge University Press.

Howarth, Caroline. 2008. "Dialogue across disciplines: Bringing politics to a social psychology of multiculture," *Journal of Community & Applied Social Psychology*, 18 (4): 349–350.

Human Rights First (HRF). 2008. *Hate Crime Survey: Racism and Xenophobia*. Available at http://www.humanrightsfirst.org/our-work/fighting-discrimination/2008-hate-crime-survey/racism-and-xenophobia/. Accessed September 1, 2013.

Hussein, Y., and Bagguley, P. 2005. "Citizenship, ethnicity and identity: British Pakistanis after the 2001 riots," *Sociology*, 39 (3): 407–425.

Huysmans, Jef. 2006. *The Politics of Insecurity: Fear, Migration, and Asylum in the EU*. London: Routledge.

IFOP (Institut Français d'Opinion Publique). Regards croisés France/Allemagne sur l'Islam. Enquête pour Le Monde (13 décembre 2010). Available at http://www.ifop.com/media/poll/1365-1-study_file.pdf. Accessed October 27, 2013.

Ignatieff, Michael. 2004. *The Lesser Evil: Political Ethics in an Age of Terror*. Princeton and Oxford: Princeton University Press.

Ignatiev, Noel. 1995. *How the Irish Became White*. London and New York: Routledge.

Imig, D., and Tarrow, S. 2001 (eds.). *Contentious Europeans: Protest and Politics in an Emerging Polity*. New York: Rowman & Littlefield Publishers.

Immigrant Citizens Survey (ICS). 2012. *How Immigrants Experience Integration in 15 European Cities*. Brussels: King Baudouin Foundation and Migration Policy Group.

Immigration Policy Center. 2011. *MIPEX III: What the Results Mean for the US*. Washington DC: American Immigration Council.

Inglehart, R., and Norris, P. 2009. "Muslim integration into Western cultures: Between origins and destinations," Faculty Research Working Papers, Harvard Kennedy School, RWP09–007: 1–38.

Institut National des Etudes Démographiques (INED). 2013. *Trajectoires et origines. Résultats de l'enquête menée en 2008 par l'INED et l'INSEE*. Available at http://teo.site.ined.fr. Accessed March 29, 2014.

International Organization for Migration (IOM). 2011. *World Migration Report*. Geneva: IOM.

Ipsos MORI. 2011. Ipsos Global@dvisor 22: Attitudes to immigration (July 2011). Available at http://www.ipsos-mori.com/researchpublications/researcharchive/2833/Too-Many-Immigrants.aspx. Accessed September 12, 2014.

Ireland, Patrick. 2011. "New ways of understanding migrant integration in Europe" (pp. 114–136), in A. E. Azzi, X. Chryssochoou, B. Kandermans, and B. Simon (eds.), *Identity and Participation in Culturally Diverse Societies*. Chichester: Wiley-Blackwell.

———. 2004. *Becoming Europe: Immigration, Integration, and the Welfare State*. Pittsburgh: University of Pittsburgh Press.

———. 2000. "Reaping what they sow: Institutions and immigrant political participation in Western Europe" (pp. 233–282) in R. Koopmans and P.Statham (eds.), *Challenging Immigration and Ethnic Relations Politics*. Oxford: Oxford University Press.

———. 1994. *The Policy Challenge of Ethnic Diversity: Immigrant Politics in France and Switzerland*. Cambridge, MA: Harvard University Press.

Irving J. P., and Doerschler, P. 2012. *Benchmarking Muslim Well-Being in Europe: Reducing Disparities and Polarizations*. Bristol: The Policy Press, University of Bristol.

Ivarsflaten, Elisabeth. 2005. "Threatened by diversity: Why restrictive asylum and immigration policies appeal to Western Europeans," *Journal of Elections, Public Opinion and Parties*, 15 (1): 21–45.

Jackson, Richard. 2007. "Playing the politics of fear: Writing the terrorist threat in the war on terrorism" (pp. 176–202) in G. Kassimeris (ed.), *Playing Politics with Terrorism: A User's Guide*. New York: Columbia University Press.

Jacobs, D., and Tillie, J. 2004. "Introduction: Social capital and political integration of migrants," *Journal of Ethnic and Migration Studies*, 30: 419–427.

Jacobs, D., Phalet, K., and Swyngedouw, M. 2004. "Associational membership and political involvement among ethnic minority groups in Brussels," *Journal of Ethnic and Migration Studies*, 30 (3): 543–559.

Jacobsen, Christine. 2005. "The quest for authenticity: Islamization amongst Muslim youth in Norway" (pp. 155–168) in J. Cesari and S. McLoughlin (eds.), *European Muslims and the Secular State*. Aldershot: Ashgate.

Jalalzai, Farida. 2009. "The Politics of Muslims in America," *Politics and Religion*, 2: 163–199.

Jamal, Amaney. 2005. "The political participation and engagement of Muslim Americans: Mosque involvement and group consciousness," *American Politics Research*, 33 (4): 521–544.

Jasinskaja-Lahti, I., Liekind, K., and Perhoniemi, R. 2006. "Perceived discrimination and well-being: A victim study of different immigrant groups," *Journal of Community and Applied Social Psychology*, 16 (4): 267–284.

Jasinskaja-Lahti, I., Liebkind, K., and Solheim, E. 2009. "To identify or not to identify? National disidentification as an alternative reaction to perceived ethnic discrimination," *Applied Psychology: An International Review*, 58 (1): 105–128.

Jasinskaja-Lahti, I., Liebkind, K., Horenczyk, G., and Schmitz, P. 2003. "The interactive nature of acculturation: Perceived discrimination, acculturation attitudes and stress among young ethnic repatriates in Finland, Israel, and Germany," *International Journal of Intercultural Relations*, 27 (1): 79–97.

Jayaweera, H., and Choudhury, T. 2008. *Immigration, Faith and Cohesion: Evidence from Local Areas with Significant Muslim Populations*. York: Joseph Rowntree Foundation.

Jenkins, Richard. 1996. *Social Identity*. London: Routledge.

Jiménez, Tomas. 2011. *Immigrants in the United States: How Well Are They Integrating into Society?* Washington, DC: Migration Policy Institute.

Jones-Correa, Michael. 2012. "Exploring discrimination: Intergroup relations, and intragroup relations among Latinos" (pp. 69–93) in L. R. Fraga, J. A. Garcia, R.

Hero, M. Jones-Correa, V. Martinez-Ebers, and G. M Segura (eds.), *Latino Lives in America: Making it Home*. Philadelphia: Temple University Press.

———. 2005. "Bringing outsiders in: Questions of immigrant incorporation" (pp. 75–101), in C. Wolbrecht and R. E Hero (eds.), *The Politics of Democratic Inclusion*. Philadelphia: Temple University Press.

Jones-Correra, M., and Joyce, P. 2001. "Discrimination and its effects on Mexican-American political preference and behavior," Western Political Science Association, Las Vegas, NV, March 15–17.

Joppke, Christian. 2013. "Tracks of immigrant political incorporation" (pp. 65–81) in J. Hochschild, J. Chattopadhyah, C. Gay, and M. Jones-Correa (eds.), *Outsiders No More? Models of Immigrant Political Incorporation*. Oxford: Oxford University Press.

———. 2009. "Limits of integration policy: Britain and her Muslims," *Journal of Ethnic and Migration Studies*, 35 (3): 453–472.

———. 2004. "The retreat of multiculturalism in the liberal state: Theory and policy," *The British Journal of Sociology*, 55 (2): 237–257.

Joppke, C., and Morawska, E. (eds.). 2003. *Toward Assimilation and Citizenship: Immigrants in Liberal Nation-States*. New York: Palgrave Macmillan.

Jost, J. T., Napier J. L., Thorisdottir H., Gosling S. D., Palfai T. P., and Ostafin B. 2007. "Are needs to manage uncertainty and threat associated with political conservatism or ideological extremism," *Personality and Social Psychology Bulletin*, 33 (7): 989–1007.

Just, A., Sandovici, M. E., and Listhaug, O. 2014. "Islam, religiosity, and immigrant political action in Western Europe," *Social Science Research*, 43: 127–144.

Kaiser, C. R., Major, B., and McCoy, S. K. 2004. "Expectations about the future and emotional consequences of perceiving prejudice," *Personality and Social Psychology Bulletin*, 30 (2): 173–184.

Kamans, E., Gordijn, E. H., Oldenhuis, H., and Otten, S. 2009. "What I think you see is what you get: Influence of prejudice on assimilation to negative meta-stereotypes among Dutch Moroccan teenagers," *European Journal of Social Psychology*, 39 (5): 842–851.

Karlsen, S., and Nazroo, J. Y. 2013. "Influences on forms of national identity and feeling 'at home' among Muslim groups in Britain, Germany and Spain," *Ethnicities*, 13 (6): 689–708.

Kay, F., and Johnston, R. 2007. "Ubiquity and disciplinary contrasts of social capital" (pp. 17–40) in F. Kay and R. Johnston (eds.), *Social Capital, Diversity, and the Welfare State*. Vancouver: UBC Press.

Kehrberg, Jason. 2007. "Public opinion on immigration in Western Europe: Economics, tolerance, and exposure," *Comparative European Politics*, 5 (3): 264–281.

Kelley, S. M. C., and Kelley, C. G. E. 2009. "Subjective social mobility: Data from 30 nations" (pp. 106–125) in M. Haller, R. Jowell and T. Smith (eds.), *Charting the Globe: The International Social Survey Program 1984–2099*. London: Routledge.

Kepel, Gilles. 2014. *Passion Française: Les Voix des Cités*. Paris: Gallimard.

Kessler, T., Mummendey, A., and Leisse, U. K. 2000. "The personal-group discrepancy: Is there a common information basis for personal and group judgment?," *Journal of Personality and Social Psychology*, 79 (1): 95–109.

Khattab, Nabil. 2009. "Ethno-religious background as a determinant of educational and occupational attainment in Britain," *Sociology*, 43 (2): 304–322.

Khrais, Reema. 2012. "How are American Muslims responding to the anti-Islam film?" *NPR*, September 22. Available at http://www.npr.org/blogs/thetwo-way/2012/09/22/161581352/how-are-american-muslims-responding-to-the-anti-islam-film. Accessed May 27, 2014.

Kinder, Donald R. 2003. "Belief systems after converse" (pp. 13–47) in M. MacKuen and G. Rabinowitz (eds.), *Electoral Democracy*. Ann Arbor: University of Michigan Press.

Kinnvall, C., and Nesbitt-Larking, P. 2011a. "Citizenship regimes and identity strategies among young Muslims in Europe" (pp. 195–219) in A. E Azzi, X. Chryssochou, B. Klandermans, and B. Simon (eds.), *Identity and Participation in Culturally Diverse Societies*. London: Wiley-Blackwell.

———. 2011b. "Global insecurity and citizenship strategies: Young Muslims in the West," *Distinktion: Scandinavian Journal of Social Theory*, 12 (3): 271–290.

Klandermans, B., van Stekelenburg, J., van der Toorn, J. 2008. "Embeddedness and identity: How immigrants turn grievances into action," *American Sociological Review*, 73: 992–1012.

Klausen, Jytte. 2008. *Public Policy for European Muslims: Facts and Perceptions*. London: The Institute for Strategic Dialogue.

———. 2005. *The Islamic Challenge*. Oxford: Oxford University Press.

Kogan, Irena. 2007. *Working through Barriers: Host Countries Institutions and Immigrant Labour Market Performance in Europe*. Dordrecht: Springer.

Koopmans, Ruud. 2004. "Migrant mobilisation and political opportunities: Variation among German cities and a comparison with the United Kingdom and the Netherlands," *Journal of Ethnic and Migration Studies*, 30 (3): 449–70.

———. 2003. "Good intentions sometimes make bad policy: A comparison of Dutch and German integration policies" (pp. 163–168) in R. Cuperus, K. A. Duffek, and J. Kandal (eds.), *The Challenge of Diversity: European Social Democracy Facing Migration, Integration and Multiculturalism*. Innsbruck: Studien Verlag.

Koopmans, R., and Statham, P. 2000. "Migration and ethnic relations as a field of political contention: An opportunity structure approach" (pp.13–56) in R. Koopmans and P. Statham (eds.), *Challenging Immigration and Ethnic Relations: Comparative European Perspectives*. Oxford: Oxford University Press.

Koopmans, R., Statham, P., Giugni, M., and Passy. F (eds.). 2005. *Contested Citizenship: Immigration and Cultural Diversity in Europe*. Minneapolis, London: University of Minneapolis Press.

Korkut, U., Bucken-Knapp, G., McGarry, A., Hinnfors, J., and Drake, H. (eds.). 2013. *The Discourses and Politics of Migration in Europe*. New York: Palgrave Macmillan.

Kosic, A., and Phalet, K. 2006. "Ethnic categorization of immigrants: The role of prejudice, perceived acculturation strategies and group size," *International Journal of Intercultural Relations*, 30: 769–782.

Kraal, K., Roosblad, J., and Wrench, J. (eds.). 2009. *Equal Opportunities and Ethnic Inequalities in European Labour Markets: Discrimination, Gender, and Policies of Diversity*. Amsterdam: Amsterdam University Press.

Kubrin, C. E, Zatz, M. S., Martinez, R. (eds.). 2012. *Punishing Immigrants: Policy, Politics, and Injustice*. New York: New York University Press.

Kugelberg, C. 2011. "Integration policy and ethnic minority associations" (pp. 264–282) in C. Shore et al. (eds.), *Policy Worlds. Anthropology and Analysis of Contemporary Power*. New York: Berhahn Books.

Kundnani, Arun. 2007. "Integrationism: The politics of anti-Muslim racism," *Race & Class*, 48 (4): 24–44.

Lahav, Gallya. 2009. "Organizing immigration interests in the European Union: Constraints and opportunities for supranational migration regulation and integration" (pp.211–230) in J. Hoschshild and J. Mollenkopf (eds.), *Bringing Outsiders In: Transatlantic Perspectives on Immigrant Political Incorporation*. Ithaca: Cornell University Press.

———. 2004. *Immigration and Politics in the New Europe: Reinventing Borders*. Cambridge: Cambridge University Press.

Lamont, M., and Nissim Mizrachi, N. (eds.). 2013. *Responses to Stigmatization in Comparative Perspective*. New York: Routledge.

Laurence, Jonathan. 2013. "Islam and Social Democrats: Integrating Europe's Muslim minorities," *Dissent*. Available at http://www.dissentmagazine.org/author/jonathan-laurence. Accessed June 19, 2014.

Laurence, J., and Vaïsse, J. 2006. *Integrating Islam: Political and Religious Challenges in Contemporary France*. Washington, DC: Brookings Institution Press.

Lee, T., Ramakrishnan, S. K., Ramírez, R. (eds.). 2006. *Transforming Politics, Transforming America: The Political and Civic Incorporation of Immigrants in the United States*. Charlottesville: University of Virginia Press.

Leibkind, Karmela. 2000. "Acculturation" (pp. 386–404) in R. Brown and S. Gaertner (eds.), *Blackwell Handbook of Social Psychology, Vol 3: Intergroup Process*. Oxford: Blackwell.

Leibkind, K., Nyström, S., Honkanummi, E., and Lange, A. 2006. "Group size, group status, and dimensions of contact as predictors of intergroup attitudes," *Group Processes & Intergroup Relations*, 7 (2): 145–159.

Leighley, Jan. 2005. "Race, ethnicity, and electoral mobilization" (pp. 143–163) in C. Wolbrecht and R. E.Hero (eds.). 2005. *The Politics of Democratic Inclusion*. Philadelphia: Temple University Press.

———. 1995. "Attitudes, opportunities and incentives: A field essay on political participation," *Political Research Quarterly*, 48: 181–209.

Leighley, J. E., Vedlitz, A. 1999. "Race, ethnicity, and political participation: Competing models and contrasting explanations," *Journal of Politics*, 61 (4): 1092–1114.

Leonard, Karen. 2003. *Muslims in the United States: The State of the Research*. New York: Russell Sage.

Leong, C. H., and Ward, C. 2006. "Cultural values and attitudes towards immigrants and multiculturalism: The case of the Eurobarometer survey on racism and xenophobia," *International Journal of Intercultural Relations*, 30 (6): 799–810.

Lewis, Phillip. 2007. *Young, British and Muslim*. London: Continuum.

Lichterman, P., and Potts, C. B. 2009. *The Civic Life of American Religion*. Stanford: Stanford University Press.

Lindekilde, Lasse. 2013. "How politically integrated are Danish Muslims? Evidence from the Muhammad cartoons controversy" (pp. 163–189) in J. Nielsen (ed.), *Muslim Political Participation in Europe*. Edinburgh: Edinburgh University Press.

———. 2010. "Soft repression and mobilization: The case of transnational activism of Danish Muslims during the cartoons controversy," *International Journal of Middle East Studies*, 42: 451–469.

Linke, U., and Smith, D. (eds.). 2009. *Cultures of Fear: A Critical Reader*. London: Pluto Press.

Lopez, Mark Hugo. 2011. *The Latino Electorate in 2010: More Voters, More No Voters*. Washington, DC: Pew Hispanic Center.

Lowy, Theodore. 1994. "American business, public policy, case studies, and political theory," *World Politics*, 16 (4): 677–715.

Luedtke, Adam. 2009. "Fortifying fortress Europe? The effect of September 11 on EU immigration policy" (pp. 130–147) in T. E. Givens, G. P. Freeman, and D. L. Leal (eds.), *Immigration Policy and Security*. New York and London: Routledge.

Lupia, A., and Menning J. O. 2009. "When can politicians scare citizens into supporting bad policies," *American Journal of Political Science*, 53 (1): 90–106.

Mähönen, T. A., Jaskinskaja-Lahti, I., and Liebkind, K. 2010. "Cultural discordance and the polarization of identities," *Group Processes & Intergroup Relations*, 14 (4): 505–515.

Makkonen, Timo. 2012. *Equal in Law, Unequal in fact: Racial and Ethnic Discrimination and the Legal Response Thereto in Europe*. Leiden: Koninklijke Brill NV.

———. 2007. *Measuring Discrimination: Data Collection and EU Equality Law*. Luxembourg: Office of the Official Publications of the EC.

Mandaville, Peter. 2009. "Muslim transnational identity and state responses in Europe and the UK after 9/11: Political community, ideology and authority," *Journal of Ethnic and Migration Studies*, 35 (3): 491–506.

Mansbridge, J. J., and Morris, A. (eds). 2001. *Oppositional Consciousness: The Subjective Roots of Social Protest*. Chicago: University of Chicago Press.

Manzano, S., and Sanchez, G. R. (2010). "Take one for the team? Limits of shared ethnicity and candidate preferences," *Political Research Quarterly*, 63(3), 568–580.

Martinez, Lisa M. 2011. "Mobilizing marchers in the Mile-High-City: The role of community based organizations" (pp. 123–141) in K. Voss and I. Bloemraad (eds.), *Rallying for Immigrant Rights: The Fight for Inclusion in 21st Century America*. Berkeley: University of California Press.

———. 2008. "Flowers from the same soil: Latino solidarity in the wake of the 2006 immigrant mobilizations," *American Behavioral Scientist*, 52 (4): 557–579.

———. 2005. "Yes we can: Latino participation in unconventional politics," *Social Forces*, 84 (1): 135–155.

Martinez, Ramiro, Jr. and Valenzuela, Abel. (eds.). 2006. *Immigration and Crime: Race, Ethnicity, and Violence*. New York: New York University Press.

Martiniello, Marco. 2009. "Immigrants and their offspring in Europe as political subjects" (pp. 33–47) in J. L. Hochschild and J. H. Mollenpokf (eds.), *Bringing Outsiders In: Transatlantic Perspectives on Immigrant Political Participation*. Ithaca: Cornell University Press.

Martinovic, B., Van Tubergen, F., and Maas, I. 2009. "Dynamics of interethnic contact: A panel study of immigrants in the Netherlands," *European Sociological Review*, 25 (3): 303–318.

Martinovic, B., and Verkuyten, M. 2012. "Host national and religious identification among Turkish Muslims in Western Europe: The role of in-group norms, perceived discrimination and value incompatibility," *European Journal of Social Psychology*, 42 (7): 893–903.

Marshall, Melissa. 2001. "Does the shoe fit? Testing models of participation for African-American and Latino involvement in local politics," *Urban Affairs Review*, 37 (2): 227–248.

Marvakis, A., Parsanoglou, D., and Psaroudakis, S. 2004. *Migrants' Experiences of Discrimination in Greece*. Vienna: EUMC.

Massey, Douglas, S. 1981. "Dimensions of the new immigration to the United States and prospect for assimilation," *Annual Review of Sociology*, 7 (1): 57–85.

Masuoka, N., and Sanchez, G. 2008. "Brown utility heuristic? The presence and contributing factors of Latino linked fate," Paper presented at the Midwest Political Science Association Annual Meeting in September. Chicago.

Mattson, Ingrid. 2003. "How Muslim use Islamic paradigms to define America" (pp. 202–209) in Y. Y. Haddad, J. I. Smith, and J. Esposito (eds.), *Religion and Immigration*. Walnut Creek: Altamira Press.

Maussen, Marcel. 2006. "The governance of Islam in Western Europe. A state of the art report." IMISCOE Working Paper, 16.

Maxwell, Rahsaan. 2013. "Assimilation and political attitudes trade-offs" (pp. 270–287) in J. Hochschild, J. Chattopadhyay, C. Gay, and M. Jones-Correa (eds.), *Outsiders No More? Models of Immigrant Political Incorporation*. Oxford: Oxford University Press.

———. 2010a. "Evaluating migrant integration: Political attitudes across generations in Europe," *International Migration Review*, 44 (1): 25–52.

———. 2010b. "Trust in government among British Muslims: The importance of migration status," *Political Behavior*, 32 (1): 89–109.

———. 2008. "Assimilation, expectations and attitudes: How ethnic minority groups feel about mainstream society," *Dubois Review*, 5 (2): 387–412.

Mayor, B., Kaiser, C. R., and McCoy, S. K. 2003. "It's not my fault: When and why attributions to prejudice protect self-esteem," *Personality and Social Psychology Bulletin*, 29 (6): 772–781.

Mazey, Judge, D. 2000. "Lobbying for migrant inclusion in the European Union: New opportunities for transnational advocacy?," *Journal of European Public Policy*, 7 (4): 620–633.

McAdam, D., Tarrow, S., and Tilly, C. 2001. *The Dynamics of Contention*. Cambridge: Cambridge University Press.

McDermott, Monica. 2013. "The importance of demographic and social context in determining political outcomes" (pp. 162–175) in J. Hochschild, J. Chattopadhyay, C. Gay, and M. Jones-Correa (eds.), *Outsiders No More? Models of Immigrant Political Incorporation*. Oxford: Oxford University Press.

McDonald, Kevin. 2006. *Global Movements: Action and Culture*. Oxford: Blackwell.

McLaren, L., and Johnson, M. 2007. "Resources, group conflict and symbols: Explaining anti-immigration hostility in Great Britain," *Political Studies*, 55 (4): 709–732.

McVeigh, R., and Smith, C. 1999. "Who protest in America: An analysis of three political alternatives—inaction, institutionalized politics, or protest," *Sociological Forum*, 14 (4): 685–701.

Meier, Kenneth. 2005. "School boards and the politics of education policy: Downstream consequences of structure" (pp. 238–256) in C. Wolbrecht and R. E Hero (eds.), *The Politics of Democratic Inclusion*. Philadelphia: Temple University Press.

Meier, K., Stewart, J. Jr., and England, R. 1989. *Race, Class and Education: The Politics of Second Generation Discrimination*. Madison: University of Wisconsin Press.

Meiksins Wood, E. 1998. *The Retreat from Class: A New "True" Socialism*. London: Verso.

Meissmer, Doris, Kerwin, D. M., Chisti, M., and Bergeron, C. 2013. *Immigration Enforcement in the United States: The Rise of a Formidable Machinery*. Washington, DC: Migration Policy Institute.

Menjivar C., Bejarano, C. 2004. "Latino immigrants' perception of crime and police authorities in the United States: A case study from the Phoenix metropolitan area," *Ethnic and Racial Studies*, 27 (1): 120–148.

Messina, Anthony (ed.). 2002. *West European Immigration and Immigrant Policy in the New Century*. Westport, CT: Praeger.

Michelson, Melissa R. 2003. "The corrosive effect of acculturation: How Mexican Americans lose political trust," *Social Science Quarterly*, 84 (4): 918–933.

Minnite, Lorraine C. 2009. "Lost in translation? A critical reappraisal of the concept of immigrant political incorporation" (pp. 48–59) I. J. Hochschild and J. Mollenkopf (eds.), *Bringing Outsiders In: Transatlantic Perspectives on Immigrant Political Incorporation*. Ithaca: Cornell University Press.

Mirza, M., Senthilkumaran, A., Ja'far, Z. 2007. *Living Apart Together: British Muslims and the Paradox of Multiculturalism*. London: Policy Exchange.

Mittelstadt, Michelle, Speaker, B., Meissmer, D. 2011. *Through the Prism of national Security: Major Immigration Policy and program Changes in the Decade since 9/11.* Washington, DC: Migration Policy Institute.

Modood, Tariq. 2009a. "Muslims and the politics of difference," (pp. 193–2009) in P. Hopkins and R. Gale (eds.), *Muslims in Britain: Race, Place and Identities.* Edinburgh: Edinburgh University Press.

———. 2009b. "The state and ethno-religious mobilization in Britain" (pp. 233–249) in J. L.Hochschild and J. H.Mollenkopf (eds.), *Bringing Outsiders in: Transatlantic Perspectives on Immigrant Political Incorporation.* Ithaca: Cornell University Press.

Modood, T., Meer, N. 2012. "Framing contemporary citizenship and diversity in Europe" (pp. 33–60), in A. Tryandafyllidou, T. Moddod, and N. Meer (eds.). *European Multiculturalisms: Cultural, Religious and Ethnic Challenges.* Edinburgh: Edinburgh University Press.

Modood, T., Triandafyllidou, A., and Zapata-Barrero, R. 2005. *Multiculturalism, Muslims and Citizenship: A European Perspective.* New York: Routledge.

Mogahed, Dalia. 2007. *Beyond Multiculturalism vs. Assimilation. Special report: Muslim World.* Princeton, NJ: Gallup.

Mogahed, D. and Nyiri, Z. 2007. "Reinventing integration: Muslims in the West," *Harvard International Review,* 29 (2): 14–18.

Moghaddam, F. M. 2005. "The staircase to terrorism: A psychological explanation," *American Psychologist,* 60: 161–169.

Mollenkopf, John. 2013. "Dimensions of immigrant political incorporation" (pp. 107–118) in J. Hochschild, J. Chattopadhyay, C. Gay, and M. Jones-Correa (eds.), *Outsiders No More? Models of Immigrant Political Incorporation.* Oxford, New York: Oxford University Press.

Mollenkopf, J., and Hochschild, J. 2010. "Immigrant political incorporation: Comparing success in the United States and Europe," *Ethnic and Racial Studies,* 33 (1): 19–38.

———. 2009. "Setting the context" (pp. 3–14) in J. L. Hochschild and J. H. Mollenkopf (eds.), *Bringing Outsiders In: Transatlantic Perspective on Immigrant Political Incorporation.* Ithaca and London: Cornell University Press.

Monforte, P., and Dufour, P. 2011. "Mobilizing in borderline citizenship regimes: A comparative analysis of undocumented migrants' collective actions," *Politics and Society,* 39 (2): 203–232.

Moore, K., Mason, P., and Lewis, J. 2008. *Images of Islam in the UK: The Representation of British Muslims in the National Print News Media (2000–2008).* Cardiff: Cardiff School of Journalism.

Morales, L., and Giugni, M. (eds.). 2011. *Social Capital, Political participation and Migration in Europe: Making Multicultural Democracy Work?* Basingstoke: Palgrave Macmillan.

Morrison, G. Wong. 2010. "Minority model or perpetual foreigner?" (pp. 165–184) in V. Martinez Ebers and M. Dorraj (eds.), *Perspectives on Race, Ethnicity and Religion.* Oxford: Oxford University Press.

Moskalenko, S., and McCauley, C. 2009. "Measuring political mobilization: The distinction between activism and radicalism," *Terrorism and Political Violence*, 21: 239–260.

Mouritsen, Per. 2012. "Beyond post-national citizenship: Access, consequence, conditionality" (pp. 88–115), in A. Tryandafyllidou, T. Moddod, and N. Meer (eds.), *European Multiculturalisms: Cultural, Religious and Ethnic Challenges*. Edinburgh: Edinburgh University Press.

Mudde, Cas. 2007. *Populist Radical Right Parties in Europe*. Cambridge: Cambridge University Press.

Mukherjee, S., Molina, E. L., and Adams, G. 2013. "Reasonable suspicion about tough immigration legislation: Enforcing laws or ethnocentric exclusion?" *Cultural Diversity and Ethnic Minority Psychology*, 19 (3): 320–331.

Muslims in the American Political Sphere (MAPS). 2004. *American MuslimPoll*. Washington, DC: Georgetown University. Available at http://explore.georgetown.edu/news/?ID=1310. Accessed February 14, 2014.

Musterd, Sako. 2005. "Social and ethnic segregation in Europe: Levels, causes and effects," *Journal of Urban Affairs*, 27 (3): 331–348.

Nagel, C., and Staehli, L. 2011. "Muslim political activism or political activism by Muslims? Secular and religious identities amongst Muslim Arab activists in the United States and United Kingdom," *Identities: Global Studies in Culture and Power*, 18: 437–458.

NBC Latino. 2012. "We are American, say most US Latinos." Available at http://nbclatino.com/2012/09/19/nbc-latinoibope-zogby-survey-we-are-american-say-most-u-s-latinos/. Accessed February 16, 2014.

Neumeyer, Matthew (Maj). 2008. *American Muslims: Living the American Dream*. Fort Leavenworth, Kansas: School of Advanced Military Studies.

Newman, B. J., Hartman, T. K, and Taber, C. S. 2012. "Foreign language exposure, cultural threat, and opposition to immigration," *Political Psychology*, 33 (5): 635–657.

Newton, Lina. 2008. *Illegal, Alien, or Immigrant: The Politics of Immigration Reform*. New York: New York University Press.

Nielsen, Jørgen. (ed.). 2013. *Muslim Political Participation in Europe*. Edinburgh: Edinburgh University Press.

Nimer, Mohamed. 2005. "American Muslim organizations: Before and after 9:11" (pp. 5–18) in P. Strum (ed.), *Muslims in the United States: Identity, Influence, Innovation*. Washington, DC: The Woodrow Wilson International Center for Scholars.

Norris, P. 2002. *Democratic Phoenix: Reinventing Political Activism*. Cambridge, MA: Cambridge University Press.

Nyiri, Zsolt. 2010. "The clash of perceptions: Comparison of views among Muslims in Paris, London, and Berlin with those among the general public" (pp. 80–98) in A. Chebel d'Appollonia and S. Reich (eds.), *Managing Ethnic Diversity after 9/11: Integration, Security, and Civil Liberties in Transatlantic Perspectives*. New Brunswick, NJ: Rutgers University Press.

————. 2007. "Muslims in Europe: Basis for greater understanding already exists," Gallup World Poll. Available at www.gallup.com/poll/27409. Accessed March 25, 2014.

Odé, A., Veenman, J. 2003. "The ethno-cultural and socio-economic position of ethnic minority groups in the Netherlands" (pp. 173–198) in L. Hagendoorn, J. Veenman, and W. Vollebergh, *Integration of Immigrants in the Netherlands: Cultural versus Socio-Economic Integration*. Aldershot: Asghate.

Odmalm, Pontus. 2004. "Civil society, migrant organisations and political parties: Theoretical linkages and applications to the Swedish context," *Journal of Ethnic and Migration Studies*, 30 (3): 471–489.

Okamoto, Dina. 2010. "Organizing across ethnic boundaries in the post civil rights era" (pp. 143–168) in N. Van Dyke and H. McCammon, *Strategic Alliances*, Minneapolis: University of Minnesota Press.

Open Society Institute (OSI). 2010. *Muslims in Europe. A Report in 11 EU Cities.* New York, London, Budapest: Open Society Institute.

————. 2004. *Aspirations and Realities: British Muslims and the Labour Market.* London: Open Society Institute.

Organization for Economic Cooperation and Development (OECD). 2013. *Employment Outlook.* Paris: OECD. Available at http://www.oecd.org/els/emp/oecdemploymentoutlook.htm. Accessed September 7, 2013.

Organization for Security and Cooperation in Europe (OSCE). 2012. *Consolidated Framework for the Fight against Terrorism.* Available at http://www.osce.org/pc/98008. Accessed September 3, 2013.

O'Toole, T., and Gale, R. 2010. "Contemporary grammars of political action among ethnic minority young activists," *Ethnic and Racial Studies*, 33 (1): 126–143.

Parvez, Fareen. 2013. "Representing 'Islam of the banlieues': Class and political participation among Muslims in France," (pp. 190–214) in J. Nielsen (ed.), *Muslim Political Participation in Europe.* Edinburgh: Edinburgh University Press.

Paxton, P., and Mughan, A. 2006. "What's to fear from immigrants? Creating an assimilationist threat scale," *Political Psychology*, 27 (4): 549–568.

Peace, Timothy. 2013. "Muslims and electoral politics in Britain: The case of the Respect Party" (pp. 299–321) in J. S. Nielsen (ed.), *Muslim Political Participation in Europe.* Edinburgh: Edinburgh University Press.

Pearson, K., and Citrin, J. 2007. "The political assimilation of the fourth wave" (pp. 217–242) in T. Lee and S. K Ramakrishnan (eds.), *Transforming Politics, Transforming America: The Political and Civic Incorporation in the United States.* Charlottesville: University of Virginia Press.

Peña, Aisha. 2007. "Protecting Muslim civil and human rights in America: The role of Islamic, national, and international organizations," *Journal of Muslim Minority Affairs*, 27 (3): 387–400).

Penninx, Rinus. 2003. *Integration: The Role of Communities, Institutions, and the State.* Migration Information Source. Washington, DC: Migration Policy Institute.

Penninx, R., and Roosblad, J. 2002. *Trade Unions, Immigration, and Immigrants in Europe (1960–1993): Comparative Study of the Actions of Trade Unions in Seven West European Countries*. New York, Oxford: Berghahn.

Penninx, R. Kraal, K., Martiniello, M., and Vertovec, S. (eds.). 2004. *Citizenship in European Cities. Immigrants, Local Politics and Integration Policies*. Aldershot: Ashgate.

Però, Davide. 2010. "Migrants' practices of citizenship and policy change" (pp. 244–263) in C. Shore, S. Wright and D. Però (eds.), *Policy Worlds. Anthropology and Contemporary Power*. New York, Oxford: Berghahn.

———. 2007. *Inclusionary Rhetoric/Exclusionary Practices: Left-Wing Politics and Migrants in Italy*. Oxford: Berghahn.

Però, D., and Solomos, J. 2010. "Migrant politics and mobilization: exclusion, engagements, incorporation," *Ethnic and Racial Studies*, 33 (1): 1–18.

Pettigrew, T. F. 1998. "Intergroup contact theory," *Annual Review of Psychology*, 49: 65–85.

Pettigrew, T. F., and Tropp, L. R. 2006. "A meta-analytic test of intergroup contact theory," *Journal of Personality and Social Psychology*, 90 (5): 751–783.

Pew Hispanic Center. 2012a. *An Awakened Giant: The Hispanic Electorate Is Likely to Double by 2030*. Washington, DC: Pew Research Center.

———. 2012b. *When Labels Don't Fit. Hispanics and their Views of Identity*. Washington, DC: Pew Research Center.

———. 2010. *Illegal Immigration Backlash Worries, Divides Latinos*. Washington, DC: Pew Research Center.

———. 2008. *National Survey of Latinos. Hispanics see their Situation in the US Deteriorating; Oppose Key Immigration Enforcement Measures*. Washington, DC: Pew Research Center.

———. 2007. *Hispanics and the 2008 Elections*. Washington, DC: Pew Research Center.

———. 2006. *America's Immigration Quandary*. Washington, DC: The Pew Research Center for the people and the Press and the Pew Hispanic Center.

———. 2004. *The 2004 National Survey of Latinos: Politics and Civic Participation*.Washington, DC. Pew Hispanic Center/Kaiser Family Foundation.

Pew Research Center. 2013. *Second-Generation Americans: A Portrait of the Adult Children of Immigrants*. Washington, DC: Pew Research Center.

———. 2012. *Partisan Polarization Surges in Bush, Obama Years*. Washington, DC: Pew Hispanic Center.

———. 2011. *Muslims Americans: No Signs of Growth in Alienation or Support for Extremism*. Washington, DC: Pew Research Center.

Pew Research Center (Global Attitudes Project). 2006. *Muslims in Europe: Economic Worries Top Concerns about Religious and Cultural Identity*. Washington, DC: Pew Research Center.

Pfaff, S., and Gill, A. J. 2006. "Will a million Muslims march? Muslim interest organizations and political integration in Europe," *Comparative Political Studies*, 39 (7): 803–828.

Philipps, Melanie. 2006. *Londonistan: How Britain is Creating a Terror State Within*. London: Gibson Square Brooks.

Phinney, J. S., Jacoby, B., and Silva, C. 2007. "Positive intergroup attitudes: The role of ethnic identity," *International Journal of Behavioral Development*, 31 (5): 478–490.

Pilati, Katia. 2012. "Network resources and the political engagement of migrant organisations," *Journal of Ethnic and Migration Studies*, 38 (4): 671–688.

Piontkowski, U., Rohmann, A., and Florak, A. 2002. "Concordance of acculturation attitudes and perceived threat," *Group Processes and Intergroup Relations*, 5 (3): 221–232.

Piontkowski, U., Florack, A., Hoelker, P., and Obdrzalek, P. 2000. "Predicting acculturation attitudes of dominant and non dominant groups," *International Journal of Intercultural Relations*, 24 (1): 1–26.

Portes, Alejandro. 1998. "Social capital: Its origins and applications in modern sociology," *Annual Review of Sociology*, 24 (1): 1–24.

Portes, A., and Rivas, A. 2011. "The adaptation of migrant children," *Future of Children*, 21 (1): 219–246.

Portes, A., and Rumbaut, R. 2006. *Immigrant America: A Portrait*. Berkeley: University of California Press.

Portes, A., and Zhou, M. 1993. "The new second generation: Segmented assimilation and its variants," *Annals of the American Academy of Political and Social Sciences*, 530 (1): 74–96.

Portes, A., Escobar, C., and Arana, R. 2009. "Divided or convergent loyalties? The political incorporation process of Latin American immigrants in the United States," *International Journal of Comparative Sociology*, 5 (2): 103–136.

Portes, A., Fernandez-Kelly, P., and Haller, W. 2005. "Segmented assimilation on the ground: The new second generation in early adulthood," *Ethnic and Racial Studies*, 28 (6): 1000–1040.

Predelli, L. N. 2008. "Political and cultural ethnic mobilization: The role of immigrant associations in Norway," *Journal of Ethnic and Migration Studies*, 34 (6): 935–954.

Princeton Survey Research Associates International. 2012. "Americans are mixed on US Muslims," *Newsweek Poll*. Available at http://www.msnbc.msn.com/id/19834255/site/newsweek Accessed April 4, 2014.

Provine, D. M., Varsanyi, M., Lewis, P. G, and Decker, S. H. 2012. "Growing tensions between civic membership and enforcement in the devolution of the immigration control" (pp. 42–61) in C. E. Kubrin, M. S. Zatz, and R. Martinez, *Punishing Immigrants: Policy, Politics, and Injustice*. New York: New York University Press.

Public Religion Research Institute. 2013. *Hispanics Religious Beliefs, Political Leanings Diversify*. Available at http://www.hispanicbusiness.com/2013/10/1/survey_hispanics_religious_beliefs_political_leanings.htm; Accessed February 16, 2014.

Pupcenoks, Juris. 2012. "Religion or ethnicity? Middle eastern conflicts and American Arab-Muslim protest politics," *Nationalism and Ethnic Politics*, 18: 170–192.

Putnam, Robert, D. 1995. "Bowling alone: America's declining social capital," *Journal of Democracy*, 6 (1): 65–78.

Qualitative Eurobarometer. 2011. *Migrant Integration. Aggregate Report.* Brussels: European Commission.

Quassoli, Fabio. 2004. "Making the neighbourhood safer: Social alarm, police practices and immigrant exclusion in Italy," *Journal of Ethnic and Migration Studies*, 30 (6): 1163–1181.

Ramakrishnan, S. Karthick. 2013. "Incorporation versus assimilation: The need for conceptual differentiation" (pp. 27–42) in J. Hochschild, J. Chattopadhyay, C. Gay, and M. Jones-Correa (eds.), *Outsiders No More? Models of Immigrant Political Incorporation.* Oxford, New York: Oxford University Press.

———. 2005. *Democracy in Immigrant America: Changing Demographics and Political Participation.* Stanford: Stanford University Press.

Ramakrishnan, S. K., and Bloemraad, I. 2008. *Civic Hopes and Political Realities: Immigrants, Community Organizations, and Political Engagement.* New York: Russell Sage Foundation.

Ramakrishnan, S. K., and Viramontes, C. 2010. "Civic spaces: Mexican home-town associations and immigrant participation," *Journal of Social Issues*, 66 (1): 155–173.

Ramirez, R., and Medina, O. 2010. *Catalysts and barriers to attaining citizenship: An analysis of ya es hora ciudadania.* Washington, DC: NCLR.

Randall, Colin. 2014. "France's Muslims drawn to far right anti-immigration party," *The National*, April 1. Available at http://www.thenational.ae/world/europe/frances-muslims-drawn-to-far-right-anti-immigration-party. Accessed June 6, 2014.

Reeskens, T., and Wright, M. 2013. "Host-country patriotism among European immigrants: A comparative study of its individual and societal roots," *Ethnic and Racial Studies*, 37 (14): 1–17.

Reichel, David. 2011. *Do Legal Regulations Hinder Naturalization? Citizenship Policies and Naturalization Rates in Europe.* EUI Working Papers (RSCAS 2011/51). Badia Fiesolana: European University Institute, EUDO Citizenship Observatory.

Reitz, Jeffrey. 2005. "In depth: French riots. Understanding the violence," *CBS News Online.* Available at http://www.cbc.ca/news/background/paris_riots/. Accessed April 4, 2014.

Rex, John. 2001. "The basic elements of a systematic theory of ethnic relations," *Sociological Research Online*, 6 (1). Available at http://www.socresonline.org.UK/6/1/rex.html. Accessed August 13, 2013.

Robins, R. W., Hendin, H. M., and Trzesniewski, K. H. 2001. "Measuring global self-esteem: Construct validation of a single item measure and the Rosenberg self-esteem scale," *Personality and Psychology Bulletin*, 27 (2): 151–161.

Röder, A., and Mühlau, P. 2012. "Low expectations or different evaluations: What explains immigrants' high levels of trust in host-country institutions?" *Journal of Ethnic and Migration Studies*, 38 (5): 777–792.

———. 2011. 'Discrimination, exclusion and immigrants' confidence in public institutions in Europe," *European Societies*, 13 (4): 535–557.

Rohmann, A., Florack, A., Piontkowski, V. 2006. "The role of discordant acculturation attitudes in perceived threat: An analysis of host and immigrant attitudes in Germany," *International Journal of Intercultural Relations*, 30: 683–702.

Rokeach, Milton. 1969. *The Open and Closed Mind*. New York: Basic Books.

Rosenblum, Marc R. 2004. *The Transnational Politics of US Immigration Policy*. La Jolla, CA: Center for Comparative Immigration Studies.

Rubaii-Barett, Nadia. 2011. "The micro-politics of immigration: Local government policies of inclusion and exclusion" (pp. 113–136) in D. F. Ericson (ed.), *The Politics of Inclusion and Exclusion: Identity Politics in Twenty-First Century America*. New York and London: Routledge.

Rudolph, Christopher. 2006. *National Security and Immigration: Policy Development in the United States and Western Europe since 1945*. Stanford: Stanford University Press.

Ruedin, D. 2013. *Why Aren't They There? The Political Representation of Women, Ethnic Groups and Issue Positions in Legislatures*. Colchester: ECPR Press.

Rumbaut, Rubén G. 2008. "Reaping what you sew: Immigration, youth, and reactive ethnicity." *Applied Developmental Science*, 22 (2): 108–111.

Rumbaut, R. and Ewing, W. 2007. *The Myth of Immigrant Criminality and the Paradox of Assimilation: Incarceration Rates among Native and Foreign-born Men*. Immigration Policy Center, a division of the American Immigration Law Foundation. Washington, DC.

Rumbaut, R. G., Foner, N., and Gold, S. J. 1999. "Transformations: Introduction, immigration and immigration research in the United States," *American Behavioral Scientist*, 42: 1258–1263.

Ryan, Bernard F. 2008. "Integration requirements: A new model in migration law," *Journal of Immigration, Asylum, and Nationality Law*, 22 (4): 303–316.

Sabatier, Colette. 2008. "Ethnic and national identity among second-generation immigrant adolescents in France: The role of social context and family," *Journal of Adolescence*, 31 (2): 185–205.

Safi, Mirna. 2010. "Immigrants' life satisfaction in Europe: Between assimilation and discrimination," *European Sociological Review*, 26 (2): 159–176.

———. 2008. "The immigrant integration process in France: Inequalities and segmentation," *Revue Française de Sociologie*, 5 (49): 3–44.

Salentin, Kurt. 2007. "Determinants of experience of discrimination in minorities in Europe," *International Journal of Conflict and Violence*, 1 (1): 32–50.

Sanchez, G. R. (2006). "The role of group consciousness in Latino public opinion," *Political Research Quarterly*, 59 (3), 435–446.

Sanders, D., Fisher, S. D., Heath, A., and Sobolewska, M. 2014. "The democratic engagement of Britain's ethnic minorities," *Ethnic and Racial Studies*, 37 (1): 120–139.

Sandovici, M. E., and Listhaug, O. 2010. "Ethnic and linguistic minorities and political participation in Europe," *International Journal of Comparative Sociology*, 51 (1–2): 111–136.

Sartori, Fabio. 2011. *Acquisition of Citizenship On The Rise in 2009*. Eurostat Statistics in Focus, 24/2011. Available at http://www.libertaciviliimmigrazione. interno.it/dipim/site/it/assets/statistiche/EUROSTAT_-_CITTADINANZA. pdf. Accessed March 12, 2014.

Schain, Martin. 2008a. "Immigration policy and reactions to terrorism after September 11" (pp. 111–129) in A. Chebel d'Appollonia and S. Reich (eds.), *Immigration, Integration and Security: America and Europe in Comparative Perspective*. Pittsburgh: University of Pittsburgh Press.

———. 2008b. *The Politics of Immigration in France, Britain, and the United States*. New York: Palgrave Macmillan.

Scheepers, P., Gijsberts, M., and Coenders, M. 2002. "Ethnic exclusionism in European countries. Public opposition to civil rights for legal migrants as a response to perceived ethnic threat," *European Sociological Review*, 18 (1): 17–34.

Schildkraut, Deborah. J. 2007. "Defining American identity in the 21st century: How much 'there' is there?" *The Journal of Politics*, 69 (3): 597–615.

———. 2005. "The rise and fall of political engagement against Latinos: The role of identity and perceptions of discrimination," *Political Behavior*, 27 (3): 285–312.

Schmitt, M. T., and Branscombe, N. R. 2002. "The meaning and consequences of perceived discrimination in disadvantaged and privileged social groups" (pp. 167–199) in W. Stroebe and M. Hewstone (eds.), *European Review of Social Psychology*. Chichester: Wiley.

Schneider, J., and Crul, M. (eds.). 2012. *Theorising Integration and Assimilation*. London and New York: Routledge.

Schneider, Silke L. 2008. "Anti-immigrant attitudes in Europe: Outgroup size and perceived ethnic threat," *European Sociological Review*, 24 (1): 53–67.

Scholten, P., and Holzhacker, R. 2009. "Bonding, bridging and ethnic minorities in the Netherlands: Changing discourses in a changing nation," *Nations and Nationalism*, 15 (1): 81–100.

Schrag, Peter. 2010. *Not Fit For Our Society: Nativism and Integration*. Berkeley: University of California.

Schrover, M., and Vermeulen, F. 2005. "Immigrant organisations," *Journal of Ethnic and Migration Studies*, 31 (5): 823–832.

Schuck, Peter H. 2009. "Immigrants' incorporation in the United States after 9/11: Two steps forward, one step back" (pp. 158–175) in J.L. Hochschild and J.H. Mollenkopf (eds.), *Bringing Outsiders In: Transatlantic Perspective on Immigrant Political Incorporation*. Ithaca and London: Cornell University Press.

Scuzzarello, Sarah. 2011. "Migrants' integration in Western Europe: Bridging social psychology and political science," *Journal of Community & Applied Social Psychology*, 22 (1): 1–19.

Sears, D. O., Fu, M., Henry, P. J. and Bui, K. 2003. "The origins and persistence of ethnic identity among the new immigrant groups," *Social Psychology Quarterly*, 66:419–43

Secretary of State for the Home Department (UK). 2011. *Prevent Strategy. Report Presented to Parliament.* Available at https://www.gov.uk/government/uploads/system/uploads/attachment_data/file/97976/prevent-strategy-review.pdf. Accessed August 14, 2014.

Semyonov, M., Raijman, R., Tov, A. Y., and Schmidt, P. 2004. "Population size, perceived threat and exclusion: A multiple-indicators analysis of attitudes towards foreigners in Germany," *Social Sciences Research*, 33 (4): 681–701.

Skrobanek, J. (2009). "Perceived discrimination, ethnic identity and the (re-)ethnicisation of youth with a Turkish ethnic background in Germany," *Journal of Ethnic and Migration Studies*, 35 (4): 535–554.

Silberman, R., and Fournier, I. 2006. "Jeunes issus de l'immigration: une pénalité à l'embauche qui persiste," *Bref*, 226: 1–3.

Silberman, R., Alba, R., and Fournier, I. 2007. "Segmented assimilation in France? Discrimination in the labour market against the second generation," *Ethnic and Racial Studies*, 30 (1): 1–27.

Simon, Bernd. 2011. "Collective identity and political engagement" (pp. 137–157) in A. E. Azzi, X. Chryssochoou, B. Klandermans, and B. Simon (eds.), *Identity and Participation in Culturally Diverse Societies: A Multidisciplinary Perspective.* London: Wiley-Blackwell.

Simon, B., and Klandermans, B. 2001. "Politicized collective identity: A social psychological analysis," *American Psychology*, 31: 717–739.

Simpson Bueker, Catherine. 2005. "Political incorporation among immigrants from ten areas of origin: The persistence of source country effect," *International Migration Review*, 39 (1): 103–140.

Singla, Rashmi. 2005. "South Asian youth in Scandinavia: Inter-ethnic and inter-generational relationship," *Psychology and Developing Societies*, 17 (2): 216–235.

Sinno, Abdulkader, H. 2009. "Muslim underrepresentation in American politics" (pp. 69–95), in A. H. Sinno (ed.), *Muslims in Western Politics.* Bloomington: Indiana University Press.

Sizemore, D. S. and Milner, W. T. 2004. "Hispanic media use and perceptions of discrimination: reconsidering ethnicity, politics, and socioeconomics," *The Sociological Quarterly*, 45 (4): 765–784.

Skitka, L. B., Bauman, C. W., Mullen, E. 2004. "Political tolerance and coming to psychological closure following the September 11, 2001, terrorist attacks: An integrative approach," *Personality and Social Psychology Bulletin*, 30 (6): 743–756.

Skrobanek, Jan. 2009. "Perceived discrimination, ethnic identity and (re)ethnicisation of youth with a Turkish background in Germany," *Journal of Ethnic and Migration Studies*, 35 (4): 535–554.

Smith, H. J., Pettigrew, T. E., Pippin, G. M., and Bialosiewicz, S. 2011. "Relative deprivation: A theoretical and meta-analysis review," *Personality and Social Psychological Review*, 16 (3): 203–232.

Smith, M. P., Guarnizo, L. E. (eds.). 1998. *Transnationalism from Below*, vol. 6: *Comparative and Community Research.* New Brunswick: Transaction.

Snellman, A., and Ekehammer, B. 2005. "Ethnic hierarchies, ethnic prejudice, and social dominance orientation," *Journal of Community and Applied Social Psychology*, 15 (2): 83–94.

Sniderman, Paul, and Hagendoorn, L. 2007. *When Ways of Life Collide: Multiculturalism and its Discontents in the Netherlands.* Princeton: Princeton University Press.

Sniderman, Paul, Hagendoorn, L., and Prior, M. 2004. "Predispositional factors and situational triggers: Exclusionary reactions to immigrant minorities," *American Political Science Review*, 98 (1): 35–50.

Sobolewska, Maria. 2013. "Party strategies and the descriptive representation of ethnic minorities: The 2010 British general election," *West European Politics*, 36 (3): 615–633.

Solomos, John (ed.). 2000. *Theories of Race and Racism.* New York: Routledge.

Somma, Nicolas. 2010. "How do voluntary organizations foster protest? The role of organizational involvement on individual protest participation," *The Sociological Quarterly*, 51: 384–407.

State Government. 2013. *Refugee Admissions program for Near East and South Asia.* Washington, DC. Available at http://www.state.gov/j/prm/releases/onepagers/202635.htm. Accessed February 13, 2014.

Statham, P., Koopmans, R., Giugni, M., and Passy, F. 2005. "Resilient or adaptable Islam?," *Ethnicities*, 5 (4): 427–459.

Stephan, W. G., Renfro, L. C., and Davis, M. 2008. "The role of threat in intergroup relations" (pp. 56–71) in U. Wagner, L. Topp, G. Finchilescu, and C. Tredoux (eds.), *Improving Intergroup Relations: Building on the Legacy of Thomas F. Pettigrew.* Malden, MA: Blackwell.

Stephan, W. G., Ybarra, O., Rios Morrison, K. 2009. "Intergroup threat theory" (pp. 43–59) in T. D. Nelson (ed.), *Handbook of Prejudice, Stereotyping and Discrimination.* New York: Psychology Press/Taylor & Francis.

Stepick, A., and Dutton, S. C. 2012. "The complexities and confusions of segmented assimilation" (pp. 7–24) in J. Schneider and M. Crul (eds.), *Theorising Integration and Assimilation.* London and New York: Routledge.

Stockton, Ronald. 2006. "Arab-American political participation. Findings from the Detroit Arab American Study" (pp. 53–79) in Philippa Strum (ed.), *American Arabs and Political Participation.* Washington, DC: Wilson International Center for Scholars.

Stürmer, S., and Simon, B. 2004. "Collective action: Towards a dual pathway model" (pp. 59–99) in W. Stroebe and M. Hewstone (eds.), *European Review of Social Psychology.* Hove, UK: Psychology Press.

Suarez-Orozco, C., Suarez-Orosco, M., and Todorova, I. 2008. *Learning a New Land: Immigrant Students in American Society.* Cambridge, MA: Harvard University Press.

Suro, Roberto. 2011. "Out of the shadows, into the light: Questions raised by the spring of 2006" (pp. 250–260) in K. Voss and I. Bloemraad (eds.), *Rallying for Immigrant Rights. The Fight for Inclusion in 21st Century America.* Berkeley: University of California Press.

Tajfel, H., and Turner, J. C. 1986. "The social identity of intergroup behavior," in S. Worchel and W. G. Austin (eds.), *Psychology of Intergroup Relations*. Chicago: Brooks/Cole.

Takle, Marianne. 2013. "Democratic mobilization in immigrant organisations," *Nordic Journal of Migration Research*, 33 (3): 126–134.

Tarrow, Sidney. 1998. *Power in Movement: Social Movements, Collective Action and Mass Politics in the Modern State* (2nd ed.). Cambridge: Cambridge University Press.

Tatari, Eren. 2010. "Institutional constraints on effective minority representation," *European Journal of Economic and Political Studies*, 3: 45–61.

Taylor, D. M., Wright, S. C., and Porter, L. E. 1994. "Dimensions of perceived discrimination: The personal-group discrepancy" (vol. 7, pp. 233–255) in M. P. Zanna and J. M. Olsen (eds.), *The Psychology of Prejudice: The Ontario Symposium*. Hillsdale, NJ: Lawrence Erlbaum Associates.

Ten Teije, I., Coenders, M., and Verkuyten, M. 2013. "The paradox of integration: Immigrants and their attitude toward the native population," *Social psychology*, 44 (4): 278–288.

The American Muslim (TAM). 2013. "The Muslims are coming." Available at http://theamericanmuslim.org/tam.php/features/articles/the-muslims-are-coming-pamela-geller-discovers-comedy-jihad. Accessed May 27, 2014.

The 1990 Trust. 2006. *Muslim Views: Foreign Policy and its Effects*. London: The 1990 Trust.

Theodore, Nik. 2013. *Latino Perceptions of Police Involvement in Immigration Enforcement*. Report for the Department of Urban Planning and Policy. Chicago: University of Illinois at Chicago.

Thomas, E., McGarty, C., and Louis, W. 2014. "Social interaction and psychological pathways to political engagement and extremism," *European Journal of Social Psychology*, 44: 15–22.

Thomas, E., Smith, G. G. E., McGarty, C., and Postmes, T. 2010. "Nice and nasty: The formation of pro-social and hostile social movements," *International Review of Social Psychology*, 23: 17–55.

Thomas, Rebekah. 2006. "Biometrics, international migrants and human rights," *Harvard Journal on Legislation*, 7 (4): 377–411.

Thronson, David B. 2008. "Creating crisis: Immigration raids and the destabilizing of immigrant families," *Wake Forest Law Review*, 43: 391–418.

Tichenor, Daniel. 2002. *Diving Lines: The Politics of Immigration Control in America*. Princeton: Princeton University Press.

Tillie, Jean. 2004. "Social capital of organizations and their members: Explaining the political integration of immigrants in Amsterdam," *Journal of Ethnic and Migration Studies*, 30 (3): 529–541.

Tilly, C., and Tarrow, S. 2007. *Contentious Politics*. Oxford: Oxford University Press.

Tilly, Charles. 2004. *Social Movements 1798–2004*. Boulder: Paradigm Publishers.

Tirman, John (ed.). 2004. *The Maze of Fear: Security and Migration After 9/11.* New York: New Press.

Todd, Jennifer. 2005. "Social transformation, collective categories and identity change," *Theory and Society*, 34 (4): 429–463.

Togeby, Lise. 2004. "It depends…How organizational participation affects political participation and social trust among second generation immigrants in Denmark," *Journal of Ethnic and Migration Studies*, 30 (3): 509–528.

Totten, Robbie. 2013. "Security and United States immigration policy: Two American immigration security traditions and an analytical framework of national security and US immigration policy," Working Paper, Rice University's Baker Institute.

Triandafyllidou, A., Moddod, T., Meer, N. (eds.). 2012. *European Multiculturalism: Cultural, Religious and Ethnic Challenges.* Edinburgh: Edinburgh University Press.

Tropp, Linda. 2003. "The psychological impact of prejudice: Implications for intergroup contact," *Group Process & Intergroup relations*, 6 (2): 131–149.

Tropp, L., and Pettigrew, T. 2005. "Relationship between intergroup contact and prejudice among minority and majority status groups," *Psychological Science*, 16 (2): 951–957.

Tsoukala, Anastassia. 2005. "Looking at migrants as enemies" (pp. 161–192) in D. Bigo and E. Guild (eds.), *Controlling Frontiers: Free Movement into and within Europe.* Aldershot: Ashgate.

US Department of Education, Institute of Education Sciences. 2010. "Detailed years of school completed by people 25 years and over by race and Hispanic origin," *Digest of Education Statistics.*

Valentine, G., and Sporton, D. 2009. "How other people see you, it's like nothing that's inside: The impact of processes of disidentification and disavowal on young people's subjectivities," *Sociologies*, 43 (3): 735–752.

Van den Bos, K., Loseman, A., and Doosje, B. 2009. *Why Young People Engage in Radical Behaviour and Sympathize with Terrorism: Injustice, Uncertainty and Threatened Groups.* Utrecht: University Utrecht (faculty of Social Sciences).

Van Deth, J. W., Montero, J. R. and Westholm, A. (eds.). 2007. *Citizenship and Involvement in European Democracies: A Comparative Analysis.* London: Routledge.

Van Doorn, M., Scheepers, P., and Davegos, J. 2012. "Explaining the integration paradox among small immigrant groups in the Netherlands," *International Migration and Integration*, 14 (2): 381–400.

Van Kempen, Ronald. 2001. "Social exclusion: The importance of context" (pp. 41–70) in H.T Andersen and R.van Kempen, *Governing European Cities: Social Fragmentation, Social Exclusion and Urban Governance.* Aldershot: Asghate.

Van Munster, Rens. 2009. *Securitizing Immigration: The Politics of Risk in the EU.* New York: Palgrave Macmillan.

———. 2004. "The war on terrorism: When the exception becomes the rule," *International Journal for the Semiotics of Law*, 17 (2): 141–153.

Van Oers, Ricky. 2010. "Citizenship tests in Germany, the Netherlands and the UK" (pp. 51–105) in R. van Oers, E. Ersbøll, and D. Kostakopoulou (eds.), *A Re-Definition of Belonging? Language and Integration Tests in Europe.* Leiden, Boston: Martinus Nijhoff Publishers.

———. 2009. "Justifying citizenship tests in the Netherlands and the UK" (pp. 113–130) in E. Guild, K. Groenendijk, and S. Carrera (eds.), *Illiberal Liberal States: Immigration, Citizenship and Integration in the EU Survey.* Aldershot: Ashgate.

Van Oudenhoven, J. P., Prins, K. S., Buunk, B. P. 1998. "Attitudes of minority and majority members towards adaptation of immigrants," *European Journal of Social Psychology,* 28 (6): 995–1013.

Van Oudenhoven, J. P., Ward, C., and Masgoret, A. M. 2006. "Patterns of relations between immigrants and host societies," *International Journal of Intercultural Relations,* 30 (6): 637–651.

Van Stekelenburg, J. and Klandermans, B. 2011. "Radicalization" (pp. 181–194) in A. E Azzi, X. Chryssochou, B. Klandermans, and B. Simon, *Identity and Participation in Culturally Diverse Societies.* London: Wiley-Blackwell.

———. 2007. "Individuals in movements: A social psychology of contention" (pp. 157–209) in B. Klandermans and C. Roggeband(eds), *Social Movements across Disciplines.* New York: Springer.

Van Tubergen, F., and Van de Werfhorst, H. 2007. "Post-immigration investments in education: A study of immigrants in the Netherlands," *Demography,* 44 (4): 883–989.

Van Zomeren, M., Leach, C. W., and Spears, R. 2012. "Protesters as 'passionate economists': A dynamic dual pathway model of approach coping with collective disadvantage," *Personality and Social Psychology Review,* 16 (2): 180–199.

Van Zomeren, M., Spears, R., Fisher, A. H., and Leach, C. W. 2004. "Put your money where your mouth is! Explaining collective action tendencies through group-based anger and group efficacy," *Journal of Personality and Social Psychology,* 87: 649–664.

Varsanyi, Monica (ed.). 2010. *Taking Local Control: Immigration Policy Activism in U.S. Cities and States.* Stanford, C.A.: Stanford University Press.

Vedder, P., Van de Vijer, F., and Liebkind, K. 2006. "Predicting immigrant youths' adaptation across countries and ethnocultural groups" (pp. 143–166) in J. W. Berry, J. S. Phinney, D. L. Sam, and P. Vedder (eds.), *Migrant Youth in Cultural Transition: Acculturation, Identity, and Adaptation across National Contexts.* Hamwah, NJ: Lawrence Erlbaum.

Verba, S., Schlozman, K. L., and Brady, H. 1995. *Voice and Equality: Civic Voluntarism in American Politics.* Cambridge: Harvard University Press.

———. 1993. "Race, ethnicity, and political resources: Participation in the United States," *British Journal of Political Science,* 23 (4): 453–497.

Verkuyten, Maykel. 2008. "Life satisfaction among ethnic minorities; the role of discrimination and group identification," *Social Indicators Research,* 89 (3): 391–404.

Verkuyten, Maykel. 2007. "Religious group identification and inter-religious relations: A study among Turkish-Dutch Muslims," *Group Process and Intergroup Relations*, 10 (3): 341–357.

———. 2005. "Ethnic group identification, and group evaluations among minority and majority groups: Testing the multiculturalism hypothesis," *Journal of Personality and Social Psychology*, 88 (1): 121–138.

Verkuyten, M., and Thijs, J. 2002. "Multiculturalism among minority and majority adolescents in the Netherlands," *International Journal of Intercultural Relations*, 26 (1): 91–108.

Voas, D., and Fleischmann, F. 2012. "Islam moves West religious change in the first and second generation," *Annual Review of Sociology*, 38: 525–545.

Waldinger, Roger. 2006. "Immigrant transnationalism and the presence of the past" (pp. 267–285) in E. Barkan (ed.), *Borders, Boundaries and Bonds: America and its Immigrants in Eras of Globalization*. New York: New York University Press.

Warner, Judith Ann. 2005. "The social construction of the criminal alien in immigration law, enforcement practice and statistical enumeration: Consequences for immigrant stereotyping," *Journal of Social and Ecological Boundaries*, 1 (2): 56–80.

Warner, C. M., and Wenner, M. W. 2006. "Religion and the political organization of Muslims in Europe," *Perspectives on Politics*, 4 (3): 457–479.

Waslin, Michele. 2009. "Immigration policy and the Latino community since 9/11" (pp. 39–51) in T. E Givens, G. P. Freeman, and D. L. Leal (eds.), *Immigration Policy and Security: US, European and Commonwealth Perspectives*. New York, London: Routledge.

Waters, M., and Jiménez, T. 2005. "Assessing immigrant assimilation: New empirical and theoretical challenges," *Annual Review of Sociology*, 31 (1): 105–125.

Weaver, Charles N. 2006. "Trust in people among Hispanic Americans," *Journal of Applied Social Psychology*, 36 (5): 1160–1172.

———. 2003. "Confidence of Mexican Americans in major institutions in the United States," *Hispanic Journal of Behavioral Science*, 25 (4): 501–512.

Weiner, Myron. 1993. *International Migration and Security*. Boulder, CO: Westview Press.

Wenzel, J. P. 2006. "Acculturation effects on trust in national and local government among Mexican Americans," *Social Science Quarterly*, 87 (5): 1073–1087.

Wiktorowicz, Quintan. 2005. *Radical Islam Rising: Muslim Extremism in the West*. Lanham: Rowman and Littlefield.

Wilamowitz-Moellendorff, Ulrich. 2001. *Türken in Deutschland*. Arbeitspapier 53. Sankt Augustin: Konrad Adenauer Stiftung.

Wiley, S., Deaux, K., and Hagelskamp, C. 2012. "Born in the USA: How immigrant generation shapes meritocracy and its relation to ethnic identity and collective action," *Cultural Diversity & Ethnic Minority Psychology*, 18 (2): 171–180.

Wiley, S., Lawrence, D., Figueroa, J., and Percontino, R. 2013. "Rejection, (dis) identification and ethnic political engagement among first-generation Latino immigrants to the United States," *Cultural Diversity and Ethnic Minority Psychology*, 19 (3): 310–319.

Williams, Michael. 2003. "Words, images, enemies: Securitization and international politics," *International Studies Quarterly*, 47 (4): 511–531.

Wilner, A. S., and Dubouloz, C. J. 2010. "Homegrown terrorism and transformative learning: An interdisciplinary approach to understanding radicalization," *Global Change, Peace & Security*, 22 (1): 33–51.

Wodtke, Geoffrey T. 2012. "The impact of education on intergroup attitudes. A multiracial analysis," *Social Psychology Quarterly*, 75 (1): 80–106.

Wong, Janelle. 2006. *Democracy's promise: Immigrants & American Civic Institutions*. Ann Arbor: University of Michigan Press.

Wrench, John. 2007. *Diversity Management and Discrimination: Immigrants and Ethnic Minorities in the EU*. Aldershot: Ashgate.

Wright, M., and Bloemraad, I. 2012. "Is there a trade-off between multiculturalism and socio-political integration? Policy regimes and immigrant incorporation in comparative perspective," *Perspective on Politics*, 1 (1): 77–95.

Wright-Neville, D., and Smith, D. 2009. "Political rage: Terrorism and the politics of emotion," *Global Change, Peace and Security*, 21 (1): 85–98.

Yildiz, A. A., and Verkuyten, M. 2012. "We are not terrorists: Turkish Muslim organizations and the construction of a moral identity," *Ethnicities*, 13 (3): 359–381.

Ysseldyk, R., Matheson, K., Anisman, H. 2010. "Religiosity as identity: Toward an understanding of religion from a social identity perspective," *Personality and Social Psychology*, 14: 60–71.

Zagefka, H., Brown, R. 2002. "The relationship between acculturation strategies and relative fit and intergroup relations: Immigrants-majority relations in Germany," *European Journal of Social Psychology*, 32 (2): 171–188.

Zapata-Barrero, R., and Gropas, R. 2012. "Active immigrants in multicultural contexts: Democratic challenges in Europe" (pp. 167–191) in A. Triandafyllidou, T. Modood, and N. Meers (eds.), *European Multiculturalisms: Cultural, Religious and Ethnic Challenges*. Edinburgh: Edinburgh University Press.

Zick, A., Küpper, B., and Hövermann, A. 2011. *Intolerance, Prejudice and Discrimination. A European Report*. Berlin: Friedrich-Ebert-Stiftung.

Zimmermann, D., and Wenger, A. (eds.). 2006. *How States Fight Terrorism: Policy Dynamics in the West*. Boulder, CO: Lynne Rienner.

Zolberg, Aristide. 2006. *A Nation by Design: Immigration Policy in the Fashioning of America*. Cambridge, MA,: London: Harvard University Press.

———. 2002. "Reflections on international migration after 9/11: Perspectives from around the world," *International Migration Review*, 36 (1): 5–6.

Zolberg, A., Witt Woon, L. 1999. "Why Islam is like Spanish: Cultural incorporation in Europe and the United States," *Politics & Society*, 27 (1): 5–38.

Index

Lightning Source UK Ltd.
Milton Keynes UK
UKOW06n1823100415

249444UK00004B/81/P

9 781137 388049